Oracle Press™

Transforming Infoglut!

A Pragmatic Strategy for Oracle Enterprise Content Management

D1472791

About the Authors

Andy MacMillan is vice president of product management for Oracle Content Management. He was with Stellent prior to its acquisition by Oracle, holding positions in consulting services, product management, and product marketing. Prior to that he was a consultant at EDS, working primarily on large Web applications for General Motors. Andy regularly represents Oracle at conferences and customer events, outlining a vision of the future of content management and highlighting strategies for implementation and adoption of content management solutions and technologies.

Andy is focused on the intersection of technology and business strategy. He believes strongly that business initiatives need to drive technology decisions and that demonstrable business results are the true measure of success of IT projects. He currently lives in Chicago with his wife, Monica.

Brian "Bex" Huff is the president and chief software architect at Bezzotech, an enterprise content management consulting firm. He was a senior Java developer on the original team that created the Stellent Enterprise Content Management product line, before Stellent was acquired by Oracle in 2007. He is the author of the textbook *The Definitive Guide to Stellent Content Server Development (Apress, 2006). He moderates the Yahoo! e-mail message boards where Oracle ECM administrators and developers can get help. He was granted the title ACE Director by Oracle for his work building up the Stellent community, and speaks frequently for Oracle at trade shows and content management–related events. In his spare time, he blogs about technology and content management at http://bexhuff.com.*

Bex is an early adopter of new technology, but insists that all innovations prove their value before introduction to the enterprise. He also believes that the abilities to communicate and teach are the most important skills that a technical person can possess. He currently lives in Minneapolis with his wife, Michelle.

ORACLE®   *Oracle Press*™

Transforming Infoglut!

A Pragmatic Strategy for Oracle Enterprise Content Management

Andy MacMillan
Brian Huff

New York   Chicago   San Francisco
Lisbon   London   Madrid   Mexico City   Milan
New Delhi   San Juan   Seoul   Singapore   Sydney   Toronto

The *McGraw·Hill* Companies

Cataloging-in-Publication Data is on file with the Library of Congress

McGraw-Hill books are available at special quantity discounts to use as premiums and sales promotions, or for use in corporate training programs. To contact a special sales representative, please visit the Contact Us page at www.mhprofessional.com.

Transforming Infoglut! A Pragmatic Strategy for Oracle Enterprise Content Management

1234567890   FGR FGR   0198

ISBN   978-0-07-160236-5
MHID   0-07-160236-4

Sponsoring Editor
Lisa McClain

Editorial Supervisor
Janet Walden

Project Managers
Aparna Shukla and Harleen
Chopra, International Typesetting
and Composition

Acquisitions Coordinator
Jennifer Housh

Copy Editor
Claire Splan

Proofreader
Jean Butterfield

Indexer
Karin Arrigoni

Production Supervisor
George Anderson

Composition
International Typesetting and
Composition

Illustration
International Typesetting and
Composition

Art Director, Cover
Jeff Weeks

To my family.
—Andy

For Michelle.
—Bex

Contents at a Glance

Contents

Foreword

Consider that 80 percent of the information within most organizations is unstructured: word processing files, e-mail, spreadsheets, Web content, images, graphics, and all the other digital assets that organizations create and use as part of their business processes. Fully 90 percent of this unstructured information remains unmanaged within most organizations— and industry estimates are that this unmanaged information is growing at a rate of 36 percent per year.

But the picture gets even more complicated. Globalization has led organizations to become more distributed than they were in the past—a trend that will only increase over time. Cross-continent, cross-culture, multi-language, hyper-collaboration environments will soon be the norm for most organizations within the next few years, if it is not already.

Furthermore, the business environment is subject to increasing regulation— not to mention it's also become highly litigious. In the U.S., post-Enron regulatory changes have mandated that organizations regard information management as an essential part of running their business.

Whether you consider it from a compliance and litigation viewpoint, through a cost-cutting lens, or from a productivity enhancement perspective, enterprise content management (ECM) technology is an integral component of the IT infrastructure within an organization. But historically, the implementation of such an infrastructure, the development of content-related policies, and the adoption patterns for ECM have tended to be very fragmented. The result has been information silos and poor interoperability of information.

As one of the principals of a consulting firm that focuses on ECM technology strategy, I've been following the ECM market space for more than 15 years, and the macro trends are quite apparent. It is the legacy, history, and the very nature of the ad hoc way that unstructured content gets created, collaboratively developed, archived, and then forgotten in organizations that make the development of an ECM strategy so critical for the types of business initiatives being undertaken today.

I've seen how organizations have tended to deploy the ECM component technologies (imaging, workflow, document management, records management, collaboration, portals, and Web content management, among others). Many organizations took the point-solution approach, deploying ECM components on a departmental basis. Others invested in an enterprise license for ECM, but deployed it to only a few departments. Neither of these makes use of the product's full functionality—not even by the departments that could benefit most. Still others rolled out ECM enterprise-wide, but user adoption is low, and they can't figure out why—so they're still not realizing those elusive economies of scale. And, finally, the chances are that none of these organizations have any idea what their content management systems are costing on an annual basis, and thus have no way of measuring the productivity impacts—and no way of providing executive management the cost justification for a wider rollout of the ECM product, either.

In fact, studies conducted by Doculabs and others have shown that upwards of 50 percent of ECM implementations are failures—projects that either went over budget, or, over time, that achieved adoption rates dismally lower than the initial projections.

So what's the problem?

The problem is 1) most organizations still take an overly tactical view toward ECM, and 2) they don't prioritize effective planning from a strategic standpoint on how to realize returns on the investment.

Many organizations continue to implement ECM tactically, to address specific business problems within individual business units, rather than strategically. In a strategic approach, ECM solutions are selected and implemented as part of a defined enterprise strategy, delivering wider benefits and greater return on investment—as well as a lower total cost of ownership. An ECM strategy takes into consideration the disparate requirements that different business units are likely to present for the various components of content-related functionality. Such a strategy also provides a repeatable process that IT can then use to provision ECM applications throughout the enterprise.

From the planning perspective, an organization that adopts the strategic approach will take the time to assess its current maturity level for ECM, defining common usage patterns and defining the requirements for content-related solutions throughout the organization. It will also undertake a cost-benefit analysis to quantify the current costs and inefficiencies of not using ECM—the hard-dollar numbers that help obtain senior executive buy-in. Finally, under the strategic approach, the organization will develop a clear roadmap that aligns the rollout of ECM applications with the organization's business priorities and maps the tactics to the vision of how the footprint of ECM usage will be expanded across the organization.

This book provides the mechanics for putting such an ECM strategy in place. But before we jump into the mechanics, it is worth pondering the benefits that a strategic approach can provide—and to understand exactly why such a strategy is critical to the effective management of an organization's unstructured content.

The strategic approach to ECM drives a wide range of business benefits. These benefits include productivity enhancements and impact on revenue generation, product innovation through collaboration, higher user adoption rates, a greater percentage of unstructured content under the management of an ECM system, and better preparedness for business continuity.

The sheer volume of unstructured content that organizations worldwide now produce in the course of day-to-day business operations (7.5 billion Microsoft Office documents annually, by one industry estimate) also makes ECM technology a significant priority from a compliance standpoint. Effective management of content throughout its life cycle is now uppermost in the minds of not just general counsel but also CEOs. The result is that ECM is no longer just a "nice-to-have" technology, but a critical prerequisite for the effective operation of a business of any size. And this cannot be achieved without methodically thinking about a strategy for how to get there.

But perhaps the most important benefit of taking the strategic approach to deploying ECM technologies is that it enables an organization to better align its rollout of technology with its business strategy. With an ECM strategy in place, an organization can effectively quantify and evaluate potential ECM applications against each other and identify the highest impact areas to focus on. An organization seeking to undertake a strategic business initiative such as outsourcing, for example, would be able to identify which ECM applications are the prerequisite to supporting the outsourcing initiative and could then prioritize them accordingly. Or an organization that faces ever-changing regulations can make it a priority to build a foundation for compliance by putting the necessary ECM technology and programs in place. Without an ECM strategy, an organization's ECM efforts tend to be more reactive, in response to individual project requests—which makes it far less likely that the organization will achieve the maximal potential return on the investments it makes in ECM technologies.

To sum it all up, ECM technologies offer many benefits, but having a strategy for how you will roll out those technologies allows you to pick a few areas and succeed at those, rather than going after too many and doing all of them poorly because of a lack of prioritization and focus. Put another way, an ECM strategy allows you to prioritize and execute those ideas that have the greatest potential impact on the business.

In most organizations, the strategic approach will involve technology consolidation—a rationalization of the multiple content-related systems that have been in use. But the long-term benefits of this consolidation include not only cost reduction (i.e., fewer systems to maintain and support), but more consistent technology-related decision-making, greater visibility into processes and approaches to business application development, and better knowledge transfer and information reuse among implementation staff. Our research indicates that organizations that undertake effective system rationalization/consolidation, along with enterprise-level, shared services-based deployments of ECM, have ended up saving as much as 25 to 40 percent of what they had been spending prior to the consolidation, supporting and maintaining all the previous ECM systems and point-solutions. This is the kind of cost reduction that gets the attention of executive management. And it is impossible to achieve without first crafting a vision through a strategy development exercise.

I've seen many ECM implementations that were less than successful—largely because the organizations in question failed to take a strategic view. In this book, Andy MacMillan and Bex Huff have together compiled the best practices to implementing ECM from a strategic standpoint. In doing so, they do a great service to anyone who seeks to manage their organization's information assets—and do so successfully.

—Jeetu Patel
Executive Vice President, Doculabs, Inc.
Chicago, Illinois

Acknowledgments

The authors would like to thank the Stellent and Oracle content management team for their work on a great set of products. Thanks to everybody who read the book, gave us feedback, and helped us gather content, including Bruce Silver, Jo Shilling, Terry Menta, Billy Cripe, Alan Baer, Joseph Stanko, and Stanley Hin. Thanks also to all of the people who wrote testimonials for us, which you will see throughout the book. Thank you as well to the team at McGraw-Hill, who helped us through the publishing processes.

Additionally, Andy would like to thank...

Thanks to the Oracle Fusion Middleware Team for welcoming the Stellent team into Oracle, and for sharing our vision of innovation and quality. Thanks to Cliff Cate, who worked with me on clarifying the "Consolidate, Federate, and Secure" strategy as part of our executive briefing series. Special thanks to the Oracle ECM Product Management team, for the collaboration and idea-sharing around the concepts and strategies outlined in this book.

Most of all, thanks to my wife, Monica, for her unwavering support for creating this book, and for always being there when I needed her.

Additionally, Bex would like to thank...

Thanks to Frank Radichel, Sam White, and Alec Kloss for constantly challenging my ideas about technology. Thanks also to Tom Chaffee, with whom I've had numerous discussions about the "right way" to implement an enterprise software strategy. Thanks to the technology bloggers who influenced my thinking and writing style, some of whom I've never met: Bruce Schneier, Clay Shirky, Kathy Sierra, James McGovern, and Mark Masterson.

Finally, thanks mostly to my wife, Michelle Huff, who is one of the most insightful people I know. She helped me clarify my thoughts, helped me make the book's concepts flow more naturally, and as usual kept my spirits up when I had writer's block.

Introduction

Enterprise content management (ECM) is a broad category of software applications, whose goal is to gain control over your "unstructured content." Unstructured content includes any kind of information that does not follow a rigid pattern: e-mails, Web content, research reports, policies and procedures, videos, and other digital assets. This is in contrast to "structured content," which is generally applied to information stored inside a rigidly defined database table, and accessible through your enterprise applications.

Unstructured content is sometimes managed centrally, but too often it is strewn about your enterprise on shared file systems, Web applications, printed documents, archives, and USB thumb drives. This kind of content has unique problems when it comes to finding it, securing it, destroying it, and ensuring its authenticity.

As Jeetu Patel mentions in the Foreword to this book, the vast majority of your content is unstructured and poorly managed, despite the fact that it is frequently critical to how you do business. To make matters worse, this unstructured content is being generated at an ever-increasing rate, making more and more management problems. Over the past 20 years, many tools and techniques have emerged to try to rescue people from this "digital landfill," but nearly half of such initiatives fail.

We feel that this failure is because of incorrect focus. Instead of point-solutions that solve one problem, you should think strategically about every unstructured content problem. You should constantly push toward enterprise-wide solutions that can help all departments. This path is not easy. You need to overcome political turf wars between departments, and also accept the fact that no single tool will solve every problem you have. True enterprise content management is an initiative, not an application. Therefore, the best solutions need to be part of an interoperable ecosystem.

In this book, we present what we call a *Pragmatic Strategy for Enterprise Content Management. Clearly, unstructured content management is a complex and constantly changing field. As a result, no single piece of software will ever be able to fulfill all of your needs. A pragmatic strategy must recognize that different departments need different systems, sometimes from different vendors. The optimal strategy will gently press you to consolidate, but will never punish you if you determine that consolidation is not cost effective. Instead, it will help you make your unstructured content problems manageable, regardless of where you choose to store it.*

This book is structured to elaborate the main points behind our pragmatic strategy. You should read Chapters 1, 2, and 3 in order to get an understanding of the scope and context of the problem. After that, you may wish to jump around in Chapters 4, 5, and 6 to see some more specifics of the strategy. Chapters 7 and 8 discuss the future of technology, how enterprise content management fits in, and how your strategy will need to evolve.

This book is intended for both strategists and implementers. It presents high-level solutions for unstructured content problems that your CIO knows all too well. In addition, it also contains limited implementation details, so that your project managers know how to get started. There are not many books that attempt to do both, which we find surprising. The critical first step in aligning business and IT strategies is to ensure that everybody is speaking the same language, and to understand the needs of others. Our intention was to facilitate this by creating one single book that provides value to every member of your team.

We strongly encourage you to write in this book. Take notes when you find something of interest, and share your ideas with your team. We would also like you to dedicate yourself to changing at least three things about your current information management strategy. Since content management is about a culture of information sharing as much as it is about technology, we believe you will find useful techniques in this book, no matter whose technology you choose to implement your strategy.

CHAPTER 1

The State of
Information
Management

What is infoglut?

Infoglut is information overload. It is the inability to find what you need. It is skyrocketing storage costs, even when storage is getting cheaper. It is not knowing where to find authoritative information assets. It is the risk of not being able to find those assets at the instant they are needed by customers, employees, and auditors. It is too much data, and too few tools to manage it.

Infoglut is the inevitable byproduct of our digital world, compounded by Internet applications and Web 2.0 technologies. In a world where anybody can create e-mail, Web sites, digital photos, instant messages, or Microsoft Office documents, it's only a matter of time before everyone is overwhelmed. As Bruce Schneier says, "data is the pollution of the information age."

Ultimately, how can you transform your infoglut into strategic assets? How can you turn this massive amount of information into a competitive edge? How can you reduce the costs associated with maintaining this data? How can you secure your information? How should you wade through all this information to find what you need, when you need it, in the format you need?

The analyst firm IDC estimated that in the year 2006 the world created about 161 billion gigabytes of information. By 2010, they predict that the world will create 988 billion gigabytes of information *in one year.* That is a six-fold increase in only four years. How much of that total is because of your organization? How much data did you create in 2006? Are you prepared to manage six times as much by 2010?

The analyst firm Gartner believes that the first organizations who learn to transform infoglut into assets will gain a significant competitive edge over those who don't:

*Gartner DL, Newman D. Spotlight on Enterprise Information Management. June 2, 2006. "Effective information management will be critical in the next decade, differentiating those enterprises that will implode under the infoglut from those that will use it to dominate the global economy."

This goes beyond simply managing the storage of data, but also determining the value of the data. What content is relevant? To whom? Why? When? And in what format?

These trends are also affecting the role of the CIO in the enterprise. In July 2008, the IBM Governance council predicted that within four years the value of data will be a line item on a company's balance sheet. The CIO will have to quantify its worth to the CFO, and guarantee that the proper governance is in place to increase value and minimize risk. The purpose of this book is to set you on the path towards transforming your infoglut. It presents a plan for the vital first step: getting a handle on your unstructured content with a pragmatic enterprise content management strategy. Unstructured content is 80 percent of the infoglut problem, and if you can properly align your strategies, you could accomplish even more.

Information Management

Every organization has problems with information management. Enterprise information management is about one thing: *organizational knowledge*. In other words, it is about the *current state and direction of your organization*. It may seem like a strange question, but where does that information currently exist? Is it stored in highly structured database tables? Is it strewn about multiple employee laptops as Microsoft Office documents? Is it locked away, undocumented, in the minds of your employees?

Is this information entirely under your control, or is some of it in the hands of your customers, partners, and competitors? In an ideal world, where would you put it? How should it be secured? What is important to keep, and when should it be destroyed? How will people find it when they need to know it? And perhaps most important, how will people find it even if they *don't know* that they need it? If your unstructured content storage will increase by a factor of six in the next four years, will your current systems be able to manage it?

Enterprise content management (ECM) helps solve this problem. ECM is not just a line-of-business application, nor a framework, nor middleware, nor infrastructure. It is all these things, plus an *initiative* about creating a culture of information sharing. It's about people first, context second, content third, and technology last.

Every ECM vendor has a slightly different offering, but overall they agree on the following definition of ECM, created by the Association for Information and Image Management (AIIM) in 2006:

"Enterprise Content Management is the technologies used to Capture, Manage, Store, Preserve, and Deliver content and documents related to organizational processes. ECM tools and strategies allow the management of an organization's unstructured information, wherever that information exists."

This book describes a set of ECM tools and techniques that you can use to solve the fastest growing and hardest to manage part of the information management problem: unstructured content.

Structured Content vs. Unstructured Content

Information management experts usually talk about placing content into two types of systems: structured content repositories, or unstructured content repositories.

The term *structured content repositories* applies to highly organized data that is typically used by enterprise applications. This includes lists of employees, customers, products, orders, inventory, and purchases. The structured data is usually stored in a relational database with a rigidly defined structure. The purpose behind them is usually to help automate well-defined business processes: make sure all invoices are paid on time, keep track of inventory, or ensure all customers are contacted once per quarter. These repositories include common enterprise applications like enterprise resource planning (ERP), customer relationship management (CRM) systems, human resource management applications, as well as a plethora of home-grown database applications.

In contrast, *unstructured content repositories* are more free-form. They include anything that doesn't fit, or wasn't put, into your structured repository. They usually contain information needed by emerging processes, projects that are rapidly evolving, or initiatives that are difficult to define. This content is frequently used for communication, and is therefore frequently delivered through multiple channels. These may contain training documents, scanned paper documents, newsletters, research reports, e-mails, spreadsheets, contracts, specifications, Web content, audio and video assets, and the like.

The terms "structured" and "unstructured" are somewhat misleading. All information has structure of one form or another; otherwise, it would be impossible to understand. So shouldn't we only need structured content repositories? No.

This distinction is important not because of the *what*, but because of the *how*. What matters is not *what* the information is, but *how* it is created and consumed. In order to benefit from a structured repository, you need to define all possible data structures beforehand, and force your users to create information with a very strict process. These usually involve Web pages or desktop clients that require a great deal of highly specific data entry. In contrast, an unstructured repository would allow a contributor to insert information in any way that is convenient to the contributor; the repository transforms the content, and extracts useful information behind the scenes to add structure.

The unstructured content repositories exist because of the inevitable gaps in larger, more rigid enterprise applications. Even if you have an enterprise application for storing financial information, your employees are likely to store vital content in loosely structured Excel spreadsheets. They will also need to refer to scanned paper documents from these systems to verify that the data entry was correct in your financial application.

Why not store this unstructured content inside your enterprise application? Simple: structured repositories take time to properly design. It is easy to add a new table in a spreadsheet, but not to your database. Doing so can cause side effects to your financial application, and as a result, your IT department has complex rules about who can change it. The necessary change-management process is usually so long and complex, that your employees are likely to prefer doing their job by sending spreadsheets around via e-mail.

However, now you have another problem. How can you secure that important data in the spreadsheet? How will people find it again? How will they be able to change it, and ensure everybody works on the most recent revision? Solving that problem is the realm of ECM.

Process Workers vs. Knowledge Workers

In general, highly structured information repositories are usually designed for *process workers*. These people follow a well-defined process in order to accomplish their jobs. Their roles are highly *tactical*: accounts receivable, accounts payable, invoicing, shipping, HR forms processing, and the like. A structured content repository helps you streamline this process, and makes it more efficient.

However, this efficiency is a paradox: once a process can be automated, soon everybody will be doing it, and it ceases to be a competitive advantage! There is some value in being an early adopter, because then you are automating processes before anybody else. There is also value in being a late adopter, because then you can benefit from the commoditization of industry-specific enterprise applications.

In general, the reliance on process instead of people is a rapid race to the bottom. Competitive advantage comes from *creating* novel processes that give you an edge, or in being able to accomplish tasks where no clear process can yet be defined. These are sometimes called a *barely repeatable process,* and it is the role of *knowledge workers* to design them, or to get things done without them.

Naturally, knowledge workers both produce and consume a great deal of unstructured content. They need to find both specific and general information on a range of topics. They need instant access to determine what action to take, whether it is a documented process or not.

There is no clear line between the process worker and the knowledge worker: many people fill both roles at different times of the day. In fact, the best way to improve your process is frequently to empower your process workers to spend more time as knowledge workers.

As a result of this blurred line, a coherent information management strategy needs to understand where the automated process ends, where knowledge begins, and how they overlap. It is also vital to ensure that both process workers and knowledge workers get the tools they need to boost their productivity. Some of this is the role of ECM applications; some is the role of enterprise applications.

The Specific ECM Problem

The challenge with unstructured repositories is in managing the content after it is created. How should the contributor find it again? How should other people find it and reuse it in the future? When should it be archived or deleted? Should it be repurposed and published to other systems? How do you make sure that this content doesn't fall into the wrong hands?

According to most technology analysts, 80 percent of the useful information in your organization is unstructured content, as shown in Figure 1-1. Unfortunately, on average only 10 percent of this content is being properly managed in a repository. The rest resides in department-specific collaboration

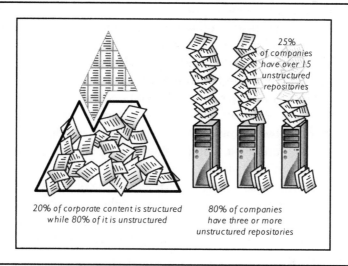

25%
of companies
have over 15
unstructured
repositories

20% of corporate content is structured
while 80% of it is unstructured

80% of companies
have three or more
unstructured repositories

FIGURE 1-1.   *The vast majority of useful content is unstructured and insufficiently managed.*

project spaces, shared disk drives, FTP servers, e-mail servers, home-grown applications, hosted applications, or desktops. All together, these systems have dozens of duplicate items; it is difficult to find content, let alone understand what's recent, and what's accurate. These systems are also not properly secured, and it's difficult for auditors or other departments to find and use this information.

In the ECM world, we call these systems *content silos*. According to industry analyst Gartner, nearly 80 percent of organizations have more than two unstructured content repositories, and 25 percent of organizations have over 15 such systems. This is why nearly 30 percent of an employee's time is spent just looking for information. If that weren't expensive enough, on average, 40 percent of your IT budget will be spent on integrations. Also, analyst firm IDC estimates that there are on average eight copies of every content item in your enterprise. Do you have the storage space for that? How about four years from now, when you need six times that?

Also, how risky is it to have so many copies of digital content sprawled around your enterprise? What happens if you are sued, and a judge demands that you produce relevant documents? The expense of finding relevant digital content—called eDiscovery—can be extraordinarily expensive: on average, one gigabyte of data will cost $2500 for a lawyer to review. Analyst firm Forrester believes that the market for eDiscovery alone will grow from $1.4 billion in 2006 to more than $4.8 billion in 2011.

If you had one unified system instead of 15, then your employees would be able to find what they need. You would have a "single source of truth," well integrated into your enterprise, allowing everyone to find the single authoritative version. You would have one system dictating who has access rights to the item and what the life cycle of the item needs to be in order to follow industry regulations. It would also properly destroy content once it is no longer relevant, minimizing legal risk. This yields significant cost saving. It means fewer IT resources spent on storage and integrations. It means knowledge workers can find what they need, when they need it, to become more efficient. And finally, it means a reduction in risk, because your content is secure, and it is retained according to the applicable business practices and industry regulations.

However, is it feasible to place all content into one single repository? Can one single system satisfy all of your content management needs? Will it continue to grow to meet all future needs? Historically speaking, the answer to this is no. Therefore, a good information management strategy needs to be dedicated to federation as well as consolidation in order to be effective in the future.

Instead of focusing on content management, your strategy should focus on *making content manageable*, no matter where it exists.

The Unstructured Content Problem

As stated, the main problem is infoglut. For many years information management centered on the goal of "information at your fingertips"—the idea that access to content and data was the key to knowledge management. Vast enterprise-wide visions were provided at leadership forums and IT conferences focusing on users that would have instant access to information from wherever they happen to be working. The state of information management 20, or even 10, years ago was such that the vision of instant access to information seemed to solve the majority of knowledge problems in the workplace.

This is understandable. Twenty years ago, most content went through an information broker of some kind, and often had a physical location. If you needed a report you went to a person who had the report in a drawer. An old memo might be in a nearby filing cabinet or perhaps down in the basement archives. The fact that information was not readily available was, by most accounts, the major barrier to collaboration and knowledge sharing.

Technology has made massive strides forward in information access. In most cases, users do have the ability to get to a massive amount of content directly and easily from their desktop, if they know where to look. Often the information that was once hidden away by information brokers and scattered across the enterprise in physical repositories is now available immediately. Provided that the information brokers are motivated to share information, and allow others to access their once hidden data, we can move beyond this problem of content "silos" that hoard information. We can instead place all of this information online in a readily accessible format.

However, this solution has led to a new set of challenges. Organizations must now contend with providing the *right* access to information. That is, more specifically, they must secure the information that is now so readily available—a problem previously solved in many cases by the existence of an information broker. They must also enable consumers to find their content quickly, and ensure that it's accurate.

Additionally, despite the fact that digital information no longer has a fixed location, people still organize it as they would organize files in a giant folder. This mentality has led to its own kind of content silos. Only those with the proper training can navigate the arcane taxonomies that were useful to information brokers, but incomprehensible to everyone else.

In short, by breaking down these content silos, you have created a flood of information that overwhelms your users. Some of it is very useful, and you would never have found it if you had to contend with an information broker. However, most of this content is not relevant, leading to infoglut. How can your users find what they need and make sure it's authoritative, recent, and secure? How can they find what they need when they don't even know if it exists?

Adding to the Problem

In almost any organization, information is scattered between hard drives on user computers, shared network drives, e-mail inboxes, databases, content management systems, miscellaneous Web and FTP servers, and within individual applications. Users have a need to store this information within the context of the places where they work. This need explains the myriad of locations across which content is scattered for any given user.

As an example, think of the way the average business document is created, such as a knowledge worker creating a presentation in Microsoft PowerPoint. They begin by creating a presentation file on their laptop computer. That file is stored on the local file system, perhaps in their

Documents folder as the user works on the document locally as the sole owner of the presentation. Multiple versions of the document may be saved as different revisions, commonly using file naming standards such as "preso_V1.ppt" and "preso_V2.ppt." This is done manually by the user since most operating systems do not currently provide standard versioning capabilities in their core file storage system. As the document nears completion others are asked to contribute to the document and also to review its contents, often by e-mail.

Now a collection of additional users collaborate on the presentation using the native application to view and edit the content, again, often saving their edits and changes as unique new files called something like "preso_V1_apm.ppt" or "preso_V1_bex.ppt" to reflect the changes made by a specific user. Those changes are then sent out to the group for review. Now, in addition to the multiple copies on the original author's local file system, we have copies of various revisions on local file systems of the different users as well as throughout the e-mail inboxes of all the participants. If the file is large, they sometimes participate via shared file systems or FTP servers instead of e-mail.

Once the document completes this review process, it may be published and distributed. This may put additional copies of the finished document in various locations within the network. It may also extend the number of copies outside the firewall if the document is e-mailed or uploaded somewhere external. Other users may store the document in locations to share with their peers. Very quickly we have different versions of the same document in different states stored across e-mail, network shares, e-mail inboxes, and even at third-party locations. In essence, the way in which we work with content today perpetuates the root problem of storing documents in decentralized, inconsistent ways.

There is also the core issue of access and process. Consider how the goals of knowledge workers conflict with the goals of process workers. A process worker needs a robust enterprise application to store highly structured data about the state of the business. These systems contain vast amounts of useful information, locked away so only a select few can access it. The information is highly structured and typically accessed via the enterprise application interface. The process workers need that level of control to secure the structured information and ensure its integrity.

Now consider the knowledge worker, who needs reports from those systems in order to plan for the future. In many cases, knowledge workers are not granted sufficient access to those systems, but they absolutely need access in order to properly do their job. This creates a strong incentive to make them violate the security policy through cajoling or favors to get access to the sensitive data. They then promptly analyze the data, save their results in a spreadsheet, and share it with their team members via e-mail or shared drives.

The result? Your highly sensitive raw data is now stored, along with an even more sensitive analysis of the data, in an unsecured spreadsheet. One misdirected e-mail, one lost laptop, or one disgruntled employee is the only thing between you and a critical security leak.

In order to make sure that your employees can find the information they need, when they need it, in the right format, and with the right security,

What's in Your Digital Landfill?

According to the Department of Commerce, US companies spend $91.9 billion in non-capitalized expenditures and $141.6 billion in capital expenditures on IT each year. What is troubling is that most of that is spent on "structured" information. But that leaves an entire world of information untouched: the world that I like to call the "digital landfill." This is the place where all the application files, images, web pages, text messages, e-mails, and a host of other bits and pieces of electronic information wind up. For the most part, these are unmanaged and out of control.

There is a growing awareness in organizations that the digital landfill is a problem. A recent IDC analysis concluded that by 2011, the "digital universe" will be ten times as big as it was only two years ago. A lot of this information is business critical, and yet poorly managed.

Our user surveys tell us that on a scale of 1 (terrible) to 10 (excellent) 54 percent would give themselves a grade of 5 or less in terms of the effectiveness of their organization in managing information. 90 percent of organizations view their ability to manage electronic information as critical to their future, yet 52 percent of organizations have "little or no confidence" that their electronic information is "accurate, accessible, and trustworthy."

ECM is emerging as a mainstream industry to help solve these problems, but it has barely begun to tap the massive opportunities available.

—John Mancini,
President, Association for Information
and Image Management (AIIM)

you need *in-context enterprise content management*. This means being able to slide content management into the normal business process of your knowledge workers. You need to ensure that they do not need to significantly alter their habits, in order to take advantage of ECM. Ensuring that your documents are up to date should be as easy as opening them up on your desktop. Securing your documents should be effortless, and they should remain secure even when taken out of the repository. An enterprise application should be able to present unstructured content to the end user, without that user needing to leave the content of their application.

Why Do I Need ECM for Unstructured Content?

Almost any database application can store unstructured content. If you treat it like binary data, you can just store it in a table and have simple rules for managing revisions. That's content management, right? Not quite. There's a huge difference between revision control and enterprise scale management of unstructured content.

Does your system encourage findability and reuse, or is it just another content silo? Does your system encourage good information architecture, or is it merely allowing content to proliferate in chaotic new ways? Do you need workflows or subscriptions to control notifications about changes in the content? Do you need to store descriptive information alongside this document—commonly called *metadata*—such as title, keywords, or department to help people find and process this content? How about allowing people to make comments or annotate the content? Can you transform the content from one format to another so people get the content however they need? What parts of your business process can you automate with unstructured content services like routing, notifications, or conversion? How easy is it to integrate your system with an externally defined security policy? Are you confident that your system can scale to a billion content items? Are you confident that you have the tools you need to properly administer a repository of that size?

By way of comparison, every enterprise application needs to manage users, passwords, and access rights. When network applications were new, it was common for every application to maintain their own user database. When new systems came online, administrators might migrate the entire user repository to the new system, or they might just re-create the users they needed.

However, as the number of systems grew, architects found that they could no longer ensure that all systems had the correct user information, nor were they confident that all systems were properly updated when employees entered or left the company. It was simply too difficult to manage user data in every application, even if every application needed user data. This ultimately led to centralized user repositories and identity management systems. Modern enterprise applications integrate with these systems, instead of trying to replicate the functionality. This ensures best-of-breed technology and easier administration.

Enterprise content management solves a parallel problem. Your enterprise has dozens of applications that need unstructured content. They need to find it, display it, and change it. They also need assurance that the content follows the proper compliance and security policies. They need content services to repurpose assets for the Web, for handheld devices, or for marketing brochures. They also need a guarantee that the item is authoritative: once one application changes the item, all should view the new revision. There should be no proliferation of copies. And finally, at the end of the content item's life cycle, these applications need assurance that the item will be properly archived or destroyed.

In short, your enterprise applications need enterprise content management.

ECM Is Empowerment, Not Control

The primary driver behind old document management solutions was to ease the burden for a small team that produced large quantities of complex documents. People needed systems that guaranteed to have the most recent version of items, along with authoring tools to assist in the creation of very large documents such as books, legal contracts, or product documentation. These tools had value in helping experts create documents, but not for average users to create or find useful information. These old systems catered to the expert creator, not the average creator, nor the consumer.

One of the primary goals behind modern content management is to empower contributors. Sometimes this takes the form of giving power users extremely complex tools that help them author complex documents. In other cases, it means allowing people to contribute content to a knowledge base or a Web site without having to be retrained to use a new tool or a new technology.

Web content management changed this ecosystem in the early part of this decade. As people placed content on Web sites for easy access, suddenly the number of Web sites proliferated. Some organizations had thousands of Web sites, and you needed to know HTML in order to update them. This turned the webmaster into a bottleneck for updating the information on those sites, and stale content proliferated.

The solution was to empower both the webmaster and the content creators. The webmaster needed powerful tools to control the overall look and feel of the site. Contributors needed simple tools that enabled them to quickly and easily modify Web content. Together, this creates the best of both worlds: Web sites that conformed to branding guidelines and IT standards, but allowed untrained users to keep the content updated.

A content management system needs to stay focused on the needs of all users of the system: contributors, consumers, managers, administrators, and developers. It needs tools of varying degrees of complexity in order to help each of them create, find, share, and manage content.

It should empower all contributors, not just the experts. It should empower consumers, so they can find information regardless of how the contributor chose to organize it. It should empower developers, by giving them the tools they need to integrate with ECM, and never again be the bottleneck in content authoring.

Centralized Policies for Decentralized Information

The goal of a pragmatic ECM strategy is not to force you to place all content into a single repository. Although this is desirable, it is not always practical. Instead, a pragmatic ECM strategy forces you to centralize your policy, and then has tools that allow you to enforce that policy wherever content may exist.

In the past, IT centralization went through a curious series of boom-bust cycles. In order to reduce costs and enforce consistency, IT laid down the rules about what information management systems to use, what languages to use, and what frameworks to use. Unfortunately, over-centralized IT usually led to insulation from the needs of the business. This meant that IT and business strategies failed to properly align themselves.

Unfortunately, non-aligned strategies inevitably lead to application proliferation. Departments install line-of-business solutions without IT approval to help them become more efficient or collaborate more effectively. These include hosted solutions, open source applications, or easy-to-install collaboration tools. This may even include applications that are difficult to secure and maintain, but are still valuable because they perform a specialized function that helps one business unit meet their objectives. Because these systems were set up without IT approval, the odds are low that the business units put sufficient thought into how IT should manage or integrate with these systems. Unfortunately, as soon as these systems become business-critical, IT will be forced to maintain them and integrate with them.

In practice, the more centralized your IT policy is, the more likely it is to not satisfy the needs of all users. As Web 2.0 collaboration tools become more commoditized, individual departments will inevitably set up systems outside of central control.

Even if your IT department has 100 percent control over all your business units, there is always the looming problem with mergers and acquisitions. What if your organization merges with another: what should you do with their content management applications? How long will it take to consolidate all the information? Is 100 percent centralization always cost-effective?

A pragmatic ECM system needs to be aware of these problems, and needs to solve it through innovation, not control. A pragmatic ECM strategy needs several pieces. It needs a repository that *could* satisfy the needs of all users and all formats, but doesn't require you to configure it this way. It needs to be an infrastructure that all your applications can use. It needs to support middleware, and act as middleware, to easily integrate with multiple systems across your enterprise. Finally, it needs simple federation tools that extend the reach of content management services to legacy applications that are difficult or cost-prohibitive to change. And finally, it needs to ensure the content is secure, no matter where it exists.

That is the core of the pragmatic ECM strategy, which is the subject of the remainder of this book.

How You Should Use This Book

The purpose of this book is to help you change your business. However, that will not happen unless you take specific action. To get the most out of this book, I would advise you to follow Seth Godin's sage advice on how to read any book about business strategy.

First, decide that you will change three things about how you work today. At least three. We will present hundreds of options in this book, but if you only change the three things that you need the most, your organization will benefit greatly from the time you spent reading. The purpose of this book is not to force you to implement a grand 10,000-point plan that you must follow to the letter in order to achieve ECM, nor is it to sell you any specific product. The purpose is to teach you how ECM is an initiative, not an application. It's about creating a culture that shares information, so it's reusable, secure, and findable. A pragmatic ECM strategy requires a good deal of initial planning, but will always be a moving target. Dedicate yourself to making three important changes, decide what those three things are while reading this book, then use the book as guidance for how to change.

Second, write on this book. Your time is far more valuable than the paper you hold in your hands, so take notes! Use a highlighter and mark up the sections that you find most important to you. At the very least, take notes on paper, and leave them in the book. What three changes seem like they would have the best return on investment? What actions should you take to get there? What might be an easy way to improve on how you are doing business today?

Third, share this information with your team. This book was designed to be primarily an ECM strategy book, but it also contains information useful for implementation. You should share this book with your ECM team to make sure that everybody is speaking the same language. This book should make sense to every member of your ECM Center of Excellence, which is a cross-departmental team that brings your ECM visions to reality (covered in Chapter 3). Your Center of Excellence is vital to keeping IT and business aligned, and this book helps you communicate and realize that value.

Takeaways

- Easy access to online information has not solved the knowledge management problem; instead, it has created *infoglut*.

- Infoglut is information overload: the inability to find what you need in the ocean of information.

- Enterprise content management (ECM) solves 80 percent of the infoglut problem: finding content, securing content, ensuring content is authoritative, destroying it properly, and reducing storage costs.

- ECM is about empowerment, not control.

- Centralized policies, along with strategic integrations and federated tools, help extend content management services beyond the ECM repository.

CHAPTER
2

A Pragmatic ECM
Architecture

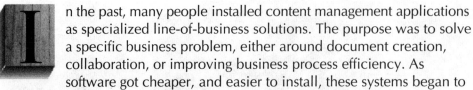n the past, many people installed content management applications as specialized line-of-business solutions. The purpose was to solve a specific business problem, either around document creation, collaboration, or improving business process efficiency. As software got cheaper, and easier to install, these systems began to proliferate across the enterprise. The problem was that nobody was thinking strategically about these applications. These line-of-business solutions had value for individual departments; however, they were not deployed strategically. The installers sometimes did not consult other departments, or even IT, before setting them up.

Content management point solutions are much more common than enterprise-wide solutions. As we will show in this chapter, solving the problem at the enterprise level is difficult because of both technical and political reasons. Some departments are quite happy with their point solutions: they help one specific team collaborate better, or they make one specific business function more efficient. A pragmatic ECM system cannot neglect these systems. Instead, it must grow out of them.

There is no single piece of software that can satisfactorily solve all information management problems. Even if you could start fresh today with the latest technologies and the best enterprise architecture, you will always have future requirements about integrating with legacy systems, business partners, and applications beyond your sphere of control. This may include old systems created without IT approval, new partner initiatives, or the inevitable pains caused when two organizations merge.

What is needed is a distributed model for information management—one that gives the option of placing all content in a single repository, but doesn't require it. Such a model would include a combination of tools that give you the power to choose when the time is right to migrate content into a unified repository. If the time is not right for consolidation, then your content management system should not punish you; instead, it should provide you with tools that empower you to store your content in any repository you wish. These tools should help you find information, secure it, and manage it, no matter where it exists.

This approach is the cornerstone of what we call a pragmatic ECM strategy, which acknowledges the reality of your heterogeneous environment. However, the goal is still the same: provide content in the right context to your user, as well as tools for IT to consistently control and manage multiple systems. This in-context content management provides seamless access to content from within the context of the appropriate application. These applications may reside on a desktop (such as Microsoft Office or Microsoft Windows Explorer), they might be e-mail clients, e-mail servers, portal servers, or enterprise applications such as Siebel, Oracle E-Business Suite, or SAP. The content may exist in a variety of underlying repositories, databases, or other storage mechanisms, but this is abstracted from the end user. The application benefits from content management in a way that's invisible to the end user; content management is something that the application or the infrastructure inherently provides. This goal is achievable with a combination of technologies, both from the Oracle stack and outside. In this chapter, we use this model to present a strategy for in-context ECM, which you can use as a template to modify to suit your needs.

Context Is King

As mentioned in Chapter 1, people don't just want access to content: they want access to the *right* content. This means analyzing the users, their common tasks, and their environment, to generate *context*. Based on this context, you then display the right information to the right user at the right time. The ability to quickly access information about a topic is substantially more valuable if that access is provided at the time it is required, in the format that is necessary, and from within the context to which that information can be acted upon.

The same rule applies when managing that information. The more context that is available around enterprise content management tools and assets, the more value they provide. Our goal here is to provide a reference architecture that provides a strategic infrastructure and tools that can be leveraged to provide ECM capabilities within the context of line-of-business applications, enterprise applications, infrastructure tools, and end-user collaboration.

Managing information in context means that users can access and edit content within the application of choice. They can also enhance content by adding feedback, or repurpose the content for different applications. There are some examples of this paradigm already in effect in some areas of enterprise content management. Web content management (WCM) is a great example. Five or six years ago most content displayed on a Web page was edited in an application far removed from the Web site. That meant that contributors would place documents in one system, then a webmaster would process those documents (often manually converting them to Web formats), and publish them to another system for viewing. In such an environment, it would take a long time for content contributors to know what their changes would look like; they would have to wait until it was fully processed by a Web developer, and the change process would be long and slow.

In contrast, today every mature Web content management system uses in-context editing. The process for changing a Web page involves a knowledge worker navigating to a Web page and editing the document directly in the Web browser. The content contributor never needs to ask a developer to make a change, and the contributor can preview the changes in the context of the entire Web site. The fact that the user works in the context of the Web site, as shown in Figure 2-1, means the process is faster, more intuitive, and less prone to error. This ensures up-to-date content, and empowers many people cross the enterprise to become contributors.

FIGURE 2-1.   *In-context editing is extremely helpful for Web content management.*

Similarly, workflows for Web content are also in context. When a contributor changes something on your public facing Web site, you will most likely want a team to review and approve those changes. Typically, these reviewers receive an e-mail that the content has changed, after which they log into the Web site and view the new content. They can approve or reject the changes from the context of the Web site. Until the new content is fully approved, all other users will continue to see the older, previously approved content.

A common example of this on the Web is the approval of comments on a Web site. In many cases, Web site managers moderate any comments from public viewers. This means that the moderator will see all the comments on the site, whereas a typical user would only see the approved comments.

However, more than just access and editing can be done in context; the metadata for the content is also available from within the context of the appropriate applications. You can also enable in-context security by wrapping an extra encryption layer around your content, as discussed in detail in Chapter 6. Finally, you can also achieve in-context records management by empowering multiple applications to apply global records management policies, which ensures compliance with regulations about document retention, no matter where those documents reside.

The key to enterprise-wide context is a unified approach to information management. This means that your enterprise applications need to be able to easily pass information between each other, so that not only can they view content from a centralized repository, but also share the context of the information request: who is making the request, for what reason, and what task are they trying to accomplish? There are several ways to ensure your applications can achieve this interoperability, such as a service-oriented architecture (SOA) and enterprise service bus (ESB), industry- or application-specific standards, or simply an enterprise-wide naming convention for resources. These options are discussed in greater detail in Chapter 4.

The Content Life Cycle

Information typically moves through a standard life cycle, beginning with the creation of the content itself and ending in the eventually permanent retention or destruction (deletion) of the content. While some aspects of the content life cycle, shown in Figure 2-2, are common in almost all content management systems, we will attempt to highlight key features and capabilities

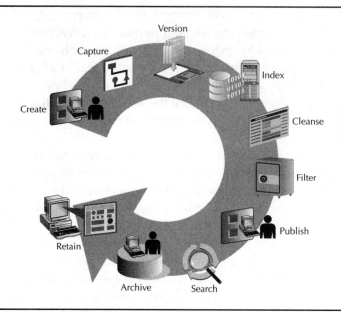

FIGURE 2-2. *The full life cycle for most business content.*

that are sometimes absent from basic content repositories in addition to outlining each aspect of the life cycle for those who are unfamiliar with the terminology. The content life cycle may span multiple systems, different integrations, and usually extends across multiple user contexts.

The content life cycle begins with the creation of content. Imagine that a member of your HR department wishes to distribute the latest policies and procedures. She would begin by creating the new document with a desktop application, such as Microsoft Word, and then manually submit it to the system. She could do this with a Web form, or more commonly with desktop tools that allow her to effortlessly save it to the repository.

Alternatively, the content could be submitted automatically by an enterprise application. This content might be in the form of reports, or a batch of images from a high-volume scanner. In the latter case, the original content is a hard copy, and needs to be digitized as part of the submission process. This is called "capture" in the content life cycle. Capture is usually accomplished by scanning a hard copy item into a digital representation. The digital representation may contain the actual text of the hard copy or it may simply be an image of the document. If the text is abstracted it is usually done through optical character recognition (OCR). Creation and capture are sometimes combined into a step called "contribution."

After the content is created and/or captured, it is stored in the content management system as a "version" or "revision." You may have submitted a completely unique content item—such as a new scanned invoice—or it may be a new revision of an existing item—such as an update to the existing HR policies and procedures. Versioning is important, so that you can refer back to older revisions of the content item as needed. Many systems also include difference analysis tools, so you can easily spot what has changed between two versions of a content item.

It is important to draw a distinction between *versions* and *renditions*. A *version* of a document represents a point in time for the document. For example, version 3 of your HR policies and procedures precedes version 4, where version 4 has new edits and changes to the document from version 3. A *rendition* of a document is a format of a document, perhaps a PDF or an HTML view of the document based on a specific branding template. Your HR department may want to generate an HTML page based on the new policies, so it can be more easily viewed on your employee portal. This HTML page is not a new version of the content; it is simply a new way of consuming the content in the existing version.

The *indexing* phase involves extracting the text from the content, and placing it in a full-text search engine. This indexing step also places relevant metadata into the index, such as title, author, comments, project, and the security classification of the item. This helps people find the content again by performing a search for specific keywords. For example, the HR policies and procedures may contain information about which vacation days your employees will receive. So, when an employee searches for "vacation days," they will find this item in their search results. Searching is an important part of being able to find content, but by itself it cannot solve all of your problems. See Chapter 5 for a longer discussion of enterprise search, and the extra tools you need.

One unique—but important—phase of the life cycle is content *cleansing*. This involves inspecting the content for hidden information that may still be embedded in your documents without your knowledge. This may include the e-mail address or user name of the person who created it, or it might also contain paragraphs that you believe you had deleted. For example, if your HR employee created the policies and procedures document with Microsoft Word with the Track Changes option enabled, all your deleted content may still be embedded in your documents! Naturally, this can cause security leaks, as well as seriously embarrassing situations. This stage of the life cycle is discussed in more detail in Chapter 6.

Once content is in the system, cataloged by the search engine, and cleansed, it is available for consumption by end users. Users can consume content either via a push mechanism, such as publishing or subscriptions, or via a pull mechanism. Pull mechanisms involve browsing for content by navigating through a Web site, searching based on text in the content, or querying content metadata such as title or project name. More recently, many systems have adopted a model of allowing their end users to comment or suggest keyword for items, so that others can more easily find it. This kind of content enhancement is commonly called *tagging*, and is covered in more detail in Chapter 8. Your users can also annotate the item by drawing notes and suggestions on it, or even ranking it on a 1–5 point scale.

As information ages it may become irrelevant, less relevant, or only relevant for historical purposes. By historical we don't mean strictly archives for the ages—in some cases your archives need to be active at an instant for auditing or compliance purposes. Some records, for example, may have a useful lifespan that is indefinite, as the information may be part of an official filing—such as a filing with the United States Securities and Exchanges Commission (SEC). Other records must be retained for a specific period of time, such as a patient medical record that must be destroyed after seven years.

In ECM terminology, *life cycle management* is intended to incorporate the entire life cycle of content. However, in some cases people who talk about life cycle management only focus on the end of the life cycle. For precision, throughout this book we use the terms "archiving" and "retention management" for the later stages of the life cycle. Retention reflects the policy governing the time period we must keep a document for, or the process by which we audit and destroy obsolete information. Archiving is the capability and model used for long-term storage of inactive content that is not ready for disposition (destruction), but is no longer actively being consumed.

In summary, all your business content is somewhere in this life cycle: e-mail, contracts, Web pages, Web sites, reports, white papers, images, and video. Either your content is being created, being captured, or it already exists in your system. Perhaps it is being published to other sites, or people are actively searching for it in your central repository. Perhaps it is no longer of use, so it is archived or destroyed. Your users may also wish to enhance the value of this content while in its life cycle, with comments, annotations, or tagging. All this content needs to be managed centrally so that you get the right information to the right people in the right context. You also need to manage the costs and risks associated with content being sprawled across your enterprise. The challenges inherent to content management are discussed below.

Primary ECM Challenges

Throughout the book we are going to discus different kinds of content management systems, content infrastructure, content-centric applications, external applications, security measures, and other content-related topics. Some of these topics may be common knowledge to ECM practitioners; others reflect the future strategy behind Oracle's ECM product line and may therefore be new concepts. Throughout the book, we will guide you towards creating a pragmatic content management strategy for your organization.

Before doing so, you will need to be able to answer several key questions about your information management needs in several key areas. You needn't have answers to all these questions right now; however, you will need to create a team that can find these answers.

Taxonomy and Metadata

Briefly, *metadata* means "data about data." Every content repository has some support for metadata, even shared file systems. In simpler repositories, you usually can only store metadata such as title, creation data, and usually the size of a file. In more advanced systems, you can use custom metadata fields such as Project Name, Comments, and Author.

The metadata is applied to the document, but the terms you use are specific to how you do business. If you are in manufacturing, you may use terms like "Part Number" or "SKU" to identify a specific item. However, do you use one term or both? Do different departments use different terms?

From a functional perspective, metadata is best described as *an investment in the findability of your information.* Your contributors spend a great deal of time creating new content, and putting it into a shared repository. However, if they want anybody to ever find their content in the future, they need to go the extra step and add metadata: a thoughtful title, some keywords, a summary in the comments field, appropriate values for your custom taxonomy, and so on.

Unfortunately, not many contributors understand the value of metadata, and find it tedious to supply it. This is especially true if your company uses a complex taxonomy for every document, and insists that people fill out large amounts of metadata for every item contributed. This problem is addressed further in Chapter 3. For now, it's important to focus on the following questions:

- What metadata fields do you typically use to describe content in your organization?

- Do different departments have different names for the same thing? Have you ever generated a thesaurus for your business units?

- Do each of your line-of-business applications organize and define information with different terms or different taxonomies? Can you rationalize these terms and taxonomies into a shared metadata model?

- Is this taxonomy meant for contributors, or consumers as well? Does your taxonomy make sense to both consumers and contributors? Are you sure?

- Do you have a controlled thesaurus for your organization, which maps non-standard words to the preferred terms? For example, assume a project name changes from Amber to Topaz. If somebody searches for information on project Amber, will they find new content, stale content, or no content?

- Do people outside your organization or department use the same taxonomy structure to describe content, or do you have to deal with multiple taxonomies?

- Do your users complain about filling in too many metadata fields? Do they leave a lot of them blank, as the default, or do they hastily fill them with unhelpful information?

- Does your metadata give a "return on investment?"

- Does your average user provide better metadata than auto-categorization software?

Findability

Findability is simply a measure of how easy it is to find content once it's in your system. Some people focus on a complex metadata model, and then encourage users to run complex search queries to find content. However, it would be a mistake to focus entirely on searching as a means to find content.

In addition to searching, you need browse-able systems where people can peruse the available information and find content that's related to their needs. Your system should monitor behavior, and make recommendations based on user history and preferences. To determine the findability of your information, ask yourself:

- Can your audience quickly and easily find the information they are looking for?

- Can they easily find content *related* to what they are looking for?

- Does your system anticipate what content your audience might need, whether or not your audience knows about it?

- How do your users prefer to browse for content? Do they prefer to look based on project, topic, task, or something else?

- Does your system allow one item to have multiple "locations" in your system, or is it locked down in an inflexible folder structure?

- Can users sort and group information to suit their needs—even as a consumer?

- How do your end users enhance the findability of information once it is already contributed to the system? Bookmarks? Recommendations? Ratings?

- Can people find content, and collaborate on it in the same system? What are their collaboration needs?

Accuracy

Having a content repository is useless, unless your users trust that the information is accurate and up to date. A common problem with having multiple content repositories is that people don't know where to go to find definitive answers. Users need a *single source of truth* in your environment to ensure that your knowledge workers are basing their business decisions on the appropriate information.

What if your engineers are designing exactly what you told them to design, but they are using last week's diagram? What if your legal team is finalizing a contract, but you just recently renegotiated for better terms? What if your sales people are presenting a product strategy to an important customer, but upper management changed that PowerPoint presentation last month? What if your salesperson is putting a quote together for a customer using an outdated price list? If people cannot find authoritative information, they will make bad decisions. After enough bad decisions, they will grow to distrust your content management system, and ultimately revert to a manual process for gathering information. This includes multiple phone calls and multiple meetings, to slowly and painfully ensure that everyone is on the same page.

Some of this is a technology problem: your system needs to make it easy for people to find authoritative information, and ideally that information would notify you when it's out of date. However, it is also a cultural problem: people need to see the value of information sharing, and the importance of keeping documents up to date.

This single source of truth is a vital component of any enterprise content management system, and should be a primary part of the architecture. You can also use client-side tools to help syndicate content to the desktop, and help notify users when their documents are out of date. See Chapters 4 and 6 for extended discussions of the technical aspects, and the end of Chapter 3 for some solutions to the social aspects. For now, keep in mind the following questions:

- How confident are you that when people find content, it is still relevant?

- What is the current business process for finding up-to-date information? Are your users comfortable connecting to an online repository, or will they need desktop clients that make things simpler?

- How do users verify the authority and authenticity of content, especially printed content?

- Do your users work offline frequently, and need pop-up reminders when content is out of date?

- What errors do you encounter with out-of-date content items, and how can you adjust your business process to reduce these errors?

- When content is out of date, should you move it out of the knowledge base and into an archive? If so, what is the life cycle of your content items?

- Is it obvious to your users when they come across an outdated document?

- Does your system guide you to authoritative content, even if you search using old terms, and old methods?

- Do you need to translate documents into other languages? If so, how can your users be certain that the translated documents are kept in sync with the originals?

- Do you have an ever-expanding intranet, where users have to wade through a sea of outdated information to find what they need?

Security

Security is a complex problem in the enterprise. Some users are hesitant to share information, for fear that it might wind up in the wrong hands. Sometimes it's confidential information that shouldn't be shared outside an organization, other times it's personal and private information about your employees, customers, suppliers, or partners. Other times, your users may be so accustomed to free and open information on the Web, that they don't see the value in spending time determining the proper security classification.

In order to trust the system, you need a security model that is powerful, flexible, and simple to use. You shouldn't force your users to make complex security decisions: the system should do as much as possible for them to prevent errors. Once content is in the system, you need to ensure that it will also be secure *outside* the system. Chapter 6 discusses most of the security problems in detail; for now, be mindful of the following challenges:

- How do you ensure that your information is secure in your information repositories?

- How do you ensure that the information is safe when *taken out* of your secure environment?

■ Is your security model both sophisticated enough for your needs, but simple enough for your users to make the right choices?

■ Can your ECM system cleanly integrate with your existing Active Directory, LDAP, or single sign-on system?

■ Who has the rights to access the information? What is the audit trail associated with your security infrastructure?

■ What are the risks associated with accidental leakage of confidential information? How likely is it, and what damage will it cause? Do you have a recovery plan?

Risk Reduction and Regulatory Compliance

Some government regulations require you to keep archives of documents for specific time periods: two years, seven years, thirty years, or even longer. Regulations or business practices that require records management dictate that you keep documents for a fixed number of years after a certain event occurs: an employee is terminated, a project is completed, a contract is signed, or your organization publicly announces some information. This practice is commonly called records management, and there are numerous regulations about how different kinds of records must be kept.

In contrast, retention management is about destroying documents according to a defined policy, in order to minimize storage costs, as well as minimize legal risk. Remember: anything that persists in digital storage is discoverable in a lawsuit, and pleading about the costs of legal discovery is rarely a viable defense. For example, during the discovery process, you will be forced to reproduce old e-mails, existing documents, information displayed on your Web site, even access logs. You will be forced to go through all this information manually, in order to find digital information that might be relevant to the case.

To put this in perspective, as of 2008 one gigabyte of data costs around $0.25 to store on a disk, but costs about $2500 for a lawyer to review. Naturally, if you could purge your e-mail archives of old, outdated, duplicate, and useless information, the costs of legal discovery are significantly reduced. Likewise, if you could have one single point of entry to search all your repositories, and "freeze" documents to prevent their alteration, you could minimize the costs of finding relevant documents in the first place. This is the role of records and retention management, covered in detail in Chapter 5.

Records and retention management may have somewhat opposing goals, but their function is remarkably similar. These are discussed in greater detail in Chapter 5. For now, keep in mind the following challenges:

■ Are you confident that your critical business documents are secured in a tamper-proof system to ensure their integrity?

■ If you are involved with a lawsuit, can you guarantee that both electronic and physical records are securely preserved, and can be quickly produced?

■ Do you have strict compliance or regulatory obligations that state how you must handle information? Can your current ECM infrastructure—e-mail, knowledge base, Web sites—easily adhere to these policies?

■ Does your existing records management policy apply equally to digital and paper documents? Or, is your current strategy to just retain backup tapes? How difficult would it be to recover old information on those backup tapes?

■ In the event of an audit, what will you need to produce? Documents? Audit trails of the documents? Evidence of the life cycle of the documents?

■ How much legal risk do you have if you keep all of your information—including old e-mails—around forever? Are you prepared to destroy potentially useful information to minimize this risk?

■ Is your retention policy providing a good return on the money being spent on storage? In other words, are you paying money to retain content that has little value, but a lot of risk?

■ Who currently sets your e-mail retention policies—your IT department or your Legal department? Are both groups in agreement on the efficacy of this policy?

■ Can you audit access to information in documents in the same way you audit access to enterprise applications or databases?

Flexibility and Manageability

Enterprise applications like ERP systems may take a long time to deploy, but they rarely need to be changed. In these kinds of applications, we have a very clearly defined problem, and a clear data structure, and flexibility is usually not a primary concern.

In contrast, the goal behind enterprise content management is to manage unstructured information, which by definition is a less well-defined problem, and requires a great deal of flexibility. Business content does not always have a clear structure, and it changes frequently. People often need to change the names of projects, alter their taxonomies, and update their keywords. In addition, your ECM system must integrate with dozens of enterprise applications in multiple ways, so that it can be the single source of truth as often as possible.

As a result, the best ECM systems are not merely applications; they are also *frameworks* or middleware for creating new content management applications. That is the only way you can guarantee that your ECM system will be able to evolve to solve tomorrow's content management problems. Other flexibility challenges are described below:

- Does this system have the correct foundation—such as a service-oriented architecture—that enables easy integration with other systems?

- Can the system easily "outsource" functionality to other enterprise systems? Such as using an existing identity management system, business intelligence system, or a workflow process management tool?

- Does your ECM system have a complete framework for extending the system with components, or application plug-ins?

- Can you easily modify both the appearance, and the behavior of your ECM system?

- Is the system easy to administer and maintain? Can you quickly change the taxonomy, alter the configuration, patch the system, and migrate content to other systems?

- Is it easy to migrate content out of the system, and into another one? Assume you centralize all content into one place, but five years later something better comes on the market. How difficult is it to move content from one system to another?

Usability

A common failing of ECM initiatives is to ignore the problem of usability. Most enterprise applications—such as ERP or CRM systems—are generally designed for *process workers* (although some of this is changing with the next generation of business intelligence driven enterprise applications). The power users for these ERP and CRM systems are people who are well trained in a specific business process, and they use a specific application in order to do that aspect of their job. In fact, it would be impossible for them to do their job unless they used the specific enterprise application. Examples of process workers include call center representatives, marketing account managers, and accounts payable processors.

In contrast, the audience of an ECM system spans both process workers and *knowledge workers*. Knowledge workers need to use a wide variety of applications in order to do their jobs, and they do not always have extensive training in all of them. They are not explicitly tasked with using an ECM system to do their jobs; rather they are simply tasked with finding information. This could be through meetings, presentations, e-mails, or phone calls. They are not incentivized to use the system; rather they are incentivized to find high quality information.

One goal of a good ECM system is to simplify this information gathering process, and empower knowledge workers to find better information, and improve general productivity. However, if your ECM system is difficult to use, then your knowledge workers will be more than happy to ignore it. They will instead revert to using shared drives, local files, e-mail, or the phone, further exacerbating the problem.

For process workers ECM systems often provide value by capturing data, archiving old content, storing reports, and displaying unstructured content during a business process. For process workers the usability of the ECM system focuses on efficiency and data accuracy, as the enterprise application typically guides the typical process flow. For these users, the key usability drivers are the ability to complete the task more accurately, or more quickly. Concepts such as batch loading scanned documents, side-by-side processing (using two monitors to view and input data), and optical character recognition are critically important.

To drive usability, you need to focus some effort into making the system intuitive and easy to adopt. You need to make it easy to contribute information to the system, and easy to accurately find content in it. Keep in mind the following challenges:

- How easy is it for people to contribute new content into the system? Does it require a significant change to their existing workflow?

- Is content management an integrated piece of the applications your process workers use? Does it allow in-context content management as much as possible?

- How easy is it for the intended audience to access the information? Does it require your users to go through massive training programs before they can find what they need? Does it intuitively improve the accuracy and speed of existing business processes?

- What is the best way to encourage user adoption? Training? Brown bag lunches? Or perhaps usability focus groups?

Reusability

The problem with reusability cuts to the core of what enterprise content management is all about. Users need to be able to place one single piece of content into the repository, then reuse is across multiple applications and Web sites.

For example, when you create a report with Microsoft Word and check it into the system, your ECM system should process it into HTML with the appropriate look and feel, then replicate it out to multiple systems. Changes to this content item should be immediately reflected wherever it is displayed: internal Web sites, external Web sites, portals, mobile devices, and even printed communications.

Content reuse is important because it is one of the key areas of efficiency gained from a content management system. Re-creating documents, reports, and other types of content causes discrepancies in information and wastes valuable resources. It is both expensive and poor business practice. If your content cannot be transformed and reused, you don't really have ECM.

Be mindful of the following challenges:

- Once the information is in the system, how easy is it to extract, and reuse elsewhere?

- Can you easily convert and repurpose the content for the Web, e-mail, kiosks, or mobile devices?

- Can you securely reuse the content in your intranet, partner extranet, and public Web site?

- Can you make one change to one piece of content, and have it be automatically updated in several places?

- Who owns the responsibility for maintaining the information, and ensuring it looks correct no matter where it is displayed?

ECM Is an Initiative, Not an Application

A successful ECM strategy requires an understanding that no single application can solve all your needs. Your enterprise will change far too quickly for any one product to satisfy all your users forever. It's an unfortunate but common error to install some monolithic application, then expect all your users to change all their habits in order to be more efficient and productive. This frequently leads to poor user adoption and failed projects.

Instead, you need to understand that successful ECM strategies require you to think about it as an enterprise-wide initiative. You need an executive team that champions ECM, as well as department heads who have intimate knowledge of content management problems, and technical people who can take you from vision to reality.

Once you think of ECM as an initiative, and not any one single application, you will achieve several benefits. Firstly, you have vendor independence: replace underperforming applications with ones that better suit your needs. Also, by blending several content-centric applications together, you can achieve a more comprehensive solution with less customization.

Every new ECM project is based on the initiative, and can build off of the success of previous projects. With each new project, your dedicated team gets more implementation and management experience, not to mention hands-on knowledge of how to maximize the benefits of ECM.

As such, your ECM system needs to be able to function as both a platform, and an application. This difference is subtle, but it's what separates enterprise content management from point-solutions that merely manage documents.

Instead of a patchwork of line-of-business applications, you need a coherent platform that you can use to create and support line-of-business applications. This enables you to achieve reusability, not just at the content level, but also at the content service level. Applications that use your content take advantage of the same features: metadata, security, records management, or even custom content services. This not only brings content services directly into your service-oriented architecture, but also ensures you only have one single system to learn, manage, and administer.

In general, you should begin an ECM initiative on a project-by-project basis: allow your team to get experience with the ECM system, and build upon that success. However, with each successive project, there is a temptation to reinvent the wheel and create entirely new metadata and security models for every system. You should resist this temptation as much as possible. Otherwise, you will end up with dozens of content silos in the same repository. At a high level, you should be asking the following questions:

- How are you currently using content in your repositories? Is it a simple data store, or do you process the content through complex life cycles?

- Do you have content in legacy systems that are expensive to maintain?

- Do you need access to that information for day-to-day activities, or just for historical purposes?

- Is it easy for other applications to reuse content in your ECM system?

- How much will it cost to migrate the content? Can you identify a small handful of repositories where consolidation would yield immediate cost benefits?

- Does your ECM strategy force your users to significantly change their behavior? If so, do they see immediate value in doing so? If not, should you change your strategy?

- What is your plan to encourage user adoption? Training? Incentives? Directives?

- What applications might you deploy in the future? What integrations are important right now?

- What is the plan to monitor usage, measure the success of the initiative, and ensure that it continues to meet the needs of your end users?

- How will you gather feedback on usability? When people have a hard time finding content, what is your plan to help the evolution of the taxonomy and/or structure?

- What is your path to success? Did you architect your system so you could build off the success of one project, and expand it to other projects?

The Solution: A Pragmatic ECM Strategy

Now that you know about the problem, and have read all the questions, what is the best way to begin a successful ECM initiative? A true ECM strategy—what we call a pragmatic ECM strategy—requires a combination of systems and people in order to meet the needs of the end users, and is quite different from the knowledge management systems of the past.

To emphasize, there is no one single solution to the information management problem. Nevertheless, there is no shortage of vendors who have promised the opposite. The past is littered with "knowledge management" systems that forced users to do everything only one way within one monolithic repository. Such "enterprisey" systems were impressive, but they rarely empowered end users. The enterprise applications of the past seemed more interested in monitoring user behavior than in empowering employees to do their job more effectively. They also were lacking in critical elements that made ECM easy to integrate into existing and future infrastructures.

Can we do better? We have to. According to some experts, content creation is occurring at a faster rate than Moore's Law. In other words, the rate at which we create content is faster than the rate at which we are designing computers to process that content. No one single system will be able to solve future content management problems: ECM needs to be able to evolve quickly.

Remember, a good ECM initiative is about empowerment; not control. In the day and age of infoglut, your users are far too busy to radically change their behavior just because you want them to. You need a combination of solutions that allows centralized control, but extends the reach of ECM beyond any one repository. You also need a cross-departmental team to constantly ensure that the system suits the needs of all users. As mentioned before, users and context are critical pieces of a successful ECM initiative; therefore, your plans should always include them.

The Drivers for ECM

There is a major shift occurring in the business world that is making ECM too important to ignore. First, because of recent economic downturns, businesses need to make their processes more efficient. Second, recent severe natural and man-made disasters have forced people to become more serious about disaster preparedness and business continuity. Third, recent corporate scandals and desires to protect personal healthcare information have both forced industries to focus more on proving regulatory compliance for digital information. And finally, concerns about the environmental and energy consumptions are moving organizations towards more efficient long-distance communications that don't rely on travel or printed paper.

By managing content throughout its life cycle, ECM can help address a lot of these drivers. By focusing on communication efficiency, it helps cut costs that arise from not finding information, or finding the wrong information. By focusing on life cycle management and archives, it helps ensure business continuity. By focusing on records management, it helps enforce document retention policies, and ensures regulatory compliance. And finally, by focusing on effective long-distance collaboration, energy costs are significantly reduced.

—Pamela Doyle,
Director, Fujitsu Computer Products of America

All together, the goal of pragmatic ECM is to empower your organization. Give your knowledge workers the information they need to make the best decision. Give your process workers simple tools that work quickly and efficiently to process information. Make sure the systems are secure, and follow records management regulations so people feel safe using them as a single source of truth. And finally, make them usable, so people enjoy working with them.

This is the power of in-context ECM. By allowing your users to take advantage of ECM from the applications they use every day, they gain the advantages of content services without having to significantly alter their habits.

A pragmatic ECM strategy is more sophisticated than simply an outline of which system belongs on which computer. It must also include a process for iterating that system to ensure it always suits the needs of your users. It's a diagram of not only where you are today, but where you want to be tomorrow, and why. At a high level, the steps are as follows:

1. **Create an ECM Center of Excellence:** this is a cross-departmental team responsible for the success or failure of all ECM initiatives.

2. **Assess your environment:** separate your systems into strategic, tactical, and replaceable, to better determine how they can work together, and if consolidation is an option.

3. **Consolidate content into strategic repositories:** migrate content from replaceable systems into it, and integrate it with other strategic systems.

4. **Federate control to tactical repositories:** use tools with a light touch to gain some control over tactical repositories and legacy systems, when consolidation is not cost effective.

5. **Secure information where it lives:** make sure your security strategy accounts for all content, whether it is in your repository or not.

6. **Bring all information management strategies together:** ensure your ECM strategy is aligned with your strategy for structured repositories and enterprise applications.

7. **Plan for the future:** ensure your ECM system can evolve to meet the content needs of the future.

If your enterprise is typical, you probably have a large gap between where you are now, and a pragmatic ECM infrastructure. You probably have multiple systems from different vendors, document sharing systems, collaboration portals, scanning applications, e-mail archives, and critical information on shared file systems. If you are like most organizations, these systems are not well integrated, so finding authoritative content is difficult. Because of this reality, you need a strategy that allows you to both leverage these systems and consolidate them, in a way that helps achieve your content management goals.

In order to do this, we have outlined the following strategy to help you get a handle on the real enterprise content management problem. We will be spending the rest of this book on the details of the pragmatic ECM strategy, with each chapter focusing on a different aspect of the above plan. Briefly, the steps are as follows.

Step 1: Create a Center of Excellence

All successful enterprise content management initiatives have some variation of an ECM Center of Excellence (CoE)—in other words, a cross-departmental group who is responsible for ensuring that current and future content management projects meet the appropriate criteria for success. This means ensuring that the individual point-solutions that your departments need can be brought together, and be properly managed across the enterprise. This team must ensure that all content management solutions are deployed strategically.

To be successful, your Center of Excellence needs to have cross-departmental representatives from at least three groups. The first group is high-level executives who are champions of information sharing and innovation. High-level support is critical to ensure that the initiative gets the resources, feedback, and power they need to help ECM projects succeed.

The team also needs department managers who understand the content needs of their groups. How do they produce information? How do they find information? What information do they frequently need to do their jobs? What are their biggest content concerns? This group is critical to understanding the needs of both content contributors and consumers.

Finally, it needs a group of technical resources who understand the gap between vision and reality, and can create a concrete list of tasks to implement the vision. This team can be made up of business analysts, but they will need feedback from enterprise architects, solution architects, and integrators. This team is critical for turning a high-level vision into a plan of action, as well as keeping the team aware of potential pitfalls and technology limitations.

Depending on your industry or the size of your company, you probably also need experts on document retention regulations. This usually takes the form of a legal advisory council, or a certified records manager.

This team should have ultimate responsibility for the success or failure of any ECM initiative. They should be champions of reusing existing content and content services to drive innovation and success. They should also review new projects for what kind of ECM footprint they will have, and prioritize which projects should be done first. They should always stay in tune to the needs of the users, to keep IT and business aligned, with a minimum of bureaucracy. Details on the organization and duties of this team are available in Chapter 3.

Step 2: Assess Your Environment

Once you put together a team, their first task is to assess the current environment to determine what content you currently have, where it exists, and how it is used.

In an ideal world, all content would exist in one place—a single source of truth—but in reality, it exists all over the place. Shared file systems, content repositories, copies on desktops and USB thumb drives, e-mail attachments in your archives, or e-mail in the archives of other companies. Your team should perform an audit of all content repositories, and categorize them in three groups:

- **Strategic** Enterprise capabilities that make up the ECM infrastructure that can integrate nicely with each other, and are a part of the long-term strategy of your organization.

- **Tactical** Legacy solutions that are less cost effective to integrate, but are important for how you do business today. They will continue to be useful in the short term, but will likely be replaced in the long term.

- **Replaceable** Legacy solutions that have few features, and can be easily replaced now.

Your ECM team would be tasked with locating all these systems, determining what content is in each of them, and how it is used. They would also be tasked with finding any content problems. Can people easily find this data? Will it be in the right format? Is the information secure and reliable throughout the enterprise? Are users adhering to the appropriate retention policies? Is your content secure? Do other departments need to access this content? Are there duplicated efforts in creating this content?

Beyond the technical challenges of consolidation lie the more difficult issues of internal politics, departmental turf wars, and individual resistance to change. Moving to an enterprise strategy for ECM and consolidating repositories, systems, and tools means changing the way users work. To be successful, we must attend to the organizational challenges as well as the technical challenges.

Your ECM Center of Excellence will need to be aware of both the technical and political challenges of consolidation, which are discussed in Chapters 3 and 4.

Step 3: Consolidate Content into Strategic Repositories

Strategic ECM is the infrastructure and middleware used by an organization to store and distribute content across applications, between systems, and amongst users. The goal of a strategic ECM infrastructure is to provide a baseline for new applications and solutions as well as a best practice and target system for the consolidation of existing legacy and non-strategic content stores.

The primary value behind consolidating all content into a single system is to achieve a single source of truth: one place where all users and all applications can go, and be ensured that they have the most recent content, in the right format, all while being properly secured and managed. All systems—whether they are Web portals, enterprise applications, or desktop clients—will use the strategic ECM infrastructure when they need to contribute or consume content.

As such, a strategic ECM repository needs to be not only an application that has content management features, but also a framework for creating new content management solutions. Your strategic ECM system needs not only to offer basic content services, but also have the ability to adapt to new content requirements.

ECM services are an important part of a services-based middleware layer. Content management services include the following:

- Manage: check-in, check-out, delete, expire

- Search: metadata and full-text

- Navigation: grouping content items, custom Web sites, suggested content

- Document information: metadata services, link management, tagging

- Transform content to PDF, XML, HTML, or RSS

- Workflow: approve, reject, comment, annotate, notify

- Subscription notifications

- Security: access control, encryption

- Compliance: records management, HIPPA, ISO

These ECM services provide the ability for enterprise applications—both off-the-shelf and custom—to interact with the strategic ECM infrastructure. Most enterprise content management systems offer a multitude of capabilities, and thus, services, for the enterprise.

Not all services are created equal, however. Often the simplest services, such as check-in and search, provide the most value. In many cases, these services may be all that an enterprise application requires. In this case, the underlying enterprise content management system takes responsibility for functions such as retention management, version management, and security behind the basic services. For many applications, providing the core content services will generate a great deal of value with a minimal amount of effort.

Consolidation of content infrastructure, storage, and middleware is a daunting task for any organization. From an IT standpoint consolidation involves many integration points. Again, thinking about our different levels of services we can identify the level of integration, the amount of exposed ECM functionality in the application, and the value derived from the core ECM infrastructure by content within the target system.

These days, many vendors are using the term *ECM rationalization* to describe this process of consolidation. Some make the mistake of believing that rationalization alone is sufficient for an enterprise-wide content strategy. However, we feel that rationalization is only one piece of a pragmatic ECM strategy. It is a vital piece, but other steps are needed as well.

To this end, a strategic content management system also includes a number of integration tools to extend the reach of your content strategy to as many systems as possible. Most ECM systems have their own APIs, including Web service–based ones, but they frequently require integrators to know a lot about the underlying application. For some cases, knowledge of the underlying system is a requirement; in others where you only need basic content services, this may be an unnecessary burden. To that end, a pragmatic ECM system needs to allow integrations in multiple ways: a robust API for advanced integrations and simpler ones for minimal integrations.

We discuss the specifics in greater detail in Chapter 4. In general, Oracle believes that ECM solutions take one of three forms: Active, Transactional, and Historical. The details about what these mean, along with the specific Oracle products for them, are outlined below.

Active Content Management

A universal content repository is critical to a strategic content management infrastructure. By definition, a single source of truth must support all kinds of content, whether it is Web content, records, documents, digital assets, or collaborative content. The system should not only support all known content assets, but it must also be easily extended to support the content management requirements of tomorrow.

For a long time, Oracle Universal Content Management (UCM) was the only truly unified platform for content management. It was designed from day one to be a service-oriented architecture. When the ECM market demanded a new feature, UCM was expanded to meet that need. Most other vendors were forced to start completely over: their systems were incapable of storing multiple kinds of content, such as Web sites and records. Their solutions were little more than a patchwork of applications, each with different interfaces, and management challenges.

Oracle UCM is a content management platform, as opposed to a line-of-business content management application. As mentioned before, true ECM needs a platform that can expand to future needs, not a patchwork. Any content being actively used will probably need to be reused in multiple places, so a single repository is needed to ensure the content is properly managed no matter where it winds up.

As such, Oracle UCM serves as the backbone for a strategic ECM infrastructure. Both middleware and enterprise applications can benefit from as many UCM content services as they require. It serves as the single source of truth in the enterprise, providing a rich set of services and capabilities to knowledge workers via a unified platform supporting document management, digital asset management, Web content management, and records management.

Transactional Content Management

As part of the strategic ECM infrastructure you will need tools for capturing, processing, and reporting on the content generated for and by process workers.

These tools will need to be integrated with the enterprise applications utilized by these workers and integrated into the content storage strategy. The goal of these tools is to improve the efficiency and accuracy of working with unstructured content within the context of these enterprise applications.

Oracle Imaging and Process Management (IPM) is designed from the ground up to enable process workers to effectively scan, process, and associate content with enterprise application functions such as accounts payables or time and expense management. Oracle IPM makes extensive use of Oracle Fusion Middleware technologies such as the Oracle BPEL Process Manager for integration with Oracle applications such as JD Edwards, PeopleSoft, and E-Business Suite as well as the management of approval processes and workflow process management.

Oracle IPM is integrated with Oracle Document Capture and Oracle Distributed Document Capture. Oracle Document Capture provides high-end document scanning and processing capabilities. For less intensive and ad-hoc scanning, Oracle Distributed Document Capture enables users to submit and process document images via multifunction and desktop scanners through a Web-based application.

Historical Content Management

Every piece of content is subject to the content life cycle. The cycle begins with content creation, and moves through the management, review, distribution, storage, and eventual disposition of the item. While all content moves through this cycle, a majority of content in the enterprise is in the final stages of the cycle, often in an archival state prior to a disposition action. At this point in the cycle, content is no longer of active interest, however, it is not possible or desirable to destroy it yet. In order to improve the performance of active content repositories, as well as minimize clutter, you should eventually migrate historical content into an archive.

Oracle Universal Online Archive (UOA) is an excellent way to provide archiving services to your enterprise. Unlike backup tapes, Oracle UOA keeps all archived content on disks, and uses life cycle management tools to reduce storage costs. In addition, it includes compression and deduplication of content, so you minimize the amount of required disk storage.

Also, since it is a universal archive, it can be the storage layer for all kinds of content: documents at the end of their life cycle, records whose life cycle dictates archiving for many years, or old e-mail messages. Keeping the archives live enables quick access, and placing them all in one system has benefits to the manageability of archived content.

Step 4: Federate Control to Tactical Repositories

The previous section raises the question, is it feasible to store all of your content in your strategic ECM infrastructure? That usually depends on the culture of your organization, and how centralized your IT department is.

Putting all content into a strategic repository means that all applications that need content should integrate with your infrastructure. This means either you build your application directly on the ECM platform, or you use ECM as a storage layer for your application. In the first case, you are extending the ECM system to include new core functionality. In the latter case, the content itself resides in the strategic repository, but the functionality for its display is hosted in a separate application.

However, in most enterprises you will have content stores that cannot easily integrate with an ECM infrastructure. These might be legacy systems that are too arcane to change, but too useful to eliminate. These might be systems that your organization inherits after a merger with another organization. Or, these might be highly specific line-of-business applications, perhaps bought as an off-the-shelf solution, in which a tight integration would be cost prohibitive. In either case, you will still need to manage the content in these systems.

To that end, Oracle provides federation tools in its ECM stack. Instead of an integration where all content resides in one repository, you should also enable people to manage content in remote repositories. Federated integrations will not have all the features built into strategic integrations, but they will allow you to enhance findability, security, and help you comply with records management policies.

This is the focus of Chapter 5, and will cover the following specific technologies.

Enterprise Search

Perhaps the most well-known example of federated ECM is enterprise search. Some organizations have content in hundreds of repositories. The first step towards getting a handle on that information is simply being able to locate it.

Oracle Secure Enterprise Search (SES) enables you to spider all the content in your enterprise, and allows your users to securely look for content. While enterprise search has been part of the enterprise infrastructure conversation for many years, not all enterprise search tools are equal. Oracle Secure Enterprise Search provides a robust and flexible security model as part of its search methodology that perpetuates the security model of each of the target systems against which it searches. Users will see all content they have rights to see, and no content that they do not. It will be automatically clustered into topic groups, and two people will see different clustering based on what items they are more likely to want. All of this is available from an unassuming, simple, Internet-style search interface.

Additionally, SES is not limited to unstructured content repositories. You can also create custom connectors to database tables, or structured repositories, such as ERP or CRM systems. That means when searching for information about a particular client, SES can also include structured data about recent support calls, and recent product purchases.

Universal Records Management

One challenge to records management is that you have records in multiple formats: e-mail archives, files on the file system, access logs, and boxes of paper gathering dust in warehouses. In order to ensure that you always comply with retention policies regardless of file format or location, you need a system that can enforce policies, no matter where the data is currently stored.

Oracle Universal Records Management (URM) uses federated tools—called *adapters*—that run inside remote systems. These URM adapters allow you to locate content in remote systems, in a manner similar to Secure Enterprise Search, but with the ability to apply enterprise-wide records and retention policies on those target systems.

For example, your e-mail archives would remain in your e-mail archiving application. However, in the event that your organization was directed to preserve old e-mails about a certain topic, you could search for relevant documents in the URM interface, and "freeze" them so the e-mail archive would not be able to delete them. Additionally, you can enforce retention policies in remote systems, to force your e-mail archive to destroy old e-mails as soon as they are no longer relevant.

URM enables you to define your records management policy in one single place, and control digital and physical records with the same interface.

This is incredibly useful when attempting to enforce an enterprise-wide records management plan.

Step 5: Secure Information Where It Lives

In a pragmatic ECM system, security takes two forms. First, you need to secure the content that exists in your strategic repository, and second, you need to secure it in federated repositories. This requires two primary kinds of technologies, both described in detail in Chapter 6.

Central Policy Management and Auditing

Securing content in a strategic ECM infrastructure would be difficult, if not impossible, without a centralized policy management system. This usually takes the form of an LDAP repository or Active Directory, coupled with a single sign-on system, or other identity management systems. This is not only important for the content repository, but for all applications that extract documents from it.

Any application that accesses content from a secure system must all follow the same rules: only certain people are allowed to read or edit a document. If you design your UCM system as a single source of truth, it will always have control over who can edit your content. However, once the content is removed from the system, the UCM repository no longer has that control.

Therefore, to ensure consistent control over document security, all applications need to integrate tightly with a centralized policy management system, and restrict rights accordingly.

To put it another way, a content management system should store content—not users, not security policies, and not access rights. It is important for an ECM system to implement basic user management for small deployments, but in enterprise-wide scenarios you should take advantage of the identity management systems already in place. Integrating one with a content management system should be nearly effortless, and the ECM system should always defer to a central policy management system to ensure proper access control.

We discuss the importance of centralized security further in Chapter 6, and give recommendations for how to integrate them.

Information Rights Management

One curious paradox about information security is that your data is only secure when it is not being used. Unstructured documents are safe when stored on a secured file system, and your structured data is protected by database security. However, that information is only safe because it is idle: nobody is currently using it. Once you access the information, the data passes through a network of computers and systems before it is displayed on somebody's desktop. At any point, somebody could copy, alter, or tamper with that content. This problem is magnified if you are storing vital information on a legacy system that is difficult to properly secure.

Now, imagine that you could protect your data no matter where it was, and add extra layers of protection when it is in use. Imagine that the information is secure, whether it exists inside the most locked-down encrypted file system, or in a USB thumb drive you lost at an airport. Imagine that you could secure a document in an e-mail attachment, no matter who gets their hands on it.

This technology is the realm of Oracle Information Rights Management (IRM). The IRM technology does not have a secure repository—it doesn't need one. Instead, you use IRM to give the same security to any document, no matter where it is stored. Initially, it encrypts your content. To access the information, you need to make a Web service call back to a central policy management system in order to get a temporary decryption key. If you do not have the proper access rights, the centralized server refuses to supply the key, and you are unable to view the content.

IRM is an important part of a secure ECM infrastructure, and it will secure your content regardless of whether you can secure the repository.

Step 6: Bring Information Management Strategies Together

As mentioned in Chapter 1, the ECM industry likes to draw a line between structured data repositories, and unstructured data repositories. Enterprise applications such as ERP and CRM are typically structured content repositories. Systems like ECM and to a lesser degree BPM fall into the category of unstructured content repositories. There is also a half-way point called *semi-structured content*, which may include documents created in an unstructured format such as a Microsoft Word document, but the information within that document is organized in a highly structured way. Often, this is represented as XML.

Naturally, these lines can get kind of blurry. You typically need to display scanned invoices in your ERP system. You may wish to display analytics on your intranet Web sites. Therefore, you need to ensure that your strategy brings together both structured and unstructured systems.

A unified strategy can take many forms. Most importantly, you need to secure the content across all systems, which is covered in Chapter 6. You also need to ensure your structured information systems can take advantage of the strategic ECM infrastructure to display content. Finally, you need a process for accessing structured content—such as business intelligence reports and analytics data—from your Web sites and unstructured repositories.

Many structured repositories allow for unstructured content storage, but it's usually to their advantage to store it in a dedicated ECM repository. This makes content more findable, more manageable, and much easier to reuse.

In other situations, it might not be cost effective for your enterprise applications to take advantage of the strategic ECM infrastructure. Perhaps your structured content repositories are difficult to integrate with, and the cost of taking advantage of a unified system outweighs the benefits. In those cases, you should use a federated approach to content management, such as secure enterprise search or URM agents.

Step 7: Plan for the Future

Lastly, you must keep in mind that technology is changing so rapidly that any plan you create will need to be reassessed on a yearly basis. Vendors will continue to add new technologies to their ECM offerings. You will also have organizational changes that will create new ECM needs as your business evolves.

Enterprise content management is tasked with managing that which is by definition barely manageable. Every year, new technology and market forces make it attractive to create new ways to store, manage, and process information in different ways, and a good ECM vendor will continue to expand their offering in radical new directions.

Some of these new features will include new Web 2.0 and Enterprise 2.0 trends. Others may include better ECM standards, which make it easier to integrate applications with a strategic ECM infrastructure. Others may include bigger and better federation tools, enabling you to extend content management features to other systems, without having to consolidate them.

Some of these systems will make an initial appearance as line-of-business applications that take advantage of an ECM infrastructure. Others may grow out of an existing unified content management system. Others may be monolithic Web applications that do not play nicely with others.

Technology is changing so rapidly, that a standard five-year plan is no longer optimal for determining content management needs. You should plan on rethinking your ECM strategy at least every three years: identify what new technology is available to bring into the fold. Your Center of Excellence should be continuously updating their best practices, and always looking out for new technology that might make their tasks easier.

Chapter 3 gives some advice on reassessing your environment, and Chapter 8 presents a few ideas on what these new trends will look like.

Takeaways

- Content is more useful when provided with a rich context.

- Enterprise content management is an initiative, not an application.

- The primary ECM challenges are: taxonomy, metadata, findability, accuracy, security, risk reduction, regulatory compliance, flexibility, manageability, usability, and reusability.

- Meet these challenges with the pragmatic ECM strategy:

    - Create a team: the ECM Center of Excellence.

    - Have the team assess your environment: content, and repositories.

    - Consolidate content into one strategic repository: a single source of truth.

    - Federate control to tactical repositories, and other non-consolidated content.

    - Secure information wherever it lives: whether in or out of a repository.

    - Bring structured and unstructured information management strategies together.

    - Plan for the future: be mindful of fast technological and organizational changes.

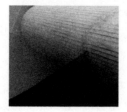

CHAPTER
3

Assessing Your Environment

ow that we've outlined a pragmatic ECM strategy for solving your information management problems, you need to determine the difference between the strategy and your current reality.

The first step in implementing a comprehensive ECM strategy is to put together a team that is dedicated to solving the ECM problem. This is an iterative process, since you won't know who needs to be on your team until you perform a complete audit of the content and environment. Nevertheless, you should be able to put together enough champions and technical resources to perform an audit.

The second step is to use your new team to survey your existing IT infrastructure, and determine how you currently use information. While this may seem like a straightforward exercise, our experience leads us to believe that you will often uncover many more systems and sources of information than you initially expect. This is okay, as part of the process of solving this problem is discovering how pervasive the need for real information management is.

We've attempted to provide some classifications and examples of different types of content stores. These classifications will be for types of repositories and for the groupings of those repositories for the purpose of implementing our comprehensive strategy. This is not an exhaustive list, but an attempt to give you some bearing on what you should be looking for as part of this assessment.

You will need to determine what kind of content is stored in each system, who uses it, and what types of benefits, costs, and risks the content brings to the organization. While determining what types of content are in a system and who uses it may sound simple, it actually poses some interesting challenges. First, you must determine not only who uses the systems, and for what purpose, via direct access, but also through various enterprise applications. Often, content stores reside beneath one or more enterprise applications, and the use of the repository by those applications may not immediately be apparent.

Once you have determined who uses the system, and for what types of content, you can then determine the benefits, costs, and risks associated with each particular system.

Benefits fit into two primary categories: "hard" and "soft." *Hard benefits* are capabilities that can be calculated based on a return-on-investment (ROI) or in the revenue or savings associated with the system over alternatives. *Soft benefits* typically do not have a hard dollar ROI, revenue stream, or savings calculation but provide intangibles such as better collaboration, enhanced productivity (which may or may not be able to be measured), and higher end-user adoption of applications.

Cost is another major aspect of our auditing of the current state of our content infrastructure. What is important here is the evaluation of the total cost of running a system. These costs include:

- Hardware and software costs, particularly if a new system is being purchased (including software licenses) or if the hardware being utilized by the system could be utilized elsewhere if it were freed up.

- Software maintenance costs—the annual fees paid to software companies for ongoing support. When evaluating software maintenance costs it is important to understand what is included in maintenance for your calculations. Sometimes maintenance includes upgrades to future versions of the software. Other times the maintenance only includes patches and incremental updates to the existing release of the software. In the latter case additional investments in new versions may be required and should be considered as a possible additional cost for that platform.

- System support provided by your own organization or your IT provider. As a line item or a collection of resources and expenditures, system support should include all costs associated with the uptime and monitoring of the system.

- Development of capabilities on the system is also a cost, which should include the staffing of the specific skill set for the particular system. While this can sometimes be a difficult cost to determine, the staffing of specialized skills can be expensive and will really add up if considered across multiple heterogeneous systems.

Along with the benefits and costs we must determine the risks associated with each system. These risks include both traditional risks, such as legal and financial risks associated with mismanagement, in addition to the risks of bad information management:

- Time and opportunities lost because of an inability to educate your customers about products and services they care about.

- Legal risk involved with keeping content long after it is useful.

- Time and opportunities lost because your employees are not working with the most recent version of a document.

- Time and opportunities lost because one department can't find content from another department.

Although the strategic ECM strategy strongly recommends a single unified repository, it's important to be mindful of the fact that multiple repositories do add value. If not, they wouldn't exist. Sometimes the benefits of local departmental control outweigh the benefits of centralized IT control. Sometimes next generation collaboration tools—such as blogs, wikis, and instant messaging—are too useful right now to wait until IT makes it a priority.

It's also important to keep in mind that having information in multiple repositories can have value: if it didn't, then it wouldn't be so commonplace. However, it's vital to assess when the negatives of distributed content outweighs the positives.

Putting Together a Team

In our experience, poor user adoption has been the primary failure behind ECM initiatives. The only way to ensure user adoption is to engage the potential audience, ensure that you can satisfy their needs. You also need executive leadership to provide the necessary incentives for adoption, and promote the successes. You need dedicated IT resources, but you also need managers and business analysts who understand the needs of their audience. This team needs to be dedicated to the value of ECM, and offered incentives to be actively involved in its success.

Some organizations call this an *ECM Center of Excellence,* a term which we will use throughout this book.

The primary goal behind a Center of Excellence is to help people break out of the project-level mindset of content management. You should not be implementing single projects; instead, you should focus on building an infrastructure that can be reused for multiple projects, multiple departments, and multiple audiences.

Part of your Center of Excellence will need to be a core team of ECM professionals who are charged with implementing the ECM strategy at an enterprise level. As we have discussed throughout the book, content systems are often in silos throughout different departments, divisions, and teams. Your team will need to collect the necessary data, categorize it, and then implement your comprehensive ECM strategy, while paying attention to the priorities and politics across the departments and systems.

This team can vary in size. For small- to medium-sized companies it might only comprise three people, and it might not be a full-time job for any of them. However, as the complexity of the project grows, you will need dedicated administrators, developers, and architects. However, at the executive level, growth of the team usually means having additional executive sponsors also putting in partial time.

No matter what the size of your team, the purpose is to prevent the "boom-bust" cycle of enterprise-wide deployments. In other words, most enterprise-wide software initiatives have an initial large push because of the clear advantages of centralization. Unfortunately, all too often the team tasked with setting up these systems becomes disconnected with the business needs of their users. This leads to individual departments feeling neglected by the centralized team, which then leads to the proliferation of line-of-business solutions. The Center of Excellence must identify these trends, and have the power to engage these departments before they feel the need to go their own way.

Preventing these "boom-bust" cycles is the primary difference between a Center of Excellence, and simply a large project team. The center stays involved in the strategy and execution of these goals over multiple projects, ensuring the long-term success of the ECM initiative.

There are many ways to create an ECM Center of Excellence. One system that has worked in the past breaks down the group into three levels: an executive steering committee, the program managers, and the project managers. Some people may belong in only one group, whereas others— like enterprise architects—may belong in all three groups. Figure 3-1 illustrates one possible way to do this breakdown, which is described further in the following sections.

Executive Steering Committee

In order to ensure broad visibility and buy-in from multiple departments, your ECM Center of Excellence should include Vice Presidents, CIOs, or COOs. This group should also contain input from department heads, and any high-level executive with a large stake in content management.

The steering committee's primary role will be to advise the Center of Excellence on the right strategy for the ECM initiative. They need to ensure that all departments will have a say in how the system is designed and used, but ultimately, the strategic decisions will rest with them.

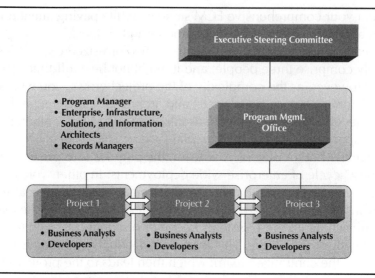

FIGURE 3-1. *The ECM Center of Excellence helps keep the ECM strategy aligned between IT and the business.*

They must also help create an environment that encourages the positive change away from project-level initiatives, and more towards an enterprise-wide mindset. They should set the metrics for what can be defined as a success, and be the ultimate arbitrators for cross-departmental turf wars. This team needs to be able to say no to projects that add to the problem. Specifically, they need to veto all content management projects that have enterprise-wide impact, and yet are still being designed by one department in a content silo.

The primary goal of the executives is to create this environment dedicated to information sharing. Without this support, your pragmatic ECM system will be ignored, and your enterprise will be doomed to a patchwork of point-solutions. Naturally, this makes your content management problem worse, and more expensive in the long run.

When this team is just getting started, they should identify some "quick wins"—projects that are in desperate need of ECM, but might be low-risk. There should be little complexity, and immediate benefits. These projects are great for being test cases for your ECM strategy. They also help build up knowledge on how to do these deployments, and help get credibility for the team.

After these quick wins, the steering committee should branch out into more strategic solutions. In general, you should start small, then slowly roll out to an enterprise-wide solution. It's safer, it has lower risk, lower cost, and helps ensure that you are asking the right questions to achieve success. In general, these projects are "low hanging fruit," such as upgrading an outdated intranet. However, you should not focus too much on quick wins that you neglect the needs of the enterprise: think strategically, act tactically.

ECM Program Management

This group contains senior technical resources, analysts, and governance experts. Their role is to take the high-level strategy from the steering committee, and design enterprise-wide policies for future ECM projects—in other words, devising the series of tactical steps involved in implementing

The Center of Excellence in Practice

I work in a very large health insurance company. In my industry, proper content governance is critical. Without constant feedback from departments, you risk dictating policies, procedures, and standards that do not fit the needs of your business.

Our ECM Center of Excellence provides the visibility we need to make appropriate enterprise-wide decisions consistent with our common platform and unified vision. It also ensures that we have an ongoing support structure for the departments using ECM solutions.

Naturally, a good Center of Excellence will be a constantly evolving system. Right now ours has a multi-level governance structure. In the steering and governance committees, we have executives from multiple departments driving the business strategy and the IT standards. We also have user groups and subject matter experts who give feedback on the executive direction. Their role is to verify that the strategy suits the needs of users and the business, it is technically feasible, and is cost effective to maintain. Our governance committee stewards participate in all levels to ensure consistency and communication.

This has helped us create a strategy for true enterprise content management, and always ensure that it will be both an effective and efficient system.

—Tom Chaffee
Principal Operations Architect

the strategy. What technology should be used to solve what problem, and what should our processes be? These tactics should be general so multiple departments can reuse them.

In practice, this means creating the infrastructure that a pragmatic ECM system will need, along with standards and best practices for future projects. The program management team should spend some time overseeing individual projects, and monitoring their progress. This team should also provide guidance for the steering committee about which projects should take priority over others. They should also oversee teams that design enterprise-wide security policies, metadata taxonomies, and content retention plans.

This team is also responsible for governance. They should not only create these policies, but enforce them as well. Since user adoption is so critical, they need a system in place to process user enhancement requests in an efficient manner. They also need a process for how to communicate this information to the rest of the CoE team, as well as the enterprise in general. The governance rules should be enterprise-wide, and not specific to individual applications.

The governance rules depend a lot on how your organization shares IT services. Do you charge usage back to individual departments, and have service-level agreements? If so, how much of this enterprise-wide analysis should be charged back to each department? If one organization uses ECM more than another, this could cause political turf wars.

Naturally, this team needs to have highly technical resources, and resources that are excellent at communicating their tactics to the steering committee and future ECM project managers. This team should have the following roles.

Enterprise, Infrastructure, and Solution Architects

These are the technical resources that are able to understand the vision behind the ECM Center of Excellence, and can anticipate the problems you will encounter when trying to bring it to reality. There is a bit of controversy about the title "architect," but whatever you call them, ensure this group can answer the following:

- How does our enterprise software currently work together? How much time is spent in integrations? Is there a better/faster/cheaper way to do it?

- What is the best enterprise-wide security model, and how should we enforce it? What systems will have a hard time enforcing the policy?

■ What is the best network infrastructure for this project, and what hardware is needed?

■ What is the best way to manage change, including patches, upgrades, and catastrophes?

■ Based on this and input from the executives, what ECM projects should we implement first?

■ How can we make success on that project repeatable for other projects, to improve speed and quality each time?

Ideally, this team could not only answer these questions, but be able to communicate those answers to higher levels, and help warring departments come to an agreement.

Input from architects is vital, but it should never trump the needs of the users. Your overall design should think about users first, then content, then context, and finally architecture. It's a huge mistake to spend a ton of time and money laying down "the ultimate" architecture, because by the time you roll it out, your users' needs will have changed. Focus on immediate needs first, then design an architecture that can accommodate current needs, but is also flexible enough to support the long-term growth of your enterprise.

How do the users want to use the system? Is that possible with the current architecture? If not, you should rethink the architecture before saying no to the users. Otherwise, you simply invite the users to take matters into their own hands, and deploy yet another content silo. A good architect should never say no to a feature request without either an alternative, or a compelling business reason why the feature is too risky. If you cannot come up with a compelling business risk–based reason for denying a feature, then you probably don't understand the problem sufficiently.

Information Architects

The role of managing the information architecture is actually much broader than it may seem at first glance. Information architecture is very important as you begin to consolidate systems or implement policies across existing ones.

The main goal is to empower people to find whatever they need, when they need it, ideally without them ever knowing that they need it. This means at least an enterprise-wide search initiative. However, this can cause problems when departments call things by different names, and organize things with different taxonomies.

Even in organizations that have relatively small taxonomies, there are often subtle differences from one metadata model to another. Tools are available to help with these mappings, including technology such as metadata profiles, which will map the appropriate term to the appropriate user at run-time. For example, to someone in finance a part number might be listed as "SKU" on the screen, while to someone in product development it might be called a "Part Number." The data is the same in either instance, but the metadata label is shown to the user in the correct context for their role, according to their information classification scheme.

Requirements around enforcement of the taxonomy will likely vary by system and by usage. For some types of content, or for some types of users, classification may be something that can be more loosely managed. Other systems, however, may have very tight and specific guidelines on the metadata that is required. The information architecture team will need to be responsible for these taxonomies and support a process for the business to request additions and modifications to the taxonomy, as it will likely be shared across a much wider array of users after consolidation.

Information architects also need to empower people to browse the repository. Ideally, people would never need to run a search: the system would guide them to what they need based on what task they are likely trying to perform. Is the user from accounting? Perhaps guide them to the accounting portal, with a list of common tasks, policies, and latest news. The ideal system would anticipate the needs of its audience, and enable them to quickly browse to information they need, without even knowing it exists.

Naturally, information architecture can be a difficult task. Oracle has tools that help manage your information architecture, but it is still important to have a resource that understands the complexity of the problem, in order to help your users find what they need.

Records Managers

Your governance team will likely benefit from a certified records manager, who can ensure that your content complies with the retention policies for your industry. This includes old e-mail records, old log files, documents about projects, paper documents, and their scanned copies. These records managers are tasked with designing records policies, but you can have another member of the team enforce them. Depending on your industry, certified records managers may be in short supply, so you may need help from outside experts and contractors.

One warning: some records managers are hesitant about the concept of using an electronic repository for a single source of truth. In their world, the single source of truth is the original paper document, and the scanned copy is a derivative. This hesitancy is understandable, but it can lead to inconsistencies in following your records management policy. In other words, some records managers properly dispose of physical records, but neglect to dispose of the electronic records. This has caused many records management policies and practices to evolve, as is evident in the ISO 15489 Information and Document Management standard, as well as the new Model Requirements for the Management of Electronic Records (MOREQ2) used throughout the European Union.

Oracle does have software tools to allow you to create policies that apply to both electronic and physical records in the same system, which is why we still believe it's important to have policies that act against physical and electronic records in a consistent way.

ECM Project Implementation

At this level, business analysts and developers will be doing the "real work" of deploying ECM solutions. They'll use guidance from the ECM program managers and the steering committee to ensure that their project conforms to the overall ECM strategy. This gets easier with each additional project, since you begin to build up the expertise with every system you deploy.

As this new ECM model is rolled out across the organization, your team will develop skills in consolidating systems, using federated tools in ECM systems, and in using ECM as middleware. Capturing this organizational knowledge is important to the ongoing success of the pragmatic ECM strategy.

The ECM program managers should come up with an initial list of policies and processes for deploying new projects. The implementation team should use this for guidance, but also help it evolve. You may also consider formal training and certifications from both your ECM vendor and a professional ECM organization, such as AIIM or ARMA.

Business Analysts

This group is tasked with analyzing the needs of their specific audience, including metadata, workflows, business process, usability, and language. Many of the key questions an analyst needs to ask are presented in Chapter 2.

This team needs to specify the goals of this project and its resource requirements, and help generate metrics for success. They should also be the key contact for change management. How will this system alter how people should do their jobs? Does it fit neatly in with the broader ECM strategy? If not, should the strategy change, should the project change, or should it be noted as an exception to the rule?

Solution Developers

This team will implement the eventual solution. They will need guidance about best practices from the architects in the ECM program management team, and in some cases they are the same people. The developers will implement the taxonomy, security, and workflows to meet the needs of the users. They will also design the Web sites, integrate this system with enterprise applications that need ECM, and perform any necessary customizations to the core system.

This team may or may not be tasked with the day-to-day maintenance of the system. In many cases, ECM solutions have tools that allow less technical people to manage the site—alter the taxonomy, create new navigation, new folders, new projects, and the like.

This team will also do all testing, both unit tests to demonstrate functionality, but also usability tests. It is vital that the implementation team be allowed to see their customers attempting to use the end result. Developers are typically highly opinionated about the correct way to create and implement software. Therefore, they tend to react with suspicion about usability problems that come from business analysts or management. Sometimes, the most useful technique for enhancing usability is to show a video of frustrated people using what the developers created.

Trainers

Again, since user adoption is critical, you will always need training. Even on a system that is easy to use, you still need training on how people should find content, and the value of sharing information in a way that others can reuse. Official training should contain screenshots of the live, customized system. You can also do informal training with brown bag seminars over lunch. Another popular technique is to use a software tool that generates a Flash animation based on screenshots, so your users can get a feel for the flow of the system.

It's a good idea to do training early on in the process, to make sure that the system will satisfy the needs of the audience. The earlier a problem is discovered, the faster and more cheaply it can be fixed.

Corporate Communications

As we said many times, the content management problem is more than just a technical problem; it's a people problem. Even if you purchase the best content management software in the world, perfectly implement it, and perfectly configure it so anybody can find anything, you still could have a content management problem. If your users don't understand the value of metadata or findability, then the overall value of the system will diminish.

Your users probably don't understand what makes content compelling. How can you make sure that your research report will be found, amongst the hundreds produced in your firm every week? What kind of human filter do you need on this content, to help connect the decision makers with the best content available?

Part of this problem is in encouraging user adoption, which we talk about at the end of this chapter. Another solution would be to engage experts in editing, copywriting, journalism, or publishing. Not only can these people teach your users to make their content compelling, but they can also help promote the best of the best. Instead of an automated e-mail about what's new, how about an internal newsletter for each department? Help people stay in touch with who is up to what, based on the content they recently created.

The Internet had an interesting effect on newspapers and television news: ad revenue plunged, people began to demand their news for free, and competition with amateur bloggers became fierce. As a result, there are many talented editors and reporters looking for more stable employment. We see this as a tremendous opportunity. As the explosion of free content on the Web made journalists less useful, the explosion of content in the enterprise made them more useful.

For example, imagine how much knowledge you could capture if you used trained reporters to conduct interviews with your employees and department heads? Perhaps this is for an employee newsletter, or daily podcast to get traveling employees up to date. More commonly, you may wish to capture information from people before they retire, or move on to other jobs. A trained reporter could make the interview process enjoyable, and create a professional product that the rest of your employees would like to watch. When combined with Digital Asset Management, discussed in Chapter 4, this can be a powerful force for sharing knowledge.

Prepare for a Content Audit

Now that you have a team, you can get started assessing your environment. You will need to enumerate all your systems that might benefit from a pragmatic ECM strategy, determine what content is in each one and how it is used, and determine the difficulty of migrating it. To do so, you will need to determine what kind of content is in these systems, how it's created, how people find it, and how they use it.

You may have several such systems, as shown in Figure 3-2. In general, your existing content repositories can be placed into three groups:

- **Strategic** Content stores that are part of our pragmatic ECM infrastructure as discussed in Chapter 2. These may or may not all be from the same vendor, but collectively these systems have been identified as the go-forward systems for the enterprise.

- **Tactical** Line-of-business content stores that are inadequate for a broad ECM infrastructure, but for various reasons will not be replaced with strategic ECM in the near term.

- **Replaceable** Content stores that will be consolidated into the strategic ECM system in the near term.

These determinations will drive the plan for each individual system. Strategic systems will be included in the ECM infrastructure and used to drive content management out into the enterprise through applications and infrastructure, as discussed in Chapter 4. Replaceable systems will be rolled into the ECM infrastructure as soon as possible.

Tactical systems are trickier: they provide a useful service, but there are strong business drivers that keep those systems in place in the near term. In lieu of replacing these content stores with strategic ECM, you should use *federated* tools from your strategic ECM to bring these systems into our pragmatic ECM framework in the near-term. These tools include enterprise search and distributed records management. These federation tools do not give you all the features of strategic ECM, but they do provide basic management, and might be more cost effective when compared to consolidation of these specific systems (see Figure 2-2).

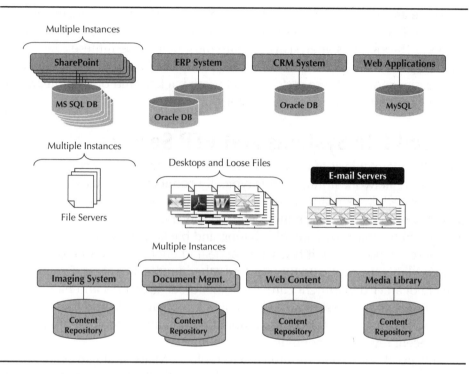

FIGURE 3-2.   *Most enterprises have content sprawled across multiple applications and repositories.*

The results of assessing your content infrastructure will likely not be very pretty. Most companies have multiple, if not dozens of pieces of major content infrastructure. This is even before including shared drives, e-mail systems, and proprietary content stores within applications.

We covered a comprehensive list of content repositories in Chapter 2. Please ensure that your team knows about all the possible content repositories that you may have. After this, we can begin to analyze them for being replaceable, tactical, or strategic.

Evaluating Your Content Repositories

Now that your ECM Center of Excellence is running, the next step is to audit your environment for content repositories. This will be the responsibility of members from the ECM program management team, who will then report back to the steering committee.

There are probably many content repositories within your organization that need to be assessed and ultimately included in your pragmatic ECM strategy. Through this analysis your team must determine if these repositories are Strategic, Tactical, or Replaceable. At a high level, here are the classifications of these systems, and some background on the integration of these content sources into this strategy.

Shared File Systems and FTP Servers

Often the main culprit of uncontrolled content in any enterprise, shared file systems are network storage that is typically connected to a user's desktop via a mapped drive. Many times these started out as a way for your IT department to quickly share files between servers, and they sometimes evolved into enterprise-wide file sharing and backup solutions.

These are useful, but it takes a great deal of energy and effort to reduce clutter, eliminate duplicate files, or find other people's content. Few people outside of an IT department care about the folder structures and naming conventions that are essential to keeping them organized. And these systems are wholly insufficient for collaboration: finding any content, let alone the most recent revision of content, is a daunting task.

In general, these systems are easy to replace. Many strategic ECM systems have simplified desktop clients that mimic the behavior of a shared file system, so your users will not have to significantly change their behavior to take advantage of the new system.

Digital Archives

Once content reaches the end of its life cycle, many times it is moved into some kind of archive. This could be a specialized digital repository that is tuned to store large amounts of static information. It might be a hierarchical storage management system that moves unused content to lower-cost media. However, in many cases it takes the form of raw data on backup tapes collecting dust in a closet.

Clearly, the challenge in content archives is being able to locate old content when needed. Perhaps you are performing a yearly audit, perhaps there is critical business information in an old report, or perhaps you are being sued and a judge is forcing you to supply old e-mails and documents. Because of this last possibility, the additional challenge in an archive is also in deleting content as soon as it's no longer business-critical information. This reduces storage costs and legal risk.

In general, these archives need to be a part of your strategic ECM system. Safe archiving is a critical piece of the life cycle of all content, so these systems need to have a tight integration with other parts of the strategic ECM infrastructure. E-mail archives are particularly important, since they contain a vast amount of useful business information that you may need in the future.

Ideally, this archive would be live, so you can easily integrate it with your strategic repository. In other words, your archives should not simply be a collection of backup tapes in your warehouse. Such systems are difficult to audit. We discuss alternatives in Chapter 5.

Specialized Content Management Systems

Your organization is likely to have several point-solutions that perform very specific functions. These include, but are not limited to content creation, collaboration, scanning, records management, Web content management, digital asset management, and archiving. These could even be very specific functional systems, such as a matter management system in your legal department, a quality-assurance application on the factory floor, or a source control system used by your IT department.

These systems need to be brought into your pragmatic ECM strategy, just like everything else. Unfortunately, they are the most difficult to categorize as strategic, tactical, or replaceable.

Is the system replaceable? If the system is no longer used, shut it down, and migrate the content into a strategic repository. If it is still in heavy use, it might be replaceable if the functionality is easy to replicate in your strategic content repository. Perhaps it only offers core content services, and its features are cheap to reimplement, or you can get by with a manual process.

Is the system strategic? It can be, if you can use your strategic repository as the back-end storage for this system. Oracle offers some tools that run inside other repositories, which essentially makes these other systems the front-end to your single source of truth. These are discussed in Chapters 4 and 5. However, not all specialized content management systems are flexible enough to allow this kind of abstraction layer.

If you cannot replace it, and you cannot make it a piece of your strategic infrastructure, then the only option is a tactical integration. This means a loose connector between the two systems, allowing some interoperability, but not as much as a strategic system.

Most of the time, you will need to do a cost-benefit analysis to determine the best way to do this integration. We cover that later in this chapter.

Legacy Web Sites and Web Applications

In the early days of the Internet, people discovered how useful it was to make documents available for download on custom-built Web sites. Some of these sites would have Web content in HTML or PDF format, perhaps generated from native Microsoft Office documents. Others may have simply been Web pages with links to download the native files.

This became so popular, that soon it wasn't uncommon for a medium-sized organization to have hundreds of different Web sites. Unfortunately, this kind of environment led to people not being able to find content, or finding outdated copies of content, or being unable to properly change the content. Suddenly, a knowledge worker needed to know how to navigate a hundred different Web sites, each with their own naming conventions and organization structure, just to do their job.

Content-rich Web sites can usually be replaced with a strategic infrastructure. If good Web content management is a core piece of your strategic repository, it is almost always cost effective to replace your intranet, dot com site, and customer sites with your strategic system. This greatly simplifies maintenance and administration issues.

However, some legacy Web applications are less easy to integrate. Ideally, you should have the legacy Web application use core services to store content in the strategic repository. That makes it easier to manage unstructured content in legacy systems. However, if this is not cost effective, a tactical integration may be the best option.

Content Stored as Files or in the Database?

The legacy Web applications mentioned above typically store their content as files on a file system. This was usually because it was much easier for a rogue employee to set up a file-based Web application, as compared to one with a database back-end. However, more sophisticated applications may be storing their content in the database as large objects (LOBs). These could be character large objects (CLOBs) or binary large objects (BLOBs), depending on the application.

However, if you store your content as LOBs, then people sometimes use the database to describe more complex information about the content. What's its title? Who made it? What are its relationships with other content items?

This information can usually be stored as metadata in your strategic repository; it's simply a bit more work and might require a custom application.

Portals and Application Servers

After the initial rush of Web servers, most enterprises began to Web-enable their back-end applications with custom middleware. This typically entailed a front end written in a JEE application server, a JEE portal server, a .NET application server, or perhaps an alternative language such as PHP, Python, or Perl.

The good news is that middleware applications fit in very nicely with a strategic ECM repository. Middleware's primary purpose is to connect with other applications, so you have many options for how you wish to do the integration. In some simple cases, all your ECM system needs to do is push content out to the application servers, where it is reassembled and displayed. You can also do a tighter integration that empowers the middleware to edit and update the content, comment on it, or process it through workflows.

The possibilities are only limited by the services that your ECM infrastructure provides, and how much time you wish to spend creating the middleware application. Oracle has multiple tools to content-enable your middleware, which are discussed in Chapter 4.

In some cases, your middleware applications may be currently integrated with a tactical content management system that cannot scale to the enterprise. The solution here is to migrate the content out of the line-of-business CMS and into the strategic system, followed by an integration between the middleware and the strategic repository.

Structured Data Repositories

The realm of ECM is in managing unstructured content, but very often the worlds of structured and unstructured come together within applications. As mentioned in the discussion of middleware in the previous section, these applications use the underlying storage mechanism of the structured data set to attempt to provide basic content management capabilities. Unlike middleware, however, these enterprise applications have fewer integration options, and they usually require expertise in the system to do an integration.

Most enterprise applications, including ERP systems, include some type of "attachments framework" for associating content with structured information. A CRM system, for example, will contain documents that have been submitted electronically or scanned paper documents from a customer that are accessible from within the system so that customer relations or support departments can access that information when necessary. From an Oracle perspective alone there are attachment-style frameworks in Oracle E-business Suite, PeopleSoft, JD Edwards, Siebel, and others. These applications will leverage Oracle ECM over time as the strategic content store, but for current customers these are sources of unstructured content within the enterprise. Below are some examples of enterprise applications, and the unstructured content they typically contain:

- **Business Process Management and Workflow Engines** Scanned documents, contracts that require approval, Web content that needs reviews.

- **Customer Relationship Management (CRM)** Help desk scripts, recent FAQs relevant to a product line, Web content for campaigns.

- **Enterprise Resource Planning (ERP)** Scanned invoices, scanned purchase orders, annotations, and comments.

- **Sales Force Automation/Sales Forecasts** Generated sales reports, successful marketing collateral, sales playbooks.

- **Human Resources Databases** Photos of employees, scanned contracts, performance reviews.

- **Lead Generation Databases** Notes about customers, scanned business cards, e-mails to/from/about prospects.

- **Product Information Management Systems** Product documentation, marketing materials, content that needs to comply with industry regulations.

- **Project Management Systems** Bug reports, feature requests, milestone reports.

In general, these enterprise applications are designed for a specific structured content purpose, and unstructured content is more of an afterthought. Ideally, unstructured content should be migrated out of these systems into a strategic ECM system, and then these applications should integrate cleanly with that infrastructure. These enterprise applications should connect to the strategic repository to find, download, and modify content.

However, some of these applications predate application servers, and lack support for several standards that make integrations easy. Most of them can be customized, but it might not always be cost effective to do a tight integration with a strategic repository. Also, each application has different needs. Some systems may be fine just accessing content items by a unique identifier, or by running a metadata query. Others may wish to process content through workflows, or enhance content with annotation, comments, or tags.

Therefore, you need to assess these on a case-by-case basis. Some of them contain vital strategic content, which needs to be managed properly, so the integration expense is worthwhile. Others are departmental and contain tactical information of little use to the greater enterprise, in which case, a combination of tactical ECM tools may yield the best value.

Either way, a pragmatic ECM strategy needs to help bring structured and unstructured content applications together. This gives you consistency across the enterprise, for following security policies and industry regulation, and for enabling the single source of truth.

Hosted Repositories and Online Communities

Online communities, such as MySpace and Facebook, are posing new challenges to IT organizations on many levels. At the most basic level it creates a new model of a mix of services that are hosted inside the organization (traditional IT) and outside (the public Internet). In many ways this is the software-as-a-service (SaaS) model taken to an extreme. These tools provide a unique challenge for IT organizations, and include the following:

- **Public Web e-mail**   Yahoo, MSN, GMail

- **Public Knowledge Bases**   Yahoo Groups, Google Groups, Freebase

- **Social Software**   Facebook, MySpace, LinkedIn

- **Polls and Forms**   Webmonkey, Wufoo

- **Presentations**   WebEX

- **Customer/Contact Management**   Salesforce.com, Highrise

- **Project Management**   Basecamp, Campfire

In general, for every piece of software used in your enterprise, there will likely be an SaaS offering that claims to do the same. Despite huge differences in quality and vague promises of security, these systems are popular in enterprises with resource-strained IT departments. If there's a six-month project backlog in IT, many departments decide that it's a better use of resources to host their applications outside the firewall.

There are two primary benefits to hosted solutions: the application is already installed, and you have a dedicated team of well-trained experts making sure it's always running. However, these come at a cost:

- *Less control over the features in the application*—Product enhancements may take much longer than in a system you own and can customize yourself.

- *Less control over data security*—Any content that leaves your sphere of immediate control might be accessed by the wrong people.

- *Less control over data access*—The SaaS repository is a content silo, but one that you have almost no control over.

- *Less control over data destruction*—Life cycle management is a manual process, and a hosted system might not fully destroy your information even when told to.

You are at the mercy of the hosted solution when it comes to content access, searching, and management. Also, since you do not own the software in question, getting enhancements to the application could be both expensive and slow to come about.

Some hosted applications have tools to give you better access to your data. Others are more like "walled gardens" that fear giving you control, because that would empower you to move your data elsewhere. Also, what happens to your content after your contract expires? Do they give it back to you, or destroy it?

Is your information safe in a hosted system? Usually the answer is yes. However, can you guarantee that your information will be properly deleted from a hosted system? If your employees make comments on Facebook, or occasionally send messages with Google Mail, then you may have increased litigation risks and costs. For example, Facebook makes it nearly impossible for people to delete their online profile. How long do you think they store your messages to your friends and coworkers? Imagine that your company was sued tomorrow, and a judge demanded to see all communications— including e-mails and Facebook messages—pertaining to a specific event. How much would it cost you to provide that information?

There are two primary solutions to this problem. One of them is to only use hosted applications that work cleanly with content behind your firewall. Some hosting companies offer an appliance that sits inside your firewall to let you display information from both your hosted system and your secure enterprise system. These allow you to see a combination of hosted and private data, without any of that information leaving your area of control.

These are sometimes called "mashup APIs" by SaaS providers, and naturally they only work if the user and the private content are both behind your company firewall. These are useful for gaining greater control over your data, although you still will not have full control.

Alternatively, if your SaaS provider does not offer a mashup API to let you have access to your data, then you can make one yourself. This technique requires some effort, but tools like Oracle WebCenter Services and Ensemble make it easier. This is discussed further in Chapter 5.

Once you have control over your information, then you can choose which integration method to use. Sometimes, it is best to simply extract all your content, and replace the hosted system with one that is 100 percent under your control. In other cases, you could do a tactical integration with tools that help you find and manage content in the hosted system. Sometimes a strategic integration is possible, where your pragmatic ECM system is the single source of truth and publishes data to your hosted system, or vice versa.

Implementing Your ECM Plan

Looking at the effort outlined in this chapter, it should be clear that a coordinated, process-driven approach is required for the successful implementation of an ECM strategy, with your ECM Center of Excellence (CoE) driving the strategy. While a CoE strategy is not specific to ECM, we do find that ECM does lend itself particularly well to such a management model.

We feel it's important to reiterate that because content management is often rolled out as a point-solution, instead of an enterprise-wide initiative. We feel it's very important to stress that a Center of Excellence provides an essential framework for consistency across the different systems and different projects. It also provides the central resources to undertake the comprehensive ECM strategy across these various departments. It also ensures governance and makes the system usable for all people in all departments.

The next steps for your CoE involves analyzing how you use content in those systems, assess the current and future technology that can help solve your problems, and also perform a cost-benefit analysis to see which systems to consolidate and which to integrate. Finally, your CoE needs to continue to assess new content needs and emerging technologies to keep the system up to date. If you do not, then you almost guarantee that departmental point-solutions will reemerge.

Gather Business Requirements

Most of the important questions about gathering business requirements are covered in Chapter 2. In brief, the most essential questions are:

- *Who are the key stakeholders?* Be sure to interview them, and ask each one who they also consider to be key stakeholders.

- *What are their information and information management needs?* Be sure to determine what they absolutely must have, and what else might make them more productive.

- *In what way does the current system fail to meet their needs?* Does the technology fail, is it difficult to use, or was the implementation poor? Is the system perfect for some users, but fails to meet the needs of others?

- *In what way does the current system fail to conform to security, compliance, or retention policies?*

- *Who will "own" this cross-departmental system?* All key stakeholders must be involved at some level; otherwise, the initiative will fail. However, the CoE should have ultimate responsibility for the key decisions.

- *What kind of system would be required to maximize inter-departmental communication and collaboration?* This includes a proper cross-department information architecture, as well as incentives for certain departments to collaborate more often.

Refer to Chapter 2 for a complete list, and assess how people are using the current system, what they need to makes themselves more productive, and what the enterprise needs to make sure proper processes are followed.

Assess Existing Technology

Your enterprise may contain only a handful of repositories, or it may contain several hundred. In either case, you have already spent time, energy, and money on these systems. Some may be begging for replacement, others may be fine as is. Assessing the current state involves looking at the technology, the value, and the people involved in each of the systems.

After your assessment, you will need to determine what technology is currently available that could replicate the functionality of your systems, but do it in a more enterprise-wide fashion. Does one ECM system better suit your needs as a strategic content store? Would one system be easier to integrate with your middleware and your tactical repositories? Which ones are easy to modify to suit your future needs? Which ones have similar features to your line-of-business solutions to better facilitate easy replacement?

Naturally, in this respect the authors are biased towards the Oracle Enterprise Content Management stack. However, because Oracle's stack was designed from day one to integrate easily with multiple systems, a full Oracle stack is never a requirement. Throughout the rest of this book we will be presenting Oracle solutions to specific problems; however, the pragmatic ECM strategy is inherently vendor-agnostic.

Prepare a Cost-Benefit Analysis

Throughout the content audit, we recommend you place your repositories into one of three categories: strategic, tactical, or replaceable. But what qualifies a system as being replaceable? How should you decide which system is tactical, and which is strategic? If money were no object, all systems should be replaced or integrated with strategic ECM. However, this is sometimes impractical, so you must weigh the costs of the integration against the benefits to the business, including lowering your risk.

ECM rationalization is very popular, because of the decreased licensing and maintenance costs. However, to achieve full rationalization, you need to spend time and money migrating content, designing and testing integrations, and replicating tactical functionality in your strategic system. This is not always cost effective.

Every organization has its own methods for measuring costs and risks. Some are in highly litigious industries, so the costs of legal discovery are important to this equation. Some measure the cost of the system based on a service-level agreement. Also, keep in mind the value of having one single vendor. Not only does this make purchasing decisions easier, but it is also helpful when getting product support. When an integration between two systems breaks, who do you call? If each system was created by different vendors, they will point fingers at each other, or at the person who designed the integration. However, if both systems and the integration were created by one vendor, then you make one phone call to one organization, which has a responsibility to fix your problem.

Despite differences in how organizations assess cost and risk, most organizations will perform similar steps in their process. As you audit your environment, keep in mind the following options you have for integrating each repository into your pragmatic ECM system:

- **Eliminate the Repository** Migrate all content into the strategic ECM, and reimplement vital line-of-business functionality natively in the strategic ECM repository.

- **Eliminate the Repository** Migrate all content into the strategic ECM, and reimplement vital line-of-business functionality with middleware tools.

- **Keep the Repository** Do a low-level integration that stores the unstructured content from the repository into the strategic ECM system.

- **Keep the Repository** Leave both content and functionality in the tactical repository, but control it from the strategic system using federated tools.

In order to decide between these options, you should determine if this repository can be completely replaced by the strategic repository. Is the repository in question expensive to maintain? Does it provide few benefits not already in the strategic system? If so, then the costs of consolidation are simply the costs of migration of the content, and retraining your users. There might be additional costs in implementing new features, but those can only be assessed on a case-by-case basis. Figure 3-3 shows common systems that you may have, along with whether they may qualify as tactical or replaceable.

What features does this repository have that are not in the strategic repository? How expensive would it be to reimplement all the features? What about 80 percent of the features? What about reimplementing just the 20 percent of features that you use 80 percent of the time, and create a manual process for the rest?

Several point-of-business repositories have highly specific features, and therefore require more money to replace. You should be able to reimplement those features in your strategic system, but that costs time and money. If reimplementation is too expensive, then an integration at the SOA level may be more appropriate, as discussed in Chapter 5.

What are the risks if the tactical system breaks? What are the risks if the strategic system fails to properly replace the functionality of the tactical system?

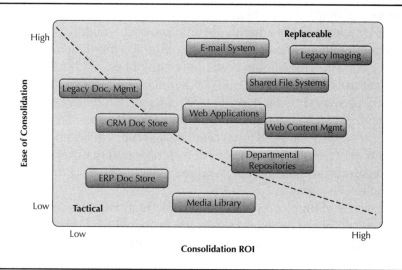

FIGURE 3-3. *The decision to replace, consolidate, or federate depends on the comparable values in each.*

Are there vital features missing in the tactical system—such as records management—that increase liability and risk? Are there lost opportunities because people can't or don't access this system? How tough is it to integrate your tactical system with a service-oriented architecture? What do you gain? Does this tactical system have content that absolutely must be findable? Is the current system only going to be running for another year, making further investment less attractive? Should that content then be migrated to the strategic system, or should the tactical system be integrated with the strategic infrastructure?

Finally, if the repository cannot be reimplemented in a cost-effective manner, and if it cannot easily integrate with your SOA in a cost-effective manner, then the best option may be to leave it as it is. In this case, it is a tactical repository, and you will not be able to bring it fully into your ECM infrastructure. However, you can still gain some control over the content with ECM federation tools, as discussed in Chapters 5 and 6.

Setting aside all arguments about the "correct" way to implement enterprise software, you should never migrate content from an existing system to a new system unless there is sufficient value-add.

If you have a system with a high cost to maintain, but it solves a simple problem, it always makes sense to consolidate. This is a nearly universal answer, regardless of the gap in features between the solutions. Some users may complain about an initial loss of features, but please remember: *It is easier to add features to strategic ECM infrastructure than it is to add enterprise scalability to a tactical ECM repository.*

Since Oracle's ECM is a highly flexible product, you have dozens of options on how to add features. Plus, when reimplementing features from a repository that you consolidated, you have the option of choosing which features are truly worthwhile. You could implement the 20 percent of features that are used by 80 percent of your users, which saves development costs and produces a system that's probably easier to use.

Any content repository of low complexity should always be migrated into the content server. Even if the system is cheap to maintain, the added value of centralized management far outweighs the costs of migrating from a low-complexity system.

Repositories of high complexity, high risk, high reimplementation cost, high value, but low maintenance costs are probably best left alone as tactical repositories. If you have an application that is mission critical, but still working fine, a loose integration with federated tools may be optimal. These systems should not be consolidated at present; but that doesn't mean that they will remain tactical repositories forever. Technology changes quickly, and the costs of consolidation get cheaper every year.

Plan for the Future

After an initial content audit, you should perform yearly audits of both your content needs and the existing technology. These audits are iterative, and therefore subsequent ones will not be as broad in scope as the initial audit.

The first reason to do yearly audits is because your content needs are always changing. New projects, new initiatives, and new campaigns all have different content needs. Some may require a lot of storage space; others may be extremely important for content reuse; others may have strict security requirements. Your CoE should evaluate the content needs for any new large initiative, and make certain that people are complying with your governance model. After a merger or acquisition, your needs will change significantly. Also, the additional departments may have their own ECM systems, and you will have to determine how best to rationalize your systems.

Also, there is the constant threat of employees bypassing strict IT rules and setting up unauthorized systems. Whether they be open source collaboration tools or a new hosted solution, there are plenty of applications that sneak by unknown to IT. That is, until such rogue systems become business-critical, at which time IT is forced to maintain a system that might not meet their approval. Ideally, the CoE would be well connected with the needs of each department and be gathering constant feedback. If so, ECM will more closely reflect the business needs of these departments, making these unauthorized systems unnecessary. However, in the event that a business-critical system snuck by both IT and your CoE, then the CoE should be tasked with assessing the new systems and determining how to best integrate with it.

Finally, there is the simple fact that ECM vendors are constantly adding new features, enhancing existing technology, and building better integration tools. Therefore, your decisions about whether a system should be strategic or tactical might change within a year. A pragmatic ECM strategy is a slow and steady push towards one consolidated, strategic repository, even as new line-of-business solutions, mergers, and acquisitions make this more difficult.

Remember: enterprise content management is an initiative, not a product. It's a constant cycle of trying to manage what is by definition barely manageable.

Another important thing to remember is not to focus entirely on the low-hanging fruit. For example, you may be able to deliver rapid ROI by focusing on just one aspect of the information management problem—such as scanning or Web content management. This will help get early buy-in from users and make the project an easy success. However, be mindful about how focusing on short-term gains may hamper long-term goals. Remember that the ultimate goal is complete consolidation, so you should not make implementation choices that limit future options. As we said earlier in this chapter, think strategically, but act tactically.

Consolidation is a never-ending process. We strongly encourage you to consolidate all strategic information into one repository, and use federated tools to manage content when a strategic integration is not cost effective. However, reevaluate every year to see what new strategic and federated tools may make your system run more smoothly.

Contribution vs. Consumption: A Trade-Off?

In the past, information management systems were forced into the false choice between empowering information creators or empowering information consumers. We are happy to tell you that you can have it both ways.

Users have access to an incredible set of tools in today's office (and personal) environment for creating information. Creating content is often not the problem, but rather how we use it.

Creating content is referred to in the content management market as *contribution*. When viewed through the model of the content information life cycle, contribution constitutes the creation and capture steps. A user contributes content by submitting it to the system, often after creating it using standard desktop tools, devices such as scanners, or through an enterprise application. As part of the contribution step, end users may provide additional context to the ECM system via the folder in which the content is submitted and the metadata provided by the user (or the end user's application). Metadata is the information about the content, such as the title or the department to which the document belongs.

Consumption is the process of delivering content to end users. From an information life cycle standpoint, consumption is largely focused around searching, browsing, publishing, syndicating, and delivering. This typically involves both the push of content to users, such as e-mail subscriptions and recommendations, as well as the pull of content from users searching and browsing.

Often in conversations around unstructured information management, contribution and consumption are outlined as opposing forces—or at least concepts that require trade-offs in effort. At a high level, the more structure and metadata a document has, the easier it is to find, both from applications and as individual end users. If a system provides for each document to have a customer ID, then searching for all of a customer's documents can be greatly simplified. A combination of metadata (each document, for example, having an associated customer identification number) and full-text searching provides the tools for locating documents. The more structured metadata you have, the easier it is for consumers of the information.

Beyond searching, other systems can also use this rich metadata to sort and organize the content into virtual folders to empower browsing. These systems could provide a different browsing structure, depending on the content, as well as the context and who the user is. If the user is a customer who would like to browse according to tasks, then you should present a browsing structure that enables this.

This metadata, however, must come from somewhere. Traditionally, this was entered by the contributor during the contribution step. The contributor would complete a form at the time of submission that described the document being contributed. Think of it as providing the information to the card catalog at the library. As you can imagine, a balance is struck between the amount of information required by consumers for efficient searching, and the time required by contributors to enter the metadata.

Oracle describes metadata as a "tax" on information. You are asking content contributors to pay this tax, in addition to creating their content. The higher the tax, the easier it is for consumers to find it. However, if the tax is too high, your contributors will rebel. They will either fill in bad metadata, or none altogether. Bad metadata is sometimes worse for consumers than no metadata at all.

While metadata entry still exists today, technology has enabled an increasing amount of metadata and context to be extracted directly from the content itself, instead of forcing a contributor to fill out long forms. For example, you can automatically extract keywords from the document, or administrators can set up special contribution services and forms that prefill the metadata. Both of these techniques are context-aware, meaning the prefilled metadata can be based on who the user is, how content is being contributed, and what kind of content it is.

We will dive into detail on how structured and unstructured content are coming together in Chapter 7, but most ECM tools today provide capabilities around metadata extraction. These tools, when used in combination with techniques for encouraging metadata entry by contributors, can help balance the effort around metadata between contribution and consumption.

Encouraging User Adoption

While the focus of this chapter has been on how to assess and manage the growing quantity of information management systems within an organization, it is also important to reemphasize that these systems exist for a reason: they help individual business units be more efficient, and enhance their ability to collaborate.

The goal in rationalizing the content infrastructure in an organization is to provide better and more consistent access to information. While there are many drivers that make a comprehensive ECM strategy a success, you must remember that users play the critical role. You should ensure your system provides the capabilities your end users require, and implement it in such a way that engages them to use it.

Therefore, your ECM Center of Excellence should spend a good deal of time discussing ways to give your users both the ability, and the motivation to embrace these new tools. They need to realize that many of these users are currently suffering from infoglut, making them feel busier than ever. Asking them to change their habits will be met with resistance, unless you can demonstrate how it will help them in the long run.

Ability

You need to ensure that the tools are simple enough that they will naturally slip into the way the majority of users do their jobs. For example, if you force them to learn entirely new tools before they can benefit from ECM, they will become frustrated, and go back to the old methods: shared drives, e-mail, and phone calls.

This is why Oracle ECM constantly tries to make it easier and easier to use the system. Why use a custom editor when Microsoft Word is so universal?

Why require heavy clients when Web forms are so simple? If a huge list of metadata fields is overwhelming for the user, Oracle lets you prefill these based on the user and the context of the request.

Desktop integration tools help significantly, especially if your users are accustomed to using a shared disk drive. However, such simplified tools can sometimes yield a repository structure that caters to the needs of contributors, at the expense of consumers. If every user is allowed to design their own folder and metadata structure, how will people be able to ever find anything again? As mentioned previously, it's up to the administrators to remember to focus energy on both consumers and contributors, so everybody benefits.

Training handbooks with real screenshots are helpful as well. Also, the sooner you create these handbooks, the sooner you will catch usability problems in your system. Poor usability is the primary enemy of user adoption. If your users find your system difficult to use, they will revert to their old habits to get their work done.

It is also useful to have a "support group" for the new users. This can be championed by the CoE, but it should also include people from other departments. They can offer each other additional help through internal e-mail lists, wikis, helpdesks, FAQs, or informal lunch seminars on "How I Use The System." Encourage those who have the most to gain from ECM to become early adopters, and encourage them to help others see the value.

Motivation

There are two primary problems with motivating your users to adjust their business process to use content management. One is the sense that there is nothing wrong with a patchwork of content silos, and that changing their habit will only slow them down. These people can usually be won over by demonstrating how the system is easy to use and how it helps them do their job faster.

If this group continues to be resistant, it may be because of Calvin Mooers' Law (1959):

> "An information retrieval system will tend not to be used whenever it is more painful and troublesome for a customer to have information than for him not to have it."

In other words, ignorance is bliss. These people may not want easy access to information, because it's easier on them personally if they remain ignorant of new ideas, new processes, new products, and new policies. This group will be difficult to win over without incentives or disincentives.

Another problem is that some people have built their careers on hoarding information and refusing to share it. Being the information bottleneck gives them both an identity and job security, so they will prefer that content remain difficult to find. This group will feel little motivation to share. They might be hard to convince, unless they feel secure in their job and see how they help the company and their coworkers by sharing what they know. They must genuinely feel that the act of sharing information directly helps *them*, otherwise they will be motivated to block adoption or refuse to comply.

For some usages—particularly compliance with legal discovery— motivation is as simple as telling people it's a required aspect of their job. However, when it comes to true information management, people need more incentives.

Once knowledge workers appreciate how they can now make better decisions because they can find the right information, they can be motivated to do the same for others. This is particularly true for the extremely busy employees who are highly regarded as information resources. If they use an ECM system, then people will go to that system to get information, which means less direct contact to the extremely busy employee, and their ideas will get a wider audience, and their influence will grow.

Another idea is to turn it into a competition. A strategic content repository keeps statistics on how often a user contributes content, and which other users access it. With a little effort, you can turn this into a great motivator for encouraging adoption. You could measure downloads, and produce a "most popular contributors" report. Ideally, you'd have separate sections for each week, each month, or by department to ensure that no one person continues to dominate the statistics. For example, to prevent dominance by your documentation department, contributors could even be judged against their peers to determine if they have above average or below average popularity. This can work wonders to encourage user adoption.

After putting such a system in place, you may get several users interested in how they can increase the popularity of their content. At this point, they may be open to information from your Center of Excellence about setting proper metadata or creating content for a broader audience.

Takeaways

- Establish a Center of Excellence for ECM at your organization:

  - Establish an executive steering committee, program managers, project implementers.

  - Design cross-departmental best practices to encourage content sharing.

  - Continue to improve based on user feedback to prevent content silos from reappearing.

- Audit all existing applications for unstructured content, categorized as:

  - **Strategic**   Content stores that are part of a pragmatic ECM strategy as discussed in Chapter 2. These may or may not all be from the same vendor, but collectively these systems have been identified as the go-forward systems for the enterprise.

  - **Tactical**   Line-of-business content stores that are inadequate for a broad ECM infrastructure, but for various reasons will not be replaced with strategic ECM in the near term.

  - **Replaceable**   Content stores that will be consolidated into the strategic ECM system in the near term.

- A pragmatic strategy needs to account for in-house applications— both structured and unstructured repositories—and hosted solutions.

- Pragmatic ECM is an initiative, not a product.

- Encouraging user adoption is critical.

  - Be sure users have the ability and motivation to use the new system.

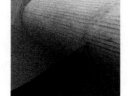

CHAPTER
4

Strategic ECM Infrastructure and Middleware

he first step in implementing a pragmatic ECM strategy is an infrastructure of one or more repositories that can handle strategic content, and strategic applications. This infrastructure will then support Web sites, portals, archived content, line-of-business applications, and any enterprise application that needs content management. This requires an infrastructure with a flexible, scalable, and extensible middleware layer. This layer offers the most basic kinds of content management services that all ECM systems provide. In addition, it offers a full suite of content services specific to your particular ECM system through a service-oriented architecture (SOA) to your unified platform. A complete content infrastructure supports document management, records and retention management, Web content management, document-centric collaboration, digital asset management, and e-mail management functionality.

In addition, the content infrastructure needs to be based on a flexible, universal repository that can add support for future content management needs. It should have a track record of expanding to meet new needs, as opposed to being just a patchwork of acquired technology. Patchworks can only achieve a federated approach to content management—multiple unique systems to configure, multiple unique systems to maintain, and multiple unique systems to learn. Federation has value, but it can never provide the solid infrastructure you'll need for the future.

Additionally, ECM solutions should support an extensible enterprise metadata model, include tools for building content-enabled vertical applications, and leverage an enterprise security model for controlling and providing access to business content.

Ideally, a pragmatic ECM solution would use nothing but strategic content stores. Unfortunately, most enterprise environments have a current state that includes not only strategic systems, but also legacy and tactical systems that must be addressed. In Chapter 5 we will look into how such systems can leverage ECM tools in conjunction with the strategic ECM system to provide a comprehensive and pragmatic ECM strategy. For now, we will deal exclusively with strategic stores and how they are used.

The Three Types of ECM Solutions

Not all content is the same. For example, Web content is updated as frequently as your Web site, sales forecasts are updated several times during the quarter, and a project blog might be updated every hour. In contrast, a scanned invoice will only have one revision, unless the scan failed for some reason. Either way, once content is no longer relevant, it should be moved out of your repository to reduce storage costs and reduce clutter.

A strategic content management infrastructure needs to be able to handle all of these kinds of content. These solutions can be categorized as follows:

- **Active Content Solutions** Primarily knowledge-worker content that is actively viewed and is frequently updated.

- **Transactional Content Solutions** Primarily process-worker content relevant to one transaction, and is rarely updated.

- **Historical Content Solutions** Digital archives stored in specialized systems for auditing purposes.

In the next few sections, we will expand on each of these types of content, the challenges they present, and which Oracle product to use to manage it.

Active Content Solutions

Active content is generally defined by the ECM industry as content needed by knowledge workers, such as Microsoft Word documents, PowerPoint presentations, or Web content. In all cases, the content is frequently accessed, edited, and enhanced. So an active content management system needs to support frequent revisions, and collaboration.

In general, active content has a large number of contributors and consumers. The content is of high current value, and clutter is a significant problem. As a result, active repositories contain fewer items than either transactional or historical repositories. Systems with a million items are common; systems with a hundred million items are less common. In most cases, old content is moved to an archive to save space and reduce clutter.

For active content, and broadly for ECM, we strongly advise unified content management. A "unified" content management system is one that provides a full compliment of content management services across content types and content uses. "Content types" can be thought of both in terms of formats (.doc, .xls, .pdf, .jpg, etc.) and purpose (full-sized image, Web-suitable image, thumbnail, etc.). "Content uses" applies to the context, delivery mechanism, or intended purpose of an item. The unified system brings these together so that we can easily mix content types and content uses in ways traditionally only available through a collection of products.

Examples of these product collections are tools specifically designed for Web content management, digital asset management, records management, collaboration management, and document management. These product categories were initially standalone products (and for some vendors still are) providing specific functionality for a targeted function. What happens in these environments, however, is that the lifecycle of the content or the processes driving the interaction with the content span these multiple content-centric systems. This is illustrated with the following example.

A global company is faced with a familiar brand management problem. Graphics are created for promotional materials through a mix of in-house and contracted graphic artists. While the initial quality of the graphics is typically very high, by the time the graphics are actually used in production advertising or marketing materials there has been significant brand-loss. Items have been recropped, resized, and in some cases the color depth has even been changed. For brand managers this is a major headache. At its core, this is a content problem that highlights the benefits of a unified ECM solution.

As stated, the quality of the initial work is usually high, likely through the use of graphic creation tools such as Adobe Photoshop. The designers create the graphics items in high-quality, multi-depth graphics formats such as Adobe PSP files (Adobe Photoshop files). Those files, however, often need to be converted to different formats and sizes for use in various online and print materials. Either the original PSP files are provided, which requires the marketing department to use the tools (Adobe Photoshop in this example) to do the conversions themselves, or the graphic designers, at the completion of their work, must go through and create multiple graphics using the tool before distributing them.

Even following this very manual process, graphics are often not in the right format for use by marketing departments, partners, etc., so they take the closest available graphic from the small subset that was created manually and will again convert it (sometimes cropping or changing color depth along the way). Through this process, we now have improperly branded graphics—and documents, and brochures, and whatever else to which the images are applied. We have a brand management issue where so much of the graphic consumption is disconnected from the original file created by the designer, since the graphics have likely been e-mailed, stored on shared drives, posted on extranets, etc.—all in various formats and states of disarray.

Similar problems exist for every department and across departments—for example, utilizing current versions of pricelists for sales people, getting accurate customer details for support teams, distributing policy documents from HR, and so on.

In addition to the document itself, active content uses highly structured database tables to store metadata that enhances the value of the item. This includes basic metadata, such as a title for the item, the name of its author, and a handful of keywords. It may also include custom metadata fields that enhance the findability of the item, such as which department created the item, its hierarchy, its taxonomy, or related content items. All of these fields are set by the creator of the content item, or by a professional information architect.

In addition to enhanced structured information added by content creators, content consumers can enhance the value of existing content items. For example, a user can rate a content item on a scale of one to five stars. They can leave comments about the item, or suggest keywords that describe the document. This latter piece is commonly called *folksonomy tagging*, and it's covered in greater detail in Chapter 8.

The key to making a useful active content management system is in the correct application of structured data. Structured data can describe what a document is by using titles and taxonomies. However, you also need structured data to help improve the findability of the content, and to allow your end user to enhance the value of the content. Who is the intended audience for the item? How does your audience search for items? By keyword? By title? By popularity? By task? Should they be allowed to modify the content? If not, can they add comments, or annotate the document with suggestions? Can they bookmark the document, and suggest keywords to improve the findability in the future?

Linking structured content with unstructured content greatly increases the value of your documents, especially if you can encourage end-user participation. However, it's important to realize that this structure is secondary to the document itself. The title, keyword, and comments are fairly meaningless if the document does not exist. Therefore, the primary value is still wrapped up in the content item.

Oracle Universal Content Management

Oracle Universal Content Management (UCM) is the flagship ECM product in the Oracle stack. It is called "Universal," because its repository is so flexible, it can manage any kind of content in one single repository: Web sites, digital assets, collaboration projects, records, scanned images, and general business documents.

At its core, Oracle UCM is an extensible platform for creating content management systems. It is not merely an ECM application; it is a framework for extending what ECM means by expanding it to include new capabilities. In general, in the enterprise this "platform" approach is superior to the "application" approach. A platform will allow you to create new applications that use content management, and extend the ECM features and functionality in new directions, while simultaneously providing a stable and proven infrastructure.

Naturally, no content management application will have all the features you require. However, it's important to remember that it's easier to add ECM features to a platform, than it is to patch-in enterprise scalability and infrastructure requirements to a specialized content application. A strategic ECM repository absolutely must have the proven enterprise scalability and integration flexibility that Oracle UCM possesses.

Every feature that UCM offers is available as a Web service, which today number well over 500. These include the core content management features in the server—contribution, consumption, workflow processing, subscriptions, conversion, and search—as well as more specialized services for extended ECM capabilities such as collaboration, digital asset management, Web content management, and retention management.

Systems that are written like UCM are commonly called service-oriented architectures (SOAs). These are popular with enterprise architects because of their superior ability to integrate with other applications. They are easy to deploy, configure, customize, maintain, monitor, and upgrade, even in complex networks. UCM was an SOA over eight years before the term even existed. A technical overview of UCM is beyond the scope of this book. For more details, please refer to *The Definitive Guide to Stellent Content Server Development* (Apress, June 2006).

Because UCM is a framework, and not an application, any time you extend its features, or modify its services, your customizations are immediately available through the standard Web services layer. This means that you can immediately take advantage of the flexibility, security, and ease of integration built in to UCM. When done correctly, you can customize the behavior of core features like contribution, without ever having to alter the enterprise applications that consume those services. UCM is an essential part of the Oracle ECM stack, for both Active and Transactional content, as shown in Figure 4-1.

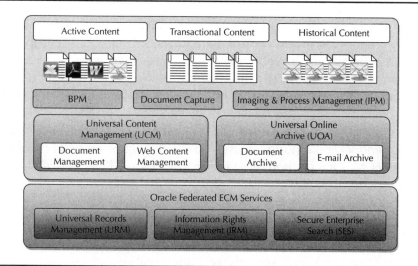

FIGURE 4-1. *Diagram of all the Oracle ECM products*

UCM started out as the first Web-based document management system at a time when very few people even had e-mail. As the ECM market matured, and demanded more features, UCM added them as application plug-ins to the core, unified repository (see Figure 4-1). Other vendors offered a patchwork of applications that created content silos, and the inevitable maintenance issues that plague enterprises with too many tactical repositories. One common problem was that if your enterprise applications needed a piece of content, they had to be aware of every possible system. Is it in a collaboration space, or in the digital asset library? Is it a record, or an ordinary business document, or on a Web site? Having a single unified repository greatly simplifies the creation of a single source of truth, and eases the integration process.

The advantage to a unified repository is clear: no matter how you contribute your content, it will receive the benefits of all ECM capabilities in one system. For example, a digital asset is not merely a digital asset; it can begin as a collection of items in a collaboration space, be served to a Web site, and be managed as a record all in the same repository. Whenever the market decides that ECM needs new capabilities, Oracle will simply extend its repository to meet those needs, as it has done many times in the past.

No matter what kind of content you are managing, all content types benefit from a core set of content management features: searching/indexing, metadata, security, revision control, workflows, subscriptions, grouping, converting documents to Web-viewable formats, replication, and general administrative services to keep the system running smoothly. Built on top of these core services are subsets that offer enhanced capabilities for specific content types.

The subsets of enterprise content management have yet to be formally defined. Vendors and industry analysts have yet to agree on what capabilities belong in ECM. Oracle chooses to group these capabilities in five broad categories, described next.

General Document Management

When we first think of content, most people think of documents: reports written in Microsoft Word, spreadsheets, presentations, notes, memos, scanned documents, and ZIP archives. Managing these kinds of documents requires a system that helps business users find authoritative content and make it easy to enhance and reuse. Ideally, this happens without much effort on the part of the contributor or the consumer.

To make it easier to contribute content, Oracle has a Desktop Integration Suite that integrates cleanly with your e-mail clients, Microsoft Office, and Windows Explorer. Through this interface, UCM appears to be no different than a shared hard drive: people see files in folders, and specialized menus display other information about the content. Editing a document through this interface creates a new revision of that item in the repository, and contributing new content is as easy as drag and drop.

If your documents are physical in format—such as signed contracts and other forms—you may want a digital copy to be available online as well. For this, Oracle Captovation offers high-volume document capture solutions that integrate with scanning devices. After which, your physical documents also benefit from the core subscription, workflow, metadata, full-text search, revision control, and security features that your digital documents have.

Naturally, it is very important to enhance documents with metadata, to improve findability and reusability. In some cases, each folder has default metadata, and the user doesn't need to fill in anything. In other cases, administrators may set up auto-categorization. This extracts titles, keywords, and project names from the document, and fills in the corresponding metadata fields based on rules and context. Power users who want precise control over all metadata, groupings, and locations may prefer the full Web interface, instead of a simplified desktop client.

General document management also includes the concepts of document creation. Sometimes your content is not in one place, it's in multiple places: snippets of word documents that need to be assembled into a final paper contract, individual PowerPoint slides that need to be assembled into a full presentation, or items grouped for easy downloads like sales kits or collateral assets. The Folios feature enables users to easily group content items into a virtual portfolio, which also contains folders and hyperlinks. This "folio" can be dynamically rendered into a single Word document, PowerPoint presentation, or PDF, XML, or ZIP file. The rendering engine is extensible, so you can modify it to suit you needs. Also, since the portfolio is virtual, documents can be in multiple collections at the same time.

Once your documents are rendered into a Web format like PDF, you can also take advantage of annotations. This means being able to draw on the Web document, commenting directly on it, highlighting certain areas, and redacting others. Even if your content is not Web-viewable, you can make comments and give feedback with the Threaded Discussions feature.

Advanced document creation includes both high-volume e-mail generation, and high-volume printing. Sometimes in this final stage of delivery, you need to pull information from multiple sources: images and copy from your ECM system, customer names and invoice data from your CRM system, or lists of inventory from your ERP system. You may need to generate a billing statement or bulk customer correspondence. At the time of this book's writing, this is a new feature of UCM that came with the recent Oracle acquisition of Skywire Software, but we anticipate a lot of growth in this area.

Other advanced features include link management, analytics to determine what content is popular, watermarks for your converted Web documents, and specialized PDF document creation.

Document-centric Collaboration Management

The term "collaboration" is something of a misnomer: all information management systems enable collaboration of one sort or another. To be more precise, we should say that Universal Content Management has document-centric collaboration capabilities.

In UCM, this means informal "project spaces" where teams of users can collaboratively set up project folders, and submit content to them. Both the teams and the content in these project spaces are temporary in nature.

Perhaps the team project is discussing a possible acquisition, vendor selection, corporate events, or ideas about a new enterprise strategy. The data stored in these project spaces may include rough sketches, outlines, memos, notes, or partial assets that are all used to generate the final content.

These teams have very precise security and workflow needs that change on the fly, and you do not want your centralized security model to be the bottleneck. Content authors need total control over who is on the team, who is allowed to view a piece of content, who needs to review it, approve it, or edit it next. When finished, the final version can be promoted to the primary UCM system, where it can reach a wider audience.

Document-centric collaboration includes ad-hoc workflows, which allow general users to design simple routing rules for approvals. It also includes ad-hoc security, so the contributor can set precisely which specific users can access the content, and whether or not they can edit it.

Since UCM provides the document-centric capabilities, you can still use the same desktop integrations to e-mail clients, and Windows Explorer for easier contribution. If an e-mail is relevant to your current project, you can share it with your team with a simple drag and drop. You can also take advantage of the discussion threads and annotations, if you need them.

Digital Asset Management

Digital asset management (DAM) is focused on the creation, conversion, and management of digital assets. This includes extracting text from video streams, which enabled people to find media assets by searching for keywords that were spoken. It also includes automatic conversion of high-resolution graphics into thumbnails, Web-optimized images, and print optimized images. This ensures that your graphics department will not be the bottleneck when users need images for Web sites, presentations, or printed collateral. It also allows your marketing department to keep track of usage, by allowing users to "shop" for copyrighted content and corporate graphics.

As disk storage gets cheaper, more and more industries are turning to video and audio assets to capture and share knowledge. Why not make videos of every important presentation and meeting, to share with future employees, partners, and customers? Why not create a video newsletter for your company by conducting informal interviews of department heads? Why not create daily podcasts for your sales team, or other employees who travel frequently, so they can stay up to date while on the road?

Most importantly, how do you intend to capture vital business information before the baby boomer retirement wave hits your company? These workers have critical information that you need to gather and share within the next few years. Since this force is retiring soon, they have little incentive to learn a new software application to help transfer their knowledge. Nor are they likely to want to spend their remaining days documenting everything they know into a formal report. Some advocate that new Web 2.0 and social software applications will encourage this knowledge transfer, but don't be complacent: unless you actively work to extract this knowledge, it might be lost forever.

To solve this problem, some organizations have decided to turn to video as a way to capture this knowledge. Some choose to film just the exit interview, to glean as much as possible about what the retiree knows about current projects. Others might find value in weekly interviews during the last few years of a retiree's employment. Videos capture a great deal of nuanced information that is lost in other media, not to mention that being interviewed is faster and more fun than writing a dry report. No matter how fun your system is, retirees simply will not be motivated to use them. Instead, make a video, and have a less seasoned employee do the work of transferring the knowledge.

Web Content Management with Site Studio

Organizations create multiple Web sites in order to communicate to different audiences: customer portals, employee portals, wikis, blogs, and partner extranets. In many cases, organizations have hundreds or even thousands of Web sites for information sharing. Unfortunately, this has led to the sprawl of content across enterprises. It has also led to one-off systems that are difficult to maintain, and to the general inability to efficiently repurpose existing content into new Web sites.

Oracle Site Studio is a multi-site management tool that helps you quickly create all kinds of content-rich Web sites. It is a framework for building, managing, and maintaining multiple Web sites, and also empowers people to create and modify these sites, regardless of their skill level. Site Studio accomplishes this by breaking down the task of site management into four groups: site developers, site designers, site managers, and site contributors.

Each group has specialized tools to help them complete their tasks: site developers create code fragments to add functionality to the site, based on any of the supported Web scripting languages. Site designers are your HTML and CSS experts, who design the look and feel of the site, and create several layouts to contain content and the code fragments. Site managers reuse the assets created by the designers and developers, maintain the navigation hierarchy, and decide what content belongs on what page. Finally, site contributors use in-context editing tools to create and edit content directly on the Web page, regardless of their knowledge of HTML.

These pieces of the Web site are stored as assets in UCM. The majority of these assets are XML, including most of the site contributor content and the project file that describes the structure of the site. Any content item stored in UCM can become a Web asset, such as audio files, video files, images, Flash animations, PDFs, or even scanned paper documents. Site Studio can also convert content that was created in a native application—such as Microsoft Word—into Web-viewable HTML that has the same look and feel of the rest of the site.

Since Site Studio is built on top of UCM, it benefits from features such as metadata, security, subscriptions, workflows, and RSS feeds as well. The workflow feature works particularly well with the in-context editing: if a user changes the Web site, workflow reviewers will see the changed content in the context of the Web page, so they know exactly what it will look like before they approve it. In contrast, other users who are not workflow approvers will only see the previously approved content item on the site.

Records and Retention Management

As mentioned earlier, records and retention management is an important part of the content life cycle. Some content needs to persist for a fixed amount of time, and then be destroyed. Other times, the content can be eliminated if it's part of a cancelled project. In either case, the proper removal of old content can reduce your business risk, and keep your active repository up to date with relevant content.

In practice, Oracle splits this task into two products: Oracle Records Manager Corporate Edition, and Oracle Universal Records Management. The former is an application that only manages retention schedules for content in the UCM system, and it is bundled with the UCM product. The latter is a fully certified records management system, which can manage the retention policy of documents anywhere in your enterprise.

Oracle Records Manager Corporate Edition allows both contributors and administrators to set retention schedules for content items. These rules are based on dates, events, or how often the content is viewed. Combined, these help reduce the clutter in your repository. By giving each item a retention schedule, you can archive it out of the system once it is no longer useful.

For example, you could base retention schedules on how popular a content item is. If nobody has downloaded it in 12 months, you can automatically archive it. Alternatively, you could trigger a workflow to determine if this item should be deleted entirely. Another option would be to use workflows to ensure that popular content remains up to date. For example, if a content item was a year old, but suddenly was accessed many times in one month, the system might want to notify the original author of this fact. Perhaps the document is very important, but no longer relevant, so it should be updated as soon as possible.

In contrast, Oracle Universal Records Management is a stand-alone product that integrates with your strategic repository. It has many more features than the Records Manager Corporate Edition included in UCM, and is discussed in greater detail in Chapter 5.

Transactional Content

Transactional content management typically empowers process workers, and not knowledge workers. Content in this realm often consists of items that are generated, and managed, as part of a highly defined process, such as accounts payable, expense management, or contract management. The content is often, but not always, scanned into the application, processed through workflow, and then stored in some type of content repository—often an archive. Besides scanned documents, transactional content can also be used for managing e-check processing, fax server solutions, or computer output to laser disk (COLD) reports.

In contrast with active content management systems, transactional systems have very few contributors and very few consumers. However, since one content item is created per transaction, they usually contain a massive number of items. Repositories with a hundred million content items are common.

The content in a transactional system is highly valuable as it moves through the process, but is then often much less valuable after the completion of the process. Using accounts payable as an example, the information in the content is usually extracted programmatically with optical character recognition (OCR) or through manual data entry as part of the process. The information is stored in a general ledger system of some kind, which becomes the system of record. The image of the scanned invoice is associated with the transaction, so it can easily be located later and reviewed if necessary.

The key difference between active and transactional content is usually in the importance of structure. An active content item has very little structure, so structure is added with metadata to enable findability, and affect the lifecycle of the item. The content item has more importance than the metadata; the metadata merely enhances the content.

In contrast, transactional documents have a great deal of structure. The primary value of managing transactional items is in extracting the structured information from them, so you don't have to refer to the original paper. The paper has value, and should be stored for auditing purposes for a period of time, but once the data is extracted from the paper, it is verified, and properly processed, the value of the scanned image declines rapidly.

In addition, there may be enterprise applications outside the content management system that need to verify the extracted data. A common transactional content process looks like this:

1. A process worker scans a paper document.

2. OCR software running at the scanning station extracts relevant data from the document, including date, description, invoice number, purchase order, and cost.

3. The process worker verifies that the scanning software extracted the correct text from the document, and then submits the form.

4. The scanned document is checked in to a content management system, usually with the extracted data.

5. In some cases, the check-in event triggers a workflow to further process the transactional content, perhaps in a remote ERP system.

When scanning medical records, contracts, or archived paper documents, this process typically ends after step 4. However, if you are scanning an invoice or a purchase order, the full solution can be significantly more complex. In those cases, you will want to trigger an enterprise workflow process to coordinate information storage across multiple applications.

For example, if you scanned an invoice, you will want to verify the extracted data by comparing it to the data in your enterprise resource planning system. The invoice should have an internal purchase order number, which you can compare against both the invoice, and the packing slip. If your supplier sent you exactly what you want, your workflow will route to the accounting department for full payment. Otherwise, it may route to a human specialist to resolve the problems with your supplier. Perhaps they shipped too little, and they only get a partial payment? Perhaps they shipped the wrong item, and they need to resend the order? In this case, your process worker will need to see the original scanned document before the process can be resolved.

Most content management systems have an embedded workflow engine to help you design the above-mentioned workflow process. In the past, these workflows were based on proprietary technology. However, Oracle is joining the movement towards the Business Process Execution Language (BPEL) workflow standard. This standard will help enterprises orchestrate workflow process between content management systems and other enterprise applications. This standard is discussed in greater detail in later sections.

Transaction content can be enhanced in the same way that active content is. You can use tagging, metadata, bookmarks, folksonomy, annotations, redaction, and the like. However, these enhancements sometimes have less value, because you are unlikely to need to refer to transactional content after the process is complete. Annotations are probably the most important, and are quite common in transactional systems since scanned invoices sometimes need visual markup to call attention to errors and oddities. Comments are likewise useful. The other features should only be used if they enhance findability of the content during a future audit.

As mentioned before, the most value in a transactional content item is in the embedded structured information. However, there are exceptions. A true ECM system can handle such exceptions, when you want to do a little bit more with your scanned documents. For example, after you scan an invoice, you may wish to publish it to a secure extranet site so your business partners can view it. That way, your partners can see which invoices you have received and paid, and which ones require resolution. You may also need to retain those documents for a fixed number of years so you remain compliant with the law, in which case records and retention management becomes vital. You may also want an employee portal, where all their expense reports and HR forms are available for viewing. You may also want medical records to be available at a nurse's kiosk.

The key to managing transactional content is to understand that the primary return-on-investment is in streamlining the process, automating paper-based workflows, and having faster resolution to processing errors. As a result, many times it is sold as a line-of-business application. However, you need to ensure that your tools are flexible enough today for your process needs tomorrow. If you cannot easily move content through your scanning solution to an arbitrary enterprise application, you should reconsider your architecture.

Oracle Imaging and Process Management

Oracle Imaging and Process Management (IPM) is an application built on top of Oracle Fusion Middleware that enables organizations to automate content-centric processes. The primary capability of IPM is to image-enable enterprise applications, such as JD Edwards, PeopleSoft, Siebel, SAP, and E-Business Suite, and to provide a platform for the creation of image-centric applications. It can capture business transactions—both paper-based and electronic—and allow your process workers to see the details of these transactions in the context of the enterprise application.

Included in the product are also predefined, out-of-the-box business processes based on best practices for accounts payable, accounts receivable, expense management, and claims processing. IPM also has certified integrations with ERP systems that enable content ingestion as well as quick access to images for data lookup and validation.

Image-enabling applications allow organizations to realize significant savings by delivering critical process documents, such as invoices, checks, faxes, and expense forms, quickly and efficiently via electronic formats. Through the integration with enterprise applications, IPM also helps reduce risk and cost by providing imaging capabilities directly in the context where your process workers perform data entry and auditing. As discussed earlier,

Transactional Content Management

Oracle Document Capture and Imaging and Process Management (IPM) are key elements in our enterprise infrastructure. IPM serves as the foundation for our transactional information repository along with with Capture, to create a seamless engine that transforms a myriad of content into valuable information for our line-of-business applications. IPM's workflow and integration tools enable data extraction, verification, and image availability from within any business application. From our ERP system, permit system, police records, or GIS, documents access is securely delivered using a variety of flexible services. This yielded fast, accurate information access, which helped us improve customer service and lower our costs.

—Jim McKenney

content in context is critical to success and often drives the value of
a content management system.

Image Management

IPM provides a set of capabilities for the management of large volumes of
images. While large active content solutions may contain *millions* of content
items, large transactional systems contain *billions* of items. For this reason,
IPM utilizes a set of image management capabilities that allow both high-
volume ingestion of documents and storage management across multiple
storage mediums including network attached storage, database, optical
systems, and archiving solutions.

Content Processing

Through the integration with Oracle Document Capture and the included
workflow and business process management (BPM) tools, IPM enables
organizations to quickly image-enable enterprise applications with an
advanced set of content processing capabilities. Work load-balancing and
parallel processing allow worklists and queues to be established and managed
across a group of process workers to optimize workforce efficiency. An
included viewer provides quick access to images directly from the enterprise
applications and the ability to mark up, or annotate, documents as part of
approval processes. Annotations allow multiple users to collaborate on an
image as part of either an ingestion or output process within the context of the
appropriate application. IPM also includes eForms to help organizations move
from paper-based processes to electronic forms processing.

Fusion Middleware and Fusion Applications

Oracle IPM has integrations with enterprise applications that go back over
a decade. The product was originally created by Optika and was called Acorde.
Optika was purchased by Stellent several years ago, and then Stellent was later
purchased by Oracle. The combination of the Optika/Stellent product and the
Oracle technology has really accelerated the solution.

   As of the planned 11*g* release, IPM will make extensive use of the Oracle
Fusion Middleware technologies, including a tight integration with Oracle
BPEL Process Manager and Oracle Enterprise Manager. The BPEL Process
Manager is discussed later in this chapter, as it is an important part of your
strategic ECM infrastructure. As of 11*g*, IPM will provide the option to use
either Oracle Universal Content Management, or Oracle Universal Online

Archive as the content repository for your transactional content management system. The use of Fusion Middleware within IPM allows enterprise applications to integrate via Oracle's Application Integration Architecture (AIA) and will be a cornerstone for how Oracle's next generation of applications, called Fusion Applications, will leverage the ingestion and processing of unstructured information.

Historical Content Management

Whether you're dealing mainly with active content, or with transactional content, after a certain period of time you won't be accessing your content often. Transactional content is useful only for as long as it takes to complete the process, after which it is primarily needed for auditors. Active content can be archived out once a newer revision is available, or once the content item is considered outdated. In either case, moving the content to less expensive storage devices can yield significant cost savings.

While a unified content management system provides depth of capabilities in a single application/repository model, and content processing systems provide tools for process workers to efficiently content-enable workflows, content archiving provides infrastructure and services for historical content across multiple applications and systems.

Archiving presents distinct challenges from an ECM platform in that archiving is focused on the long-term storage and management at an infrastructure layer of information that often naturally resides elsewhere. For example, e-mail archiving provides for the categorization and long-term storage of e-mail that typically resides on an e-mail server, such as Microsoft Exchange or Lotus Notes. The purpose of archiving is not necessarily to provide additional functionality to e-mails or to the e-mail server, but rather to offload the infrastructure requirements into a centrally managed, highly available, back office environment.

Why have one system for archiving, and a different system for active management? Archiving solutions need to be optimized for high volumes of infrequently accessed content. Active repositories need to be optimized for frequently accessed content, usually in smaller quantities. These are different problems. Place frequently used content in an active repository; place large volumes of rarely used content in the historical repository.

This is highly advantageous from the end user's perspective. The archives are only useful for auditors or for historical research. However, users insist that their active content system be free of clutter, so they can more easily find authoritative content. Content flagged as archived should not show up in the day-to-day active content management system.

In general, there are two kinds of historical solutions: archive-centric and policy-centric. Archive-centric solutions focus on making connectors to large repositories, and making it easy to move content into, out of, and around the system. They focus on ease of deployment, configuration, and maintenance. They are excellent for general digital archives.

In contrast, a policy-centric solution is much more sophisticated. It is focused around retention policies for the digital content. For example, the policy-centric solution will retain contracts and e-mails for a fixed amount of time, and then destroy them. They may need to conform to certain industry regulations, as well as customized life cycles. These systems are a combination of hardware and software, and require much more configuration.

Oracle has several solutions for both policy-based and archive-based repositories for historical content management. These are discussed in the sections that follow.

Oracle Secure Files

Storing files in the database is fairly common. As mentioned in Chapter 2, it's typical for enterprise applications to store unstructured content as Large Objects in the database. This greatly simplifies your architecture, and allows you to easily associate structured information with your unstructured files, but it comes at a performance and storage cost. In the past, accessing files stored in a database took longer than accessing them on a shared file system, and it required more disk space for your database.

Recognizing this, the Oracle database team spent many years trying to optimize how they store unstructured data. Finally, in 11g they released Oracle Secure Files, which completely changes the conventional wisdom about storing unstructured content. From a performance perspective, it is comparable to a shared file system, even when you include the performance costs of the additional security and storage features that file systems lack.

Besides performance, there are three other compelling reasons to store content in Secure Files. The first is compression, which means that the binary data is automatically compressed to save space. Oracle Database 11g provides compression levels of approximately 30 percent for typical archived content. The second is encryption, which means that the file will be automatically encoded so that your database administrators will not be able to read the files. The third feature is called deduplication, which means that it never stores two copies of the same file.

In practice, when you add a file to the system, it checks to see if that file was already added. If so, the database records that there are two copies, but on disk it only stores one copy. It also compresses it and encrypts it, all while maintaining better than file-system performance. In addition, de-duplication occurs at the *block* level, as opposed to the file-level. That means that when you store a new revision of the file, it won't store an entirely new file: only the blocks that are different. In practice, this reduces your file storage needs even further, especially for multiple revisions of the same document that only contains minor changes.

Since this is done at the infrastructure level, the deduplication, compression, and encryption occur regardless of which user or application stored the content in the database. In other words, if the same document is attached to an e-mail in thousands of mailboxes, in different project spaces, and even contained in different enterprise and custom applications, the underlying infrastructure across all those applications only stores *one single copy* of the item. The applications themselves are not aware of the de-duplication being done at the infrastructure layer—each application believes it has stored the document independently.

All together, enabling these features still ensures file-system quality performance, additional security, and the potential of an 80 percent reduction in storage costs. Also, since this is built on top of the Oracle database, you can take advantage of built-in Oracle life cycle management tools. You can distribute the file storage across multiple types of media: high-performance disk, low-cost storage disk, and a read-only storage tier. You can use this tool to move content to cheaper storage, if it is accessed rarely.

By itself, Secure Files is not a content management system: it is simply a way of storing files in the database. However, this feature can be used in two ways to create a strategic historical content repository.

Oracle Universal Online Archive

The Universal Online Archive (UOA) is a recent addition to Oracle's ECM product line. It is an archiving solution built on top of Secure Files, with the ambitious goal of enabling enterprises to store digital archives that are always available. Instead of using expensive specialized hardware, or locking data away in a backup tape, your archives are always online and live.

The advantage to keeping archives online is instant access: since it is available right in the database, your applications can always read the data. Auditors and knowledge workers will always need to research information in your archives, so you need some kind of process to enable that. The movement towards business intelligence, data mining, and other analytics is pushing us towards faster and easier access to these archives. These processes are slow and expensive if your archives are on backup tapes, and in some cases these expenses are increasing. In contrast, the cost of an always online archive is getting cheaper, while its value is increasing.

The primary cost of an online archive is disk storage. However, since UOA sits on top of Oracle Secure Files, it reduces disk storage needs significantly. Because of this reduction, and the fact that disk storage continues to be cheaper, online archives are significantly more cost effective than in the past.

For an archive to be successful it needs to be transparent, manageable, and highly scalable. Oracle Universal Online Archive works across multiple content types, multiple content stores, and includes e-mail archiving. The Universal Online Archive is an important piece of the pragmatic ECM strategy covered in Chapter 2. It was designed to be an online archive for any kind of digital content, however, the first release is focused on being an archive for e-mail systems, such as Microsoft Exchange or Lotus Notes.

The UOA solution is best classified as an archive-centric solution. As a stand-alone product, it does not provide comprehensive retention policies. In order to accomplish a true policy-based archiving solution, you will need Universal Records Management (URM) as well. The URM solution is a records and retention policy engine that uses adapters to enforce policy in other repositories. This is discussed in greater detail in Chapter 5.

When UOA is combined with URM, your e-mail archiving policy is no longer dictated by IT. Your records managers can say when an item should be archived, and how long it should be retained based on events, instead of simply time and size constraints. For example, e-mails could be deleted two years after project completion, six months after employee termination, or twelve months after you lose a specific customer. Policies like this will further reduce your e-mail space requirements, and will significantly reduce your legal risk.

In the future, Oracle plans to extend this archive to other repositories. For example, assume you have a large document in SharePoint, and you determine that it should be archived. A UOA connector in SharePoint could move the document to the archive, and leave a placeholder file. When the end user downloads the document from SharePoint, the UOA connector would retrieve it from the archive, and deliver it to the user behind the scenes.

In other words, you would be using a secure, compressed, deduplicated, encrypted archive without ever noticing!

From the point of view of a user, the archived document still exists in SharePoint, so they need not be retrained. In the event that 20 people all place the same document in different SharePoint folders, the deduplication in Secure Files ensures that only one copy is placed on the disk. If used along with Universal Records Management, you can also be ensured that you are complying with whatever regulations and laws your organization requires.

Oracle UCM and Secure Files

If you already own Oracle Database 11*g* and you do not need a new e-mail archiving solution, another option for strategic historical content management is a combination of Oracle UCM and Secure Files.

Since version 10gr3, Oracle UCM can be configured to store files in nearly any repository: a shared file system, the database, or even custom hardware. This is called the File Store Provider, which stores content in different places, depending on the metadata. This is important, because sometimes using a single storage system is not optimal for performance or compliance reasons.

For example, it is best to store old content and large files in Secure Files. This is because such content is only accessed rarely, or one item at a time. In contrast, in order to deliver a Web page with Site Studio, you sometimes need to display dozens of content items: JavaScript files, HTML, Cascading Style Sheet (CSS) files, Flash animations, images, and text in XML or HTML format. This would mean a dozen database requests per page. In some setups, this can hurt performance, especially if your Web server is far away from your database in your network. It doesn't matter how fast the database is; the performance would be limited because of the latency involved in one computer making a request to another.

In other words, small files that don't require security, and that are accessed frequently, should be statically published to your Web server. Luckily, all this takes in UCM is a custom metadata flag that signifies content as "public Web content." A properly configured File Store Provider will store Web content locally and all other content in Secure Files, giving you the best of both worlds.

Using Strategic ECM in the Enterprise

There has been a debate of sorts for some time in the content management community about how to classify ECM. Is it infrastructure? Is it an application? Is it middleware? What features do you need for each?

Thinking of ECM as an *application* leads to the proliferation of line-of-business solutions. In other words, vital, useful, strategic information is locked away in content silos. People make copies, information becomes outdated, and your security policy is not followed. People have a hard time finding the content they need, and when they do find it, it is outdated, or of questionable authenticity. However, we cannot ignore the fact that these line-of-business applications exist for a reason. As mentioned in Chapter 2, if you do not have an ECM Center of Excellence, it's likely that the centralized IT system did not suit the needs of the end user of unstructured content applications. Therefore, individual departments felt the only solution to their specific information management problem was with a content silo. It's a sub-optimal solution, but they could never achieve an optimal solution until the IT department fully appreciates what the business needs.

One solution to this problem is to think of ECM as *infrastructure*. Design a set of basic content services, and create applications that consume those services. Then you can place all content in your strategic ECM infrastructure, which you can then integrate with your line-of-business applications.

Unfortunately, the idea of basic content services is fraught with danger. Every vendor, every partner, and every customer has a different idea of what services should be include in "basic content services." It is true that most of the time, your organization would only use 20 percent of the features in an ECM system. However, the problem is that every organization will use a different 20 percent of the features in a system. Therefore, they will never agree to what "basic content services" actually means. This fundamental lack of agreement will mean that an infrastructure approach to ECM is a good start, but will ultimately be insufficient.

Therefore, ECM also needs to act as *middleware*. This means that not only should it support other middleware applications, but it should also act as middleware and integrate directly with enterprise applications. This means that it should integrate with portals and applications servers, but it should also connect directly to ERP and CRM systems.

To be maximally useful, your strategic ECM system should be able to act in all three ways: as an application, as infrastructure, and as middleware. All three methods have their uses, so in order to truly be a strategic ECM system, you need to support all three. The specifics of each method is described in greater detail in the sections below.

ECM as an Application

When you install ECM as an application, you usually only care about one specific use: a public-facing Web site, a departmental knowledge base, collaborative project spaces, document scanning and processing, enterprise publishing, or highly structured content authoring environments—for example, United States Federal Drug Administration (FDA) approval documents or technical manuals. Newer varieties of these applications have a content management system as back-end data storage; however, older versions may be locked away in a hard-to-access content silo. These are sometimes called *content-centric applications*, or *content-enabled vertical applications*, which are covered in greater detail in Chapter 7.

In the past, many ECM solutions were only deployed as applications. However, this can exacerbate the content management problem, because these systems were usually deployed as silos. When you deploy ECM as an application, there is a strong tendency to put insufficient thought into maximizing the future reusability of your content. You tend to think tactically about your current problem, but not strategically about the future needs of the whole organization.

A better strategy is to create multiple content-centric applications that use a strategic ECM system as a repository. For example, let's consider a common ECM use case: a high-volume scanning application for processing invoices. This is a common application, and provides tremendous value through greater processing efficiency. However, the primary value of this ECM system is not the content; the value is its ability to extract structured information, and pass it off to an enterprise application like Oracle E-Business Suite or SAP.

Those tools have the appropriate features to complete the business process. ECM is the tool that scans the content and stores it for later use. In an ideal integration, a process worker would be able to view the original scanned content—perhaps even with notes and annotations—from the content of the E-Business Suite application. This in-context viewing ensures that the process worker need never use two interfaces or learn two applications.

This is how pragmatic ECM applications should be created, which is the model that Oracle Imaging and Process Management follows.

Not to pick on the imaging aspects of ECM, the same can be said for "persuasive" or "collaborative" content management systems. These systems are for knowledge workers, as opposed to scanning applications, which are meant for process workers. These systems enable complex document authoring, information sharing, archiving, and tools for solving Web content and records management problems. These systems provide tremendous advantages for organizations for creating and sharing content—but again, it is the context in which this content is created and shared that provides much of its value. The ability for a call center agent to access a manual, a customer, or a FAQ is greatly enhanced when users can seamlessly interact with the content through enterprise applications and standard desktop tools. ECM is at its best when users don't realize they are using it; instead, they benefit from centralized security, version control, search, tagging, and records management simply by using the applications they already know.

In some cases, it is a good idea to initially roll out a strategic ECM system as an application to a business unit. This allows you to start small, and scale up and out as needed. Oracle UCM is excellent for this, because it can be used as the unified repository for multiple line-of-business applications, and migrating content between them is simple.

However, as mentioned before, you should be cautious about deploying ECM as an application. Be mindful about the metadata, taxonomy, security, and information architecture problems that might limit future reuse of the system. There is also the danger that a department would add unnecessary security policies to lock away content so other departments could not access it. In other words, after all the time and energy you spent breaking down content silos, they might emerge again because of unnecessarily strict security policies.

Your ECM Center of Excellence should be wary when people think of ECM as an application. This usually means new content silos are emerging, either with custom applications, custom configuration, or a locked-down security model. Your CoE needs to have the influence to break down both existing and emerging content silos.

In general, ECM as an application works great for department-level solutions, solutions for small- to medium-sized enterprises, or as an initial roll-out. It's a good way to get accustomed to your system, but you need to be mindful of future requirements.

ECM as Infrastructure

The role of ECM as an infrastructure is to provide content management tools and capabilities to be used by IT. Your IT administrators would configure the system for the proper life cycle management, metadata, records and retention policies, high availability, redundancy, backup, and general storage management.

In contrast, your users would never notice that they were using a content management system; instead, they would be dragging files into a special shared folder, as they always have. This gives you greater control over the content, but it has little to no effect on existing processes and workflows.

All applications rely on infrastructure of one form or another. An ECM application will need to store information in some combination of the database, the file system, and some kind of backup media. Large ECM deployments typically leverage shared databases and shared file systems that are a piece of the enterprise infrastructure.

Expanding that raw storage a step further gets us to the concept of ECM infrastructure. ECM infrastructure provides services and capabilities on top of the enterprise storage layer. This infrastructure may provide some basic life cycle management, deduplication, or even smart storage technology to optimize retrieval times while minimizing costs.

ECM infrastructures are built on top of basic file systems, optical systems, tape-based systems, WORM (write once, read many) storage devices, and databases. Traditionally, there have been clear trade-offs between these different options. File systems offered the best performance, but were more expensive than tape drives, and lacked many of the management capabilities of databases or WORM devices. Optical systems were generally expensive but provided volumes not available by traditional means (going back ten years or so). Databases provided the most manageability, but historically lagged in read/write performance behind file systems. As with any technology area, recent advances blurred these distinctions, and may require us to reevaluate our assumptions.

As mentioned earlier, Secure Files is a feature of Oracle Database 11*g* that provides the ability to manage large blocks of raw digital content in the database with access speeds comparable to file systems. For small files the two systems are equivalent, but for large files the database can significantly outperform the file system. Oracle achieves these speeds without sacrificing the infrastructure management capabilities of the database, such as high availability, redundancy, backup and restore, replication, and Real Application Clusters (RAC).

Naturally, Secure Files is just one important piece of ECM as infrastructure. By itself, Secure Files does not provide any of the necessary content services that an ECM infrastructure would need. Instead, you need the Universal Online Archive or the Universal Content Management system on top of Secure Files to provide those services and capabilities.

The UOA provides the basic services needed for archiving historical content, such as e-mail archives. Whereas UCM can provide the basic search, download, and edit services that active content needs. Unfortunately, there may be a problem with using just the core content services—needs vary based on department and project. Some may only need searching and downloading; others may need subscriptions and workflow; still others may need transformation and taxonomy services.

Therefore, basic services are a good start, but a pragmatic ECM strategy should never restrict you to them. It should allow you to use basic services if that's all you need. However, once you get past the basic services, you need to move towards providing comprehensive ECM as part of your middleware layer.

ECM as Middleware

The push to ECM as middleware grew out of necessity. Enterprises needed a system that could provide infrastructure, but at the same time was much more than infrastructure. Enterprises needed a system that was a useful application, but at the same time would be able to grow into much more. What enterprises needed was ECM as middleware.

Middleware contains the key building blocks for creating custom applications, and extending off-the-shelf enterprise applications. These include application servers, portals, and rich Internet applications for the user interface layer; enterprise search; business intelligence; developer tools; and, of course, a coherent security infrastructure with single sign-on. The complete offering of Oracle Fusion Middleware is illustrated in Figure 4-2.

Content management is positioned squarely in the middle of the Oracle Fusion Middleware stack; it is a key component providing critical information management services. Most modern middleware strategies focus on service-oriented architecture (SOA) and the ability for components to be reused easily across both the infrastructure and the target application within the enterprise.

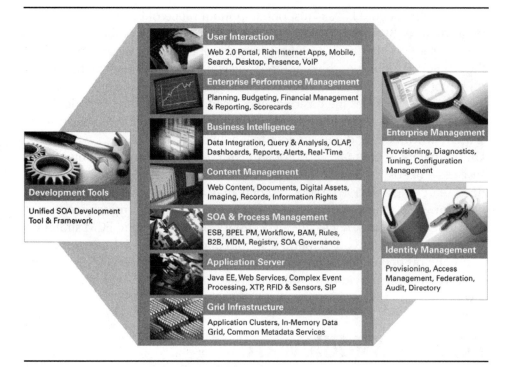

FIGURE 4-2. *Content management provides an ever-expanding set of services both to and through Fusion Middleware.*

Content management as middleware also plays a major role in what is often now called the User Interaction (UI) layer. Whether the UI layer is a portal, a Web site, an iPhone, a customer service kiosk, or an enterprise application front-end, content plays a critical role in the user experience. When looking at content management as middleware, the ability to deliver content into multiple user interaction layers is critical. An ECM system must be able to transform content "for purpose," allowing native content such as Microsoft Word documents to be transformed, dynamically, in real time, into the appropriate format for the appropriate application and with the correct branding.

Content management functionality can be provided, via this SOA approach, for use by enterprise applications via an enterprise service bus, or accessed directly via SOA to the ECM system itself. When using a service bus model, the middleware services are responsible for interacting with the content infrastructure. As such, services provided by an ECM system through a middleware strategy can be categorized in two simple ways: core services and specialized services.

ECM as Middleware

Oracle UCM provides a tremendous amount of versatility in every role it takes in an organization. We've had great success implementing it as the front-end of a Web site, as the back-end of a portal, and as a collaborative environment for document management. The common element in probably all UCM implementations seems to be the desire to manage a single source of content and then allow that content to be transformed or delivered in a number of different formats or methods. What sets UCM apart is its capability to meet all these requirements through one of the most functional and flexible service-oriented integration frameworks available.

—David Roe, Ironworks
contentoncontentmanagement.com

Core content services include only the essential features of ECM, such as finding content, downloading it, grouping it, and editing it. These services only scratch the surface of what is possible with ECM, but it may be all you need for high-volume scanning applications, or an e-mail archive. Many attempts have been made to create a standard for basic content services, but all have struggled for different reasons.

There are a number of content management standards that may play a role in your pragmatic ECM strategy and may provide some of these basic services. JSR-170, also called the Java Content Repository (JCR), is a Java-centric industry standard that provides very core content services to Java applications. Its newer iteration is JSR-283, which adds several features missing from JSR-170, but has not yet achieved significant adoption. Unlike the JSR specifications, WebDAV is a Web-based protocol for revisioning content items in a folder structure. As such, it works with non-Java repositories such as Microsoft SharePoint. WebDAV is useful, but it has problems dealing with metadata and dates. Syndication feeds such as RSS and ATOM are also used in lieu of content management standards, but feeds are primarily used for distributing content items, rather than finding or managing them.

The latest content management standard is called the Content Management Interoperability Services specification, or CMIS. At the time of this book's writing, this specification has just been submitted to an OASIS committee for consideration of becoming a standard. It is backed by many major software vendors, including Oracle, IBM, Microsoft, EMC, Open Text, and SAP. Instead of being a Java-specific standard, CMIS is a protocol standard. This means that you can consume standard content management services from any application that can consume Web services. This standard is only at version 0.5, but it will likely become the de-facto ECM standard in 2009.

Nevertheless, most of these standards tend to be pretty limited in their abilities. In our opinion, they have a place in an ECM strategy, but in practice they have always needed supplementary ECM features that are outside the standard. Some enterprises would prefer to integrate their applications directly with ECM using SOAs. This is a nice loose-coupling of applications, but it requires every enterprise application that needs ECM to create a custom ECM connector. Another approach would be to integrate ECM with an enterprise service bus (ESB), and then integrate each system with the bus. In this case, each application only needs to create one integration to the bus, after which the bus orchestrates messages between the different enterprise applications. However, the ESB option requires a greater investment in hardware and software for your enterprise.

In contrast to basic content services, specialized content services provide more advanced capabilities such as content tagging, transformation, in-context editing, digital asset management, workflows, subscriptions, annotations, or retention management. In almost any ECM system the number of specialized services greatly outnumbers the core services. For example, Oracle Universal Content Management has over 500 content services available out-of-the-box as Web services. Of these, barely a dozen qualify as core services.

The reason for this distinction is essentially the familiar 80/20 rule. A majority of applications—especially those that are not content-centric, but rather just utilize some small basic set of content—do not need access to high-value ECM services. Bringing the core services into an enterprise service bus, as shown in Figure 4-3, greatly simplifies the complexity of integrating basic content management with multiple applications. The lack of extended features is the price you have to pay for this simplicity.

In contrast, integrating high-value specialized content services requires a greater understanding of the problem and the features available in the ECM application. It doesn't usually make sense to wire specialized content services into the bus, because specialized services are used by only a few specific applications. Instead, it may make more sense for those applications to connect directly to the ECM system to access those services. For any

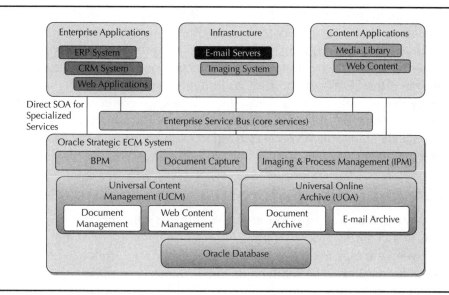

FIGURE 4-3.   *ECM as middleware provides services to multiple applications according to their needs.*

organization a decision on the mix of core and specialized services should be made on an application-by-application basis.

Beyond the SOA approach to ECM discussed above, there are also significant connections between content management and other areas of middleware that provide solutions with compelling value propositions. Middleware is used to build enterprise and custom applications, usually through the assembly of multiple middleware capabilities and enterprise services into a solution. Following are a few examples of how content management relates to other areas of Oracle Fusion Middleware.

Strategic ECM Middleware Integrations

Integrating ECM requires thinking about it as middleware. This means two primary options: ECM acts as middleware, or ECM is hidden behind middleware. In the first case, your ECM system connects directly to the applications you need: ERP, CRM, e-mail archives, and the like. This is a good option if your system has very specific content needs. In contrast, if you want to provide a common set of ECM services across a variety of applications that is beyond core services, providing ECM through middleware is a good option.

There are many ways to create these integrations. Probably the most common is the SOA approach, either through an enterprise service bus, or directly to the content server. These integrations are common, because they expose everything that the UCM system can offer. Besides SOAP, Oracle offers specialized tools if you only need to expose one aspect of your strategic content repository.

SOA Suite and Enterprise Service Buses

Let's assume that you need to integrate multiple applications at several points in a business processes flow. For example, if you are hiring a new employee, you may need to update several systems in sequence before the process is complete. The same holds true for when you update the price of a product or add a new customer. This is called a *composite application*, because it ties together multiple smaller applications in order to run a specific service. In this case, it would be quite challenging to create a plug-in to each environment so every system can communicate with every other system. Instead, in these cases it is desirable for all systems to make one integration to an intermediary, which then orchestrates the connections between systems.

You could create this intermediary with middleware. Such a beast would typically be written in an application server, with custom Java connectors to each back-end application. The process flow would be coded in the Java code itself. This is a common approach, but sometimes it is too inflexible: most changes to the process flow would require a Java programmer to alter, test, and deploy the new code. If your system needs to be tuned frequently, and is too mission critical to make frequent code changes, this can become a challenge.

Alternatively, you could use an ESB. These are based on two concepts: first, encourage every application in your enterprise to use a semi-standard messaging interface to enable inter-application communication; second, use an easily configured workflow engine instead of custom Java code to help "orchestrate" the communication between applications.

These days, most ESBs use some kind of Web service for messaging, which helps them promote and leverage a service-oriented architecture. Different ESBs use different workflow engines, but the most common standard thus far is the Business Process Execution Language, described in the next section.

Business Process Execution Language

As mentioned above, a messaging protocol like SOAP is only one part of an enterprise service bus. The other part is some kind of easy-to-configure workflow engine to "orchestrate" what the applications do. These days, the most common standard for defining and processing workflows is the Business Process Execution Language (BPEL).

BPEL is an XML-based standard language for designing and executing workflows and composite applications. It allows you to control the flow of the process from one step to the next, determine which message to send to which application, spawn new processes, join two processes together back into one, and even automate human tasks. Also, the XML document that defines your workflow is a nice audit trail to ensure your process meets specific requirements.

Since BPEL is a workflow standard, there's less vendor lock-in. You can orchestrate a BPEL process between two systems that use a different BPEL Process Manager, as shown in Figure 4-4. The advantage here is that two business partners can automate a BPEL process between them, even if they run completely different BPEL engines in their respective enterprises.

Many applications support some kind of workflow process. The workflows built in to Oracle UCM are more document-centric, whereas the ones in Oracle IPM are more task-oriented. These built-in workflows can be used in combination with an enterprise business process management tool, or as stand-alone content-centric workflows.

For example, if you were looking to implement a basic workflow to approve content before it is published to the Web, the document-centric workflows built into UCM services are ideal. If, however, your workflow needs to be integrated with other systems, or leverage another enterprise process—such as a standardized out-of-office escalation policy—then you should install the BPEL Workflow add-on for UCM, and use Oracle's BPEL Process Manager to run your document-centric workflows.

BPEL Challenges

BPEL is still an emerging standard. Many new features were added to BPEL 2.0, which not all BPEL process managers support. In June 2007, a consortia that included Oracle published the BPEL4People specification, which extended BPEL to include a standard way to define human interaction tasks. However, BPEL4People has not yet been ratified as a standard, and at

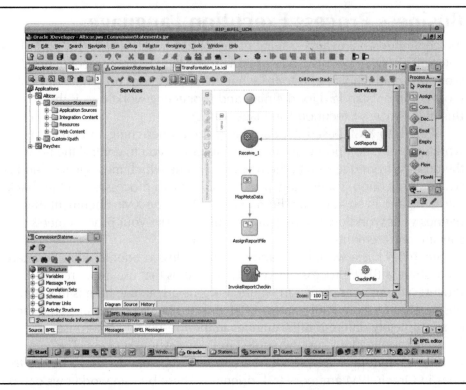

FIGURE 4-4. *Developers create BPEL process flows with familiar workflow terms.*

present it is mainly used for application-to-application communication. These additions served as a stern reminder that BPEL is not a programming language: rather, it is an *orchestration* language. It enables what is called "programming in the large," and is lacking features possessed by other languages like Java.

In short, BPEL enhances middleware, but does not replace it. You do not write applications in BPEL; rather, BPEL empowers non-programmers to chain together prebuilt applications into composite applications. This distinction is subtle, but very important. In practice, it is difficult to know beforehand if your business process is too complex to be modeled purely with BPEL. As a result, it is important to know how to extend BPEL with languages like Java to fill in the functionality gaps. Likewise, if a process flow is difficult to describe with BPEL, but easy to describe in Java, you should perhaps write part of it with Java.

By enabling non-programmers to create composite applications, you can make adjustments to your process flow more quickly and more safely. In exchange for this ease, you must sacrifice some functionality that exists in complete programming languages. For the most part, the speed with which composite applications can be created and modified is worth this trade-off.

Oracle Open Web Content Management

As mentioned in Chapter 2, one of the most exciting additions to the federated ECM toolset is Open Web content management (Open WCM*). The goal behind Open WCM is to manage and display any Web content—HTML, XML, images, and text—from any Web-enabled application anywhere in your enterprise.

This means that a consistent Web editing experience is possible from any type of Web application. For end users, they always use the same tools to click-and-edit content directly from within the Web application. IT departments, application designers, and site owners can now freely choose the underlying technology they wish to use for building the site without impacting the end-user experience for content owners.

Oracle UCM's core WCM capability is Site Studio. Similar to Universal Records Management, Site Studio is an application plug-in to the UCM platform. All of the Web content—fragments of code, Web page layouts, native documents, navigation lists, images, HTML and XML content—are all stored in the content server and rendered with Site Studio. In this way, the UCM servers act as both the content repository and the application that renders the Web page. This includes content and code fragments written in any supported Web scripting language.

Rendering dynamic Web pages in context with the content server yields several advantages. Firstly, it allows you to use any UCM feature within the content of the displayed Web page: workflows, subscriptions, RSS feeds, annotations, and metadata. However, running the system in-context with the server is limiting when you want to display this content in a remote portal, application server, or other Web application.

For example, assume you have a fully functional Web application that allows you to submit time sheets and expenses online. Most of the work in creating this system is in the custom application code to store structured data. However, some of this application is Web content: images, disclaimers,

---

*Open WCM is an active Oracle project targeted at the Oracle 11 release timeframe. At the time of this book's writing, it is a yet-to-be-released roadmap item.

policies and procedures, help files, and the like. Ideally, all this Web content would originate from your single source of truth, so if you update the branding in your strategic repository, it will be immediately reflected in all these Web applications.

A common solution to this problem is a publishing model: download the Web content out from the strategic repository on a set interval, and push it to the appropriate location in the remote Web application. This way, you can merge your static Web content with your application code, and have a vey rich and well managed Web site. This is a common model, used by many, and Site Studio has several tools for exactly this.

However, the publishing model is limited because you lose *in-context editing*. This is the ability to see your content on a Web page and edit it directly on that page. In-context editing eliminates the need of using specialized tools to update Web content. It also empowers content owners, rather than application programmers, to own and manage the content on a Web site. Site Studio uses in-context editing as part of its core set of capabilities; however, in order to use it, the entire site must exist in Oracle UCM.

In contrast, Open WCM allows you to have in-context editing even in remote applications, regardless of how that application was created. This includes JEE Application Server and Portals, Oracle WebCenter and WebLogic servers, and even SharePoint. Open WCM, shown in Figure 4-5, has the ability to extend Site Studio's functionality so that it can enable in-context editing on any Web application in the enterprise. It uses an adapter-driven architecture to allow in-context editing on any application in your enterprise. All systems can benefit from your strategic repository, with extremely little configuration.

Open WCM is focused on the editing, transformation, workflow, and delivery of content into Web applications. To utilize Open WCM, an application developer simply replaces the editable content of a page with a tag. Server-side tags are currently planned for JSP and ASP.NET, allowing programmers to choose either language. For all other languages, including pure HTML pages, a set of DHTML and Ajax tags are being developed to allow the tags to be used with any scripting language (such as PHP).

The developer must also run an Open WCM adapter in their Web application. This adapter is triggered whenever the application renders a page with an Open WCM tag. The adapter then renders the Web content and injects it into the page. The end user can edit the Web content without ever leaving the context of the page, and therefore never be aware that Oracle UCM is managing their content.

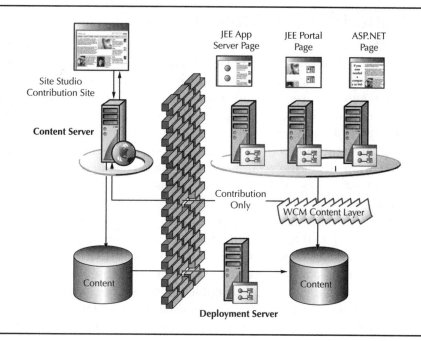

FIGURE 4-5.   *Open WCM empowers Web content management,*
regardless of application.

This tag approach allows application developers to use the design
environment of choice, their Web application architecture of choice,
programming language of choice, and delivery infrastructure of choice
while still providing best-in-breed, consistent, in-context editing and review
of content.

For the end user, Open WCM offers consistent in-context editing
capabilities, regardless of how the developers choose to implement the
application. If your IT department has a Java portal, as well as several .NET-
based applications, your content contributor in HR always has a consistent
process for updating content in these systems. There is no need for them to
understand the difference between Java and .NET, not even the difference
between two different Web applications; it all just works.

As you can see, content-enabling your existing Web applications just got
a whole lot easier with Open WCM. This allows you to easily push a
tremendous number of content services directly into the enterprise user
interaction layer.

ECM and Identity Management

To be effective, information security must span across the realm of access points from which information can be gathered, downloaded, or shared. Identity Management (IdM), generally speaking, provides capabilities such as user management, user authentication, application security, and single sign-on. A centralized IdM system is essential to the security and simplicity of any enterprise architecture. As such, your ECM applications need to seamlessly integrate with your centralized identity management system.

While IdM manages the security around enterprise applications and enterprise infrastructure, such as data warehouses, we often lose control over information security once it is moved from one repository to another. For example, you may have extensive controls over access to sales data when it is in a financial application. However, if you are like most businesses, access to financial data is very important for knowledge workers. Thus, the tighter the control you have over access to these applications, the more likely it is that the data will be copied into insecure formats for easier access. This includes text files, Excel spreadsheets, or e-mail messages.

In other words, your highly secure repository has all but guaranteed the insecurity of your data.

A content management system needs to both cleanly integrate with Identity Management, and also expand document security beyond the reach of the repository. Luckily, Oracle ECM can meet both needs simultaneously. These topics are covered in greater detail in Chapter 6.

Tools for Creating Custom Integrations

The tools discussed earlier are prepackaged applications that enable content services to be extended into systems and to be leveraged by other pieces of middleware. All of Oracle's ECM products have a Web services integration layer, including URM, UOA, IPM, and IRM. However, Web services are not the only options.

If you need more advanced content services in your applications, you may wish to use the content management APIs to get direct access to richer functionality and capabilities. For example, you may be creating a digital media library for the marketing department that uses extensive transformation and presentation services. Perhaps you are creating a specialized forms routing solution that is heavily dependent on a forms capability in the content management system. Perhaps your application needs to enrich the content item with annotations, comments, metadata tagging, and the like, and needs to ensure that other applications can share this data as well. In either case, you may need to create your own custom integration using one of the following available tools.

Because Oracle's UCM was designed from day one to be a service-oriented architecture, there are well over 50 ways to integrate applications with the content server. A full technical overview is beyond the scope of this book; however, we illustrate some general options below. For more information, refer to the technical documentation for UCM.

Loosely Coupled Integration Tools

Oracle UCM has several simple integration paths. These range from basic command-line tools, to file system integrations, to controls that you can embed in custom applications.

If you need to put content into the system, perhaps the easiest method is a protocol called WebDAV, short for Web Distributed Authoring and Versioning. This is a common standard that integrates with the file system in Microsoft, Apple, and UNIX environments. Creating a new content item in UCM is as simple as dragging documents and dropping them into a WebDAV folder. This is perhaps the simplest method for contributing new content to the system, after which you can see the item in a search result, in a virtual folder hierarchy, and even on a Site Studio Web page. This means that updating your public facing Web site can be as simple as drag-and-drop.

WebDAV is useful, but as mentioned earlier, the protocol is extremely limited. A better approach is to use the Oracle Desktop Integration Suite feature—included in UCM—which offers more functionality than a pure WebDAV connection could. These include the ability to view and change metadata, view information pages about the content item, as well as processing it through workflows. All of this functionality is available on both the file browser interface, and in e-mail clients like Lotus Notes or Microsoft Outlook.

Once CMIS becomes a well supported standard, it might become the most common method for doing a loose integration with content management systems. Besides support for SOAP connections, it also supports a lightweight URL-based Web services. Some people are calling this lightweight connection ReST, after the architectural style known as Representational State Transfer. However, it is best described as ReST-inspired, since it lacks several features typical in a ReST-based interface.

All of these tools are useful for placing content into the UCM system, and can be somewhat helpful for finding content in folders. If instead you would like to extract content from the system, perhaps the simplest method is by using syndication feeds like RSS. This "feed" is a simple XML file containing a list of items, along with limited metadata about them. It usually also contains some HTML about how to display the item, or in some cases, the RSS feed can contain the entire content item.

The UCM system has many lists of items, such as search results, items in your workflow queue, or items you have previously checked out (meaning a user has a lock on editing that item). There are also lists of items on Site Studio Web pages and the administrator's error logs. Fortunately, any list inside the content server can be instantly converted into an RSS feed. That means that if you have a system that understands RSS feeds, the content server should be able to integrate with it in minutes. We cover RSS feeds in greater detail in Chapter 8, along with some sample integrations.

RSS feeds are useful for getting content out of a system. Unfortunately, that only covers a fraction of the hundreds of services that UCM offers. If you'd like to do more, you might need to create a custom application in Java or .NET and run Web services.

In some special cases, you may be able to use one of Oracle's command-line utilities to perform additional administrative services. These tools perform the Web services from a simple command-line interface, which can be easily integrated with scripts or legacy systems. These are not typically used for complete integration solutions, but can be very useful for day-to-day maintenance, or one-time migration applications. These command-line tools include the Batchloader utility, IdcCommand, IdcCommandUX, and IdcClient. Each is best for different tasks; please refer to the documentation for a more complete overview.

Tightly Coupled Integration Tools

In other cases, you may need a more sophisticated integration than what these tools offer. You may have a robust Java or .NET application, and would like more functionality than what Open WCM has to offer. In which case, you will need to create custom integration yourself with some of the more advanced ECM integration tools.

The most popular integration option is to connect to the content server via SOAP, which is an XML-based Web protocol for executing services—not to be confused with SOA. Again, any functionality offered to the end user is available through a Web service call, and is therefore available through SOAP. As stated before, all Oracle ECM products—UOA, IPM, IRM, and URM—all support SOAP-based Web services for integrations.

The main advantage to SOAP is its simplicity: since it's built upon standards like XML and the Web, there are SOAP toolkits available in every programming language. This includes modern languages like Java and .NET, workhorse languages like C/C++ and PL/SQL, and even Web-centric languages like JavaScript and Adobe Flash. Oracle also supports the Web Services Description Language (WSDL) to assist in creating applications to execute Web services, but WSDL support is not required.

The main disadvantage is security. Since the Web is "stateless," you need to pass authentication credentials with every request. In other words, in order to connect your server with the content server, you will need to provide a password, or some other kind of authentication token: a cryptographically secure cookie, a Kerberos token, or a SAML token. As you can see, an enterprise-wide SOAP initiative is best when coupled with an enterprise-wide single sign-on initiative.

Another popular option is the Content Integration Suite (CIS), which is included with UCM. CIS is a Java application that can run inside a JEE application server, a servlet engine like Tomcat, or in a stand-alone Java application. The CIS server module connects to the content server and can run any available Web service. It also performs caching of the response data to boost performance on heavily used systems. You can connect to the CIS server via a number of Java standards, such as EJBs, RMI, JMS, or JCA.

Unlike SOAP, you can configure CIS to have a trusted connection with the content server, so you don't need to pass in authentication credentials: you simply need to pass in the name of the user. You can also opt to encrypt the entire connection with CIS. While this is possible in SOAP, it is easier with CIS.

Pragmatic Consolidation

Just because you can place all of your content into one single repository, doesn't mean you should. The pragmatic ECM strategy emphasizes users first, content second, context third, and architecture last. Always keep in mind what your users need, and in what context, and design the best architecture you can to serve those needs. Ideally, all strategic content will be in one strategic repository, meaning one system to learn, patch, and maintain.

However, in practice you will probably also have a handful of tactical repositories that must be included in your strategy.

Repositories of strategic content take multiple forms. You may have more than one dedicated ECM repository. You may also have strategic content in enterprise applications like Siebel or PeopleSoft. You may also have strategic content in legacy applications, or custom Web portals. Finally, you may have strategic information sitting on shared file systems.

The first step is to migrate all this strategic content into your strategic repository. This enables you to have a single source of truth for your enterprise.

The second step is to integrate core content services into the applications that do not have a need for advanced features. These include scanning applications, some ERP integrations, and some Web portals. You can achieve this integration with existing ECM standards, or with basic content syndication tools. Another option is to use the interface to UCM's service-oriented architecture, with or without an ESB, to content-enable your applications.

The third step is to integrate high-value content services into content-centric applications. These include desktop applications, Web content systems, and anything that needs more advanced ECM capabilities such as workflows, digital asset management, or transformation. You can achieve some of this with UCM's content services, but sometimes you can get what you need with Open WCM.

Remember: your ECM system needs to be rolled out in a way that empowers the line-of-business content applications that your users need. As mentioned in Chapter 2, a good approach is to look for some quick wins: consolidate expensive, replaceable systems that are not serving the needs of your users. Roll out these line-of-business solutions on a project-by-project basis, but continue to abide by the best practices and enterprise requirements laid out by your Center of Excellence. This will enable you to gain experience, while keeping an eye on the overall ECM strategy of your company.

But what about consolidating systems with functionality that is missing in Oracle's ECM stack? Should these be left alone in every case? Again, you should make your decisions by thinking of the users first. Who uses those features? How much value do they provide? Are they essential features? Is it worth replacing those features with manual processes in order to have centralized access and management of your content? Will these features be essential in the foreseeable future?

If the features are essential, now and in the future, then you need to know how much value ECM would provide, compared to leaving the repository as a content silo. Do other people need this content? Who are they, and why do they need it? Are they knowledge workers, process workers, or auditors? How much value is there in consolidation? How about a tight integration? How about a loose integration?

In general, for enterprise applications, an ECM platform is superior to a line-of-business application. A platform allows you to extend the ECM features and functionality to suit current and future needs, while simultaneously providing a stable and proven infrastructure. Naturally, no enterprise application will have all the features you require. However, it's important to understand that it's easy to add new features to an ECM platform; it's difficult to add infrastructure to an ECM application.

In short, unless you have a compelling business reason, err on the side of consolidation. For cases where you have a compelling reason to keep your silo, Oracle has a group of ECM tools that allows you to extend some level of control over those silos. These are called ECM federation tools, and are the subject of the next chapter.

Takeaways

- Strategic ECM should provide capabilities across the spectrum of ECM needs.

    - Active content for knowledge workers: Oracle Universal Content Management (UCM)

    - Transactional content for process workers: Oracle Imaging and Process Management (IPM) with UCM or Universal Online Archive (UOA)

    - Historical content for enterprise archiving: Oracle Universal Online Archive

- Pragmatic ECM provides strategic middleware, applications, and infrastructure.

- Most applications access the strategic ECM system with core content services, usually through a service-oriented architecture (SOA), perhaps delivered via an enterprise service bus (ESB).

- Content-centric applications access it with specialized content services.

  - Such applications may require direct integrations, also via SOA.

  - There are multiple ways to integrate. Look for common approaches that can be used across multiple applications for consistency.

- ECM middleware plays a critical role across enterprise applications and can be leveraged with other middleware capabilities.

- Consolidation is the ideal, but federation is sometimes more cost effective, and therefore needs to be included in your strategy.

CHAPTER
5

Managing Legacy
and Non-strategic
Content Stores

y now you should have a list of all your existing content repositories. Strategic stores must be combined to form your ECM middleware infrastructure. You should eliminate replaceable stores and migrate the content into your strategic infrastructure. Tactical stores can be slowly eliminated or maintained indefinitely.

It is easy to classify which systems are replaceable, but it's more difficult determining which ones are tactical versus strategic. The previous chapter covered what a good strategic ECM system should have to be effective. If you have an essential content management repository that cannot grow to become a part of your strategic ECM infrastructure through middleware, then you should consider it to be a tactical content repository.

Ideally, you would replace it with a system that can be strategic ECM. However, this is not always an option. It may be a highly customized and useful system, and replacement might not be cost effective in the near-term. Perhaps the solution has a significant ROI. Perhaps it significantly enhances one team's productivity, so much so that the added costs of maintenance are worth it.

Keep in mind that what systems qualify as strategic ECM is based on many factors, which we covered in Chapter 2. These include cost, but also must consider existing integrations, the technical capabilities of the system, and the future potential of the product. Whatever you deem is the strategic infrastructure, everything else is either replaceable or tactical.

The question about consolidation versus federation was covered in detail at the end of Chapters 3 and 4. Briefly, in some cases, it is more cost effective in the near-term for these businesses to leave tactical systems as they are.

However, keeping these systems around makes the enterprise content management problem a bit tougher to solve. You still have problems with finding content, securing it, and ensuring it follows proper records management policies. This chapter covers the problems you will have managing content in tactical repositories, and offers some tools and tips for solving those problems.

ECM Challenges for Tactical Repositories

Once you have decided that a tactical repository is worth the additional costs of maintenance and upkeep, and that consolidation is not an option, you still have specific content needs. In general, these are the problems involved with finding content, and making sure that your content management policies are maintained. These needs include

- The ability to find and modify information in tactical stores.

- The ability to secure content according to an enterprise-wide security policy.

- The ability to ensure ISO, HIPPA, and other regulations are followed in tactical systems.

- Enforcing retention policies based on content usage, updates, and metadata.

- Enforcing records policies based on corporate classifications and legal processes.

- Implementing policies without disrupting users or business processes.

- The uniform and consistent application of policies across content stores.

Applying records and retention policies in place within existing content stores allows companies to leverage their investments in existing infrastructure, while reducing content clutter and storage costs. Also, and perhaps most importantly, companies can minimize risk by managing content in legacy data stores according to corporate policies for legal discovery and destruction where and when it is appropriate.

More information about these specific needs follow. In the next section, we cover tools that can help you manage these problems in tactical repositories.

Policy Management

In a unified system, you will have, by the very nature of a unified system, a single location where content is stored (and content metadata) allowing you to search for content and implement enterprise policies for records, retention, and knowledge management in a single location. If, however, you are in a decentralized system you need a model that allows you to set policies in a single location and have them executed in-place across the various infrastructure pieces.

Policy management includes any policy to which content is subject. For most organizations this is a combination of regulatory requirements, ISO requirements about reporting and quality management, and corporate policies.

Our goal is to universally implement and execute these policies across the various content stores in the enterprise. To do this, we must define the policy in a single location, then execute that policy uniformly, in place, wherever we store content.

Retention Management

As mentioned in Chapter 1, the enterprise is going through a content explosion, causing a tremendous amount of content clutter throughout corporate systems. Users are unable to sift through content quickly to find relevant information, and often once information is located no one is sure if the information that was found is still relevant or accurate.

The solution to clutter reduction, in ECM terms, is called retention management. *Retention management* is the process of defining life cycle schedules to documents. This schedule enables actions to be taken on the document to help reduce clutter, which in many cases reduce liability and cost associated with storing old, outdated documents. Retention management actions include deleting the document, deleting previous (usually outdated) revisions to a document, archiving, labeling (changing metadata, watermarking, etc.), or making the content item a record.

The retention schedule of a content item is typically driven by one or more of the following variables:

- **Calendar-Based** A schedule against which documents must be acted upon due to a specific date. For example, a document may need to be kept for seven years after the date it was first created. This is sometimes called a *retention period*, or a *retention duration*.

- **Event-Based** An event is an occurrence, usually not known at the time of document creation, which drives the retention schedule. For example, an event could be the end of a project (keep all documents for two years after a project ends) or when a building is demolished (keep all documents for ten years after the building is torn down). The project end date or the date of demolition for a building may not be known when the documents are created, but may still be used in determining the retention schedule for the documents.

- **Users** User activity or inactivity can also drive retention schedules. For example, a retention schedule may say that all content on the intranet that has not been viewed by at least three people in the last year should go through a workflow for archival consideration.

These schedules are typically defined as a "disposition." A disposition is the life cycle through which a document progresses, typically referring to the later stages of the process. Disposition process actions include

- Retain permanently
- Present for review
- Destroy automatically
- Destroy after authorization from the administrator
- Transfer to archive or another repository

When a document is a formal record, it cannot be deleted or modified and has a legally certified and auditable control placed around the document to ensure it has not been changed in any way.

Since retention management is about both saving storage costs and reducing legal risk, the odds are good that you will benefit if the majority of your content has a retention schedule. When possible, this schedule should destroy the content after it is no longer relevant, in order to reduce legal risk. In other cases, it should be moved to an archive for future use. The process of determining business value is called "records appraisal," and is an important step in the creation of a formal records management policy. Indeed, as mentioned in Chapter 1, IBM believes that in the next few years, all CIOs will need to quantify the value of their data, so that it can be placed on the CFO's balance sheets. If the content cannot prove its value, and stale content has legal risk, you can guarantee that the CFO will be encouraging people to destroy outdated content.

One of our major objectives with a retention management strategy is the ability to centrally define our retention policies and then execute them uniformly across all content storage locations. To do this, we need to utilize ECM tools across the non-strategic and legacy systems as well as our strategic system(s). These tools will need to implement our retention policies in context, meaning the content items on which we desire to place a retention schedule must be able to continue to exist in their current location and have those policies implemented on those target systems.

Records Management

There is considerable debate about whether records management is a subset of retention management, or vice versa. In the opinion of the authors, all content benefits from a retention schedule. Also, all content that persists needs to be findable and subject to the appropriate records policies.

Regardless of the details of that particular argument, records management and retention management are closely linked. While retention management typically deals with the end of a life cycle of a document, records management is the enforcement of a policy that ensures the integrity of an existing document. Many records also contain an explicit retention management schedule.

Documents that are records typically cannot be changed. Documents are declared records for various reasons, typically driven by policy or by legal requirement, or by the execution of a legal hold. A document that is a record cannot be changed and the system in which such a document is held must be able to demonstrate that the document has not changed since it was declared a record. The most common standard for certifying an application as a records management system is the United States Department of Defense 5015 Chapter 2 and 5015 Chapter 4 records management certification, often referred to as DOD 5015.2 and 5015.4.

Records policies often define both a period under which the document cannot change and also the destruction or retention policy that must be followed once that period ends. An example of a records policy would be a medical document that must be kept, unaltered, for a predefined number of years after a patient visit and then must be demonstrably destroyed.

There are several challenges to records management, especially for electronic records, that makes solving this problem so critical. During a lawsuit, the process of discovery involves your organization producing any documents relevant to the case. One gigabyte of storage may only cost 25 cents to purchase, but on average it costs $2,500 for a lawyer to review. Some additional challenges include

- Any information that persists—even electronically—is discoverable:

  "Today it is black letter law that computerized data is discoverable if relevant."
  Anti-Monopoly, Inc. v. Hasbro, Inc., No. 94CIV2120, 1995 U.S. Dist. LEXIS 16355 (S.D.N.Y. 1995)

- The difficulty of doing electronic discovery is not a valid excuse:

  "Deficiencies in the retrieval system cannot be sufficient to defeat a good faith request to examine relevant information."

"If a party chooses an electronic storage method, the necessity for a retrieval program or method is an ordinary and foreseeable risk."
Kaufman v. Kinko's Inc., 2002 WL 32123851 (Del. Ch. 2002)

- The cost of going through electronic archives to provide discovery documents is generally not a valid excuse:

  Plaintiff sought 800 backup tapes from Toshiba. Claimed cost of processing tape (analyzing data, identifying and restoring files, searching, producing specified data) would have been $1.5 to $1.9 million. Toshiba asked plaintiff to split or cover the cost. Trial court ordered Toshiba to produce at their own expense.
  Toshiba v. Superior Court of Santa Clara County, 124 Cal. App. 4th 72 (Cal App. 2004).

- Inability to provide relevant records can be extremely—even fatally—costly:

  Adverse inference instruction contributed to $1.45 billion judgment against Morgan Stanley. Finding Morgan Stanley grossly negligent in failing to produce e-mails, overwriting e-mails after twelve months in violation of an SEC order, failing to conduct proper searches for backup tapes that may have contained e-mails, and failing to notify plaintiff or the Court when it discovered new e-mails.
  *Coleman Holdings v. Morgan Stanley & Co., No. CA 003-5045AI, 2005 WL 674885, at *9-10 (Fla. Cir. Ct. March 23, 2005).*

- Don't retain more content than is absolutely necessary:

  There is nothing wrong with a policy of destroying documents after the point is reached at which there is no good business reason to retain them.
  Arthur Andersen, LLP v. United States, 125 S. Ct. 2129, 2131–35 (2005); Fidelity Nat. Title Ins. Co. of New York v. Intercompany Nat. Title Ins. Co., 412 F.3d 747, 750 (7th Cir. 2005)

- Apply policies consistently and universally: electronic content and paper content must conform to the same rules:

  "Destruction of data pursuant to valid document retention policy" did not warrant spoliation sanctions.
  Hynix Semiconductor, Inc. v. Rambus, Inc., No. C-00-20905 RMW (N.D. Cal. Jan. 4, 2006).

If all records are in one repository, performing discovery is simple. However, the existence of federated repositories poses some very unique challenges to our ability to solve this problem. What we need is one unified system in which we define our policy, and then force all federated systems to follow that policy.

In some cases, content will have records policies that include a disposition rule that will need to supersede the retention policy. As was mentioned, there are arguments over which is a subset of the other, but records and retention management are closely linked, and ideally both driven by a cohesive set of centralized policies and executed uniformly across the entire content ecosystem in the enterprise.

Content and Application Proliferation

As mentioned in Chapters 1 and 2, the early adopters of knowledge management believed that by having all applications and content in one place, and instant access to all information, you could solve the infoglut problem. This means e-mail, discussions, collaboration, and document management in one enormous system. Typically, as these applications matured, their components became more and more interdependent, which made upgrades and additional features difficult to implement. As a result, these knowledge management features ceased to be best-in-breed, and the system could no longer serve the needs of their users.

At first, these problems went unnoticed. People had few alternatives for collaboration and document management. However, the early days of the Internet boom allowed departments to quickly deploy Web sites, and entire Web applications with much greater ease. If the centralized IT system could not serve the collaboration needs of a department, each department would implement its own solution. This problem is still very much alive today, as is evident by the proliferation of SharePoint systems.

This trend not only leads to content proliferation, but also *application proliferation*. Not only were individual departments allowing people to access content over the Web, but they were developing their own Web-based solutions to help them increase their own productivity. The departments would use an outsourcing budget to create these systems, or in some they would utilize in-house programming talent to create them.

The effect is clear: if an employee wanted to research a problem or perform an audit, he would have to understand the nuances of hundreds of different systems. In the event of an audit, or a legal hold, there would be thousands of manual steps to ensure that the relevant content was properly discovered and secured. Clearly, this is not an ideal situation.

A common solution to this problem is enterprise search. This allows you to use one single interface to scan hundreds of repositories. This simplifies the problem, in that the user doesn't need to go to each of the hundreds of systems to perform a search. The usefulness of enterprise search is not limited to auditors; every employee who needs to find content in tactical silos would benefit from one single system that can search all repositories simultaneously.

A complete discussion of application proliferation is beyond the scope of this book. However, one aspect of this problem is very important to content management. Assume you are keeping a tactical repository around because the application is highly useful, but it would not be cost effective to re-implement that functionality. Can we solve this content proliferation problem by solving the application proliferation problem?

The traditional answer would be no, because the traditional solution would be to reimplement the functionality in a portal or application server, and use a strategic ECM system as the content store. As we just said, in our case, this solution was deemed not cost effective.

However, what if you solved the application proliferation problem in an entirely non-standard way? What if there was a tool that made re-implementing the application significantly easier, and thus more cost effective? One alternative approach is discussed later in this chapter in the section "Oracle WebCenter Services: Ensemble."

The Solution: Federated ECM

Some organizations choose to solve this problem by not solving this problem. In other words, they use training and manual processes instead of integrating content management across their enterprise. All employees are expected to learn to navigate the dozens of systems they need to do their jobs. If they cannot find something, they use the phone or e-mail to track down information, or they make decisions with incomplete information. Maintaining records and retention policies is also a manual process. Unfortunately, these manual processes lead to unnecessary cost, complexity, and risk.

As mentioned in Chapter 2, in an ideal world you would consolidate every piece of content into one single repository. This would be a completely unified ECM solution, but unfortunately 100 percent centralization is rarely practical. Because of the inherent complexity with integrating existing code bases and legacy systems, it is rarely cost effective to consolidate everything all at once.

Even if you do not have a heterogeneous environment at present, the odds are good that you will have one in the future. Your organization may merge with another organization that uses an ECM infrastructure different than your own. Alternatively, you may suffer from a common side effect of IT centralization: too much separation between IT and the businesses they are supposed to support. This leads to a patchwork of line-of-business solutions that IT is later forced to support. In either case, you will need a pragmatic ECM strategy to handle multiple repositories.

Understanding this reality, Oracle designed its ECM tools, shown in Figure 5-1, to support both centralized and federated approaches to information management. This includes the ability to manage security, findability, records, workflows, or Web content even in remote repositories. The best strategy is to consolidate the most important content immediately, consolidate the rest when cost effective, but always manage content outside the repository with federated tools.

Keep in mind that a federated approach lacks several key advantages to a fully consolidated system. A unified approach will always have more

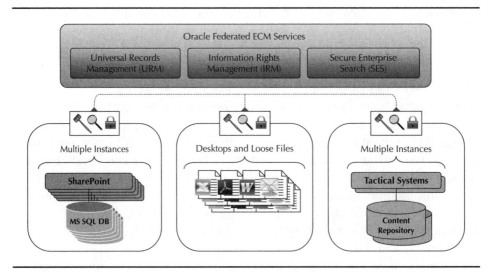

FIGURE 5-1. *Use federation tools to get some control over sprawled content.*

features, and will be easier to administer and maintain. However, in the event that immediate consolidation is cost prohibitive, federated tools can help tremendously. Next, we cover several tools in detail, and how they fit into the pragmatic ECM strategy outlined in Chapter 2.

Oracle Universal Records Management

Records management, as discussed before, is an essential piece of a pragmatic ECM strategy, and Oracle implements it with their Universal Records Management (URM) product. URM is an application plug-in to the core UCM repository, which means that URM uses the same unified repository as UCM, except it gives content items new life cycles. URM is DOD 5015.2 and 5015.4 certified, and it serves as a single location for setting records and retention policies across your enterprise.

What is unique about Oracle URM is its federated approach to implementing records management policies. This means it can manage a content item as a record, even if it doesn't exist inside the URM repository!

By using records management adapters, as shown in Figure 5-2, Oracle URM can enforce disposition rules for documents, no matter where they are in your enterprise. For example, your legal department may have a disposition rule to delete all e-mails about a particular project one year after the project is completed. To implement this policy, you would define it

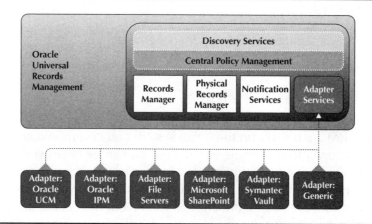

FIGURE 5-2. *Oracle Universal Records Management uses adapters to manage content as a record, no matter where it exists in the enterprise.*

inside the Oracle URM, and run a records management agent inside your e-mail archive system. This agent would be responsible for deleting the item when the disposition event occurs.

In addition, assume that you are involved in a lawsuit in which e-mails about this project are relevant. In this case, your records manager would place a "freeze" on all content about this project. From this point on, the records management agent would protect the old e-mails and refuse to let anybody delete them in the remote archive. In the event that the remote archive is not sufficiently secure to prevent this deletion, URM moves the content item into its own repository for protection.

This adapter-driven architecture uses the central URM server to store the policies, and communicate them to adapters running elsewhere in your enterprise. Oracle has generic adapters that integrate with any Java- or .NET-based application. As of this book's writing, Oracle has expanded these generic adapters to support the following repositories:

- Microsoft SharePoint 2003 and 2007

- EMC's Documentum

- IBM's FileNet

- Symantec e-mail vault

- Oracle Universal Online Archive and Oracle E-mail Archive Service

- Oracle Universal Content Management

- Oracle Imaging and Process Management

- Oracle Content Database

- Content on shared file systems

These URM agents run on the target system and communicate with the URM policy server to determine when a record can be destroyed. As mentioned above, if a user attempts to alter or delete a record in violation of the retention policy, the URM agent will block this behavior. Unfortunately, some repositories are not secure enough to prevent the accidental deletion of content. In those cases, once a document is flagged as a record or "frozen," the URM agent moves the record to the UCM repository for safe keeping. The agent leaves a "stub" document in the original system that describes where the document was moved, and why. Alternatively, you also extend the generic adapter to place a "sealed" version of the content item in the remote system, and use Oracle Information Rights Management to control alteration and deletion. This is covered later in this chapter, but in greater detail in Chapter 6.

Oracle Records Management

The landscape of records management, legal, and IT was severely altered with the recent amendments to the Federal Rules of Civil Procedure (FRCP). The newly amended rules change how discovery of electronically stored information (ESI) is performed and because of those changes, records management must become a strategic partner with legal, IT, and business. However, it isn't just about risk; it's about improving productivity, eliminating lost information, and managing information through its life cycle.

The changes to the FRCP have caused organizations to shift their traditional thinking of "records and information management" to "retention management." This dynamic change is critical in order to manage ESI content, as recommended by the amended FRCP. Additionally, many organizations are streamlining and simplifying their retention programs in order to accommodate the huge masses of content that are being developed and stored across the enterprise.

We currently use Oracle's UCM application (Fixed RM) for our records centers and active offices that create a great deal of hardcopy records. In both instances, we utilize barcode technology to streamline processing and workflow.

The success of our program in and out of court is attributed to our people, but the work horse behind the success is the Oracle UCM application. The Simplot Company realizes the value of managing its electronic records and is evolving its traditional records program to do just that.

The ability to create content has outstripped our ability to manage it. Oracle understands the value of records management and the need to manage all content across the enterprise. Oracle's suite of applications gives you the ability to gain control of your organization's informational assets.

—David McDermott, CRM
Records Manager
J.R. Simplot Company

The federated approach to records management yields several advantages that other systems cannot offer. These include

- You can set your records and retention policy in one central location, and have all other repositories (file systems, e-mail archives, content management systems) follow that policy.

- You can use adapters to search across your entire enterprise from the URM server to find relevant records.

- After you find content with an enterprise search, you can apply a "legal hold" or a "freeze" on it to prevent its deletion, no matter where it resides.

- You can enforce an enterprise-wide retention policy from one interface.

This federated approach is superior to other models, because it allows in-context records management. Instead of forcing people to move all important documents into one single repository, Oracle URM allows you to use the application you're comfortable with to access your information.

Oracle Secure Enterprise Search

Finding content across the enterprise is a very different problem than finding content on the Internet. The primary difference is that Web content is mainly Web pages and images, which are tied together with hyperlinks. Many search engines use these links and keywords around these links to determine what a document is about, and the number of links to a document determines its relevance. This is fine for Internet research, because on the Web most people are looking for information *in general*, and not necessarily a *specific* piece of content.

In addition, most public-facing Web sites have resources dedicated to helping search engines and new users find and navigate their site. They spend lots of money on search engine optimization, information architects, corporate communications, and public relations in order to boost the page rank, and make the site more readable.

The enterprise is quite different. Sometimes you search for information in general, however, most of the time you're looking for something specific. Also, this specific item needs to be authoritative. It cannot simply be a copy of an older revision—it needs to be recent. Finally, the content creators are not communication experts: they frequently do not know, or do not care to know, about how they have to change their habits to make their content easier to find.

Adding to this problem, most enterprise content is not natively in a Web format, therefore the number of hyperlinks is very few. You might not even be searching for a document; you may be more interested in a record in a database or an old e-mail message. It is therefore more difficult for a search engine to determine what a document is about and how important it is. Also, since each system uses its own security model for information access, you must also ensure that people do not find content they are not allowed to see. Finding information in such an environment is quite a challenge, and in some industries it might even be heavily regulated.

And finally, there is a tremendous amount of important information that isn't even stored as a document. It might be chunks of XML files that need to be assembled in a proper way before they are meaningful, or it might be customer information stored in multiple database tables.

Solving the "enterprise findability" problem requires a number of tools. These tools are collectively called information access technology tools, and include content classification, text extraction, taxonomy management, as well as enterprise search. Oracle Secure Enterprise Search solves many of these problems out-of-the-box, and can be customized to solve many more.

Similar to records management, Oracle Secure Enterprise Search (SES), shown in Figure 5-3, is an adapter-driven architecture that allows you to search multiple information repositories from one simple interface. SES uses its connectors to crawl—or "spider"—information repositories, extract the text of content along with metadata, determine the security level required to access it, and store all of this into a local index.

In practice, SES is easy to set up and integrate with existing content repositories, such as EMC Documentum, SharePoint, FileNet, Lotus Notes, and Oracle Universal Content Management. To integrate with other systems, SES supports several generic spiders, including one for Web pages, one for file systems, and one for RSS feeds. Finally, SES has a robust Java API so you can create more advanced connectors, such as JDBC connections to the database that holds your product information, your customer information, or your project management information.

For example, let's assume you'd like to empower your customer service by giving people a single search point for customer information. You have content in UCM, a legacy content management system, and customer information in database tables.

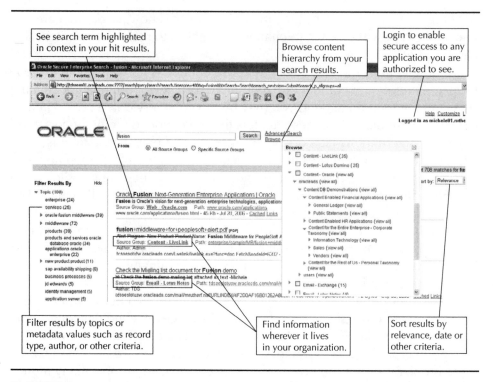

FIGURE 5-3. *Secure Enterprise Search can find and index content from anywhere in your enterprise.*

Integrating UCM is simple, since SES already has a connector out-of-the-box. Integrating a legacy content management system is trickier. If most of the content is available over the Web or the file system, you could use one of SES's generic crawlers. This would extract the text and limited metadata from the content, and place it all in the SES search index. The SES administrator can configure this spider to run every week or every hour as needed.

Another option would be to create a tighter integration with the tactical repository. If the repository has a Java API, SES can extract even more information about the content, including title, author, date, and a richer security context. SES also supports a federated search approach, where SES sends the query to the remote application, and lets the application run the search. This is an excellent idea for large repositories that already have a robust search engine. This way, you won't have two copies of the search index, which decreases the storage and maintenance costs. The federated approach works well for applications like text-based e-mail archives. It will also offload some of the effort of searching to the legacy system, improving the performance of SES.

Finally, you can configure SES to connect directly to a database, and extract structured information from it. This kind of integration is sometimes more difficult, because you need to be very familiar with the structure of the back-end database. You also need a way to validate that the current person searching should be able to view the raw data in the database, in order to keep this system secure. You can store this information in the database with Oracle Label Security, which is covered in more detail in Chapter 6.

We must always be mindful of ensuring that the content is secure when people search through SES. Ideally, your organization would have a single sign-on system throughout the enterprise, which would enable all your applications to use the same authentication credentials, and follow the same security policy. In this case, SES is a natural extension of your existing security policy.

However, especially when integrating legacy systems, this is not always a possibility. In those cases, you have multiple options. The simplest option is to do the integration with SES as only one user. This means anybody with access to SES gets to see the same content in the legacy system. If you'd like to see more secure content, you need to go directly to the legacy system. Another option is to spider all the content from the legacy system, place it in

Intuitive Enterprise Search

We installed Secure Enterprise Search for a number of global financial services organizations. In most cases, users felt immediately at ease with the intuitive interface. Virtually everybody who got their hands on the search had overwhelmingly positive feedback. In one instance, it caused a bit of angst among senior managers when they found content that they previously thought was permanently hidden away. That was a firm reminder of the importance of secure repositories, and proper destruction of outdated digital content. SES also gave us a way out of the never-ending cross-departmental debates about metadata, taxonomy, and organizing content. Since your view of the results depends on security profiles defined in Active Directory, every user sees a slightly different organization of the results. Uniformly, the users loved this approach, since it allowed each department to organize their content however they wanted.

—Morgan Sheehan,
Principal, FILPAX Consulting Limited

the SES index, and use SES alone to secure the content. Finally, you can do query-time authentication to the legacy system, and run all queries in the legacy system as that user.

Lastly, you need to configure the system so SES knows what kind of content will be relevant. The search engine does a good deal of "Google-style" link analysis to find which content items are linked to most frequently. This is useful to help relevant pages stand out more, but in the enterprise it is rarely sufficient.

In addition, SES performs content *clustering* to help users automatically find related content items. An administrator needs to configure the search engine to know about the taxonomy and keywords in other systems, so that it can better place them into topic categories. If your content repository has well-defined metadata—such as content in UCM—clustering can be very effective at helping people find similar content. However, if you have very loosely defined metadata—such as raw files on a file system or e-mail archives—SES can do on-the-fly analysis of keywords in the data and attempt to cluster it for you. At present, this clustering is a hierarchical taxonomy, so it requires regular maintenance by an administrator whenever your hierarchy needs clean-up.

Finally, because Secure Enterprise Search has its own Web-services API, you can embed it in just about any application in your enterprise. In other words, you could embed a small "search everything" Web form on your intranet portal, and nobody would ever know that it was running SES.

Challenges to Enterprise Search

One of the biggest challenges to finding content across the enterprise is human language itself. It hinders not only the ability to find information, but also to properly secure it.

The first such challenge you will face is probably the easiest to fix. Assume you are integrating SES with a department-level repository. Some content is labeled as "internal." Does that mean internal to the department, or to the organization as a whole? Naturally, you will need to map department-level security specifications to a global specification that works across all systems. If you are lucky, this will be straightforward and easy to implement.

Unfortunately, solving this problem in general for all metadata is an incredibly daunting task. For example, each department in your organization may have a different word for "project." One group may call it an "initiative," others may call it a "program." These terms are used by your content contributors. How should a content consumer know what proper terminology to use in order to find the content they need?

This problem is difficult to solve even for small Web sites. The problem boils down to this: your content contributors do not know their audience well enough to use familiar names. Secure Enterprise Search has thesaurus and synonym capabilities, so with the proper amount of effort and maintenance, you can let each department use their own terminology. However, this places a large burden on the administrator to keep the thesaurus up to date.

You could also employ a "brand manager" to encourage everybody to use the proper terminology everywhere. However, this also can fail because your audience uses multiple terms for the same thing, just like your contributors do. In other words, if you enforce everybody to use the term "project" instead of "initiative" or "program," then users on the Web looking for "initiatives" will never find your content. Therefore, this approach will not work well for content on a public Web site, where everybody uses different terms and everybody is battling for relevance. Although SES allows thesaurus and synonym matches, public search engines ignore them completely in order to minimize irrelevant pages.

An ultimate solution to this problem is difficult. Perhaps instead of forcing your contributors and consumers to have a consistent language, we should create tools that allow them to name things whatever they wish? Then the challenge becomes knowing more about the audience, and trying to present them with words they might understand. Part of the solution is a controlled thesaurus, which is covered in Chapter 7. Another part is called a folksonomy, which is covered in greater detail in Chapter 8.

Oracle Information Rights Management

Another problem with content in federated repositories is the difficulty in securing them. How can you effectively secure an item once it moves from one repository to another? Even if all repositories have integrations with your centralized identity management system, you still have problems when people download content and send it around via e-mail.

As mentioned briefly in Chapter 2, Information Rights Management (IRM) is an extra layer of security embedded directly in your content that protects it anywhere in the world. It doesn't matter if your documents are in a content management system, on your desktop, or on the thumb drive of somebody on the other side of the planet, your content is still secure.

The policy determines who can view your content, who can print it, and who can edit it. IRM uses a plug-in to common applications, such as Microsoft Word, Excel, or PDF, to password-protect your content. When you attempt to open it, IRM prompts you for your username and password, and authenticates back to the policy server to determine your rights. If you use single sign-on, this authentication process is automatic. If you have sufficient rights, the IRM server gives you a temporary decryption key and allows you to view the content.

All content items are encrypted, and contain the *classification* of the content. If users have access rights to that specific classification, they can view it. Otherwise, the content remains encrypted.

This book covers the specifics of an IRM strategy in greater detail in Chapter 6. Suffice it to say, the ability to federate the security model is an extremely powerful way to control access to content. This works all across the enterprise, whether your items are in a consolidated repository, a legacy system, or even when they exist outside your organization's firewall.

Oracle WebCenter Services: Ensemble

The content proliferation problem frequently goes hand-in-hand with the application proliferation problem. Not only is it easy to sprawl useful Web content across hundreds of sites, it is also easy to sprawl hundreds of useful Web applications across hundreds of sites.

In the past, people chose to solve this problem with a JEE portal server. The theory was that if you created your application as a standards-compliant "portlet," then you could run it anywhere: a department-centric portal server, an enterprise-wide portal server, or a partner extranet portal. This solves the application proliferation problem by ensuring that your application is portable to another physical server, for use in another user interface.

Unfortunately, this only solved part of the problem. It's a reasonable solution if you can always enforce the policy that applications only be created as a standards-compliant portlet. However, this policy is difficult to enforce. There are hundreds of other ways to create Web applications, not to mention the thousands of legacy Web applications that could not be re-written as a portlet in a cost-effective way. Some of them may be valuable and complex .NET or PHP applications that run fine, but it would be nice if users could access their functionality within the context of a different application.

Use Mashups Instead of Portals

Ensemble solves the portal problem in a slightly different way. Instead of forcing people to rewrite their application as Java *portlets*, Ensemble allows you to turn any application—regardless of language—into a reusable *pagelet*, as shown in Figure 5-4. You can then reuse these pagelets on other Web applications.

In other words, Ensemble lets you embed existing Web applications into any Web page in your enterprise! This is commonly called a *mashup*, since you are mashing the HTML from two applications into a single, combined interface.

This sounds radical, but the idea is simple: Ensemble acts as a proxy between you and the legacy Web application. When you submit an HTML form in the pagelet, your request actually goes back to Ensemble. Next, Ensemble forwards your request back to the legacy Web application. The legacy application processes the request, and sends back an HTML response page back to the Ensemble server. Finally, the Ensemble server transforms the legacy response data into a simpler chunk of HTML, and the Ensemble client libraries draw the response HTML in the hosted pagelet. This technology is primarily based on Asynchronous JavaScript and XML (Ajax), so it works regardless of how you originally created the Web applications.

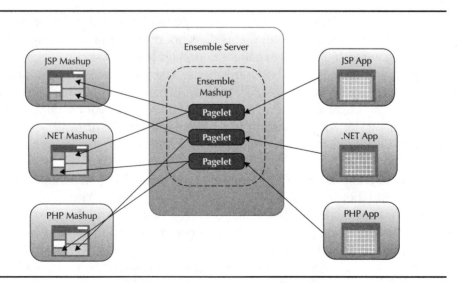

FIGURE 5-4.   *Ensemble allows you to mashup applications anywhere in your enterprise.*

For example, let's assume you have a legacy project management system that is only used by one department in your company. You would like more people to use it, so you decide to embed it in an employee portal. Your employee portal can be anything: a Site Studio page, SharePoint, or a JEE Portal Server. Your legacy project management application can also be written in anything: Java, .NET, PHP, or Perl. The process is still the same.

After generating a pagelet for your application, you embed a small XML tag onto your employee portal. This is a tiny bit of configuration, which tells Ensemble to replace the XML tag on the Web page with HTML from the project management application.

When the user loads the employee portal in her browser, at first all she sees is the standard employee portal. However, behind the scenes her browser makes an Ajax request to the Ensemble server, asking for it to provide the HTML from the project management pagelet. Next, Ensemble makes a Web request to the legacy project management application, and gets the HTML for its home page. Ensemble then adjusts this HTML if needed—perhaps inserting or transforming the HTML—and sends it back to the user's browser. Once the browser gets this extra HTML, Ensemble's client-side JavaScript draws it on the page, wherever the developer placed the XML configuration tag.

The added benefit is that Ensemble can also secure the legacy application. Since Ensemble acts as a proxy, it can enforce a perimeter-based security model: people will need to have authentication tokens from their enterprise before accessing the application. This does not provide full and complete security features, but it is an excellent option for legacy systems.

Another more advanced option is to act as a proxy between you and your software-as-a-service (SaaS) vendors. As mentioned in Chapter 3, your SaaS vendors might not give you sufficient control over your secure content, so you might not want to store some content outside the firewall. However, you would still like to display this secure content within the content of your SaaS application.

Ensemble allows you to do precisely this by making a "mashup" behind your firewall, between the SaaS and your secure content. You could use Ensemble to turn your SaaS application into a pagelet, and then insert it into your employee portal. Alternatively, you could create a pagelet of your employee portal, and insert it into the SaaS application.

As you can see, Oracle Ensemble is almost the exact opposite of Oracle Open WCM. As mentioned in Chapter 4, Open WCM allows you to embed Web content assets into an application-centric Web site. In contrast, Ensemble allows you to embed Web application assets in a content-centric

Web site. Both adhere to a similar pragmatic philosophy: people want to reuse content and services, but they don't want to redo everything from scratch. So don't force them.

No matter what kind of Web application you are trying to create, you will almost certainly benefit from some combination of Open WCM and Ensemble.

Tactical Integration Tools for Legacy Systems

In addition to the above options, you can use Oracle's ECM integration tools to create your own custom federated solutions. These kinds of solutions generally take the form of inserting new content into the system, or extracting it out.

For example, assume you have a legacy application that generates database reports. It would probably be useful to automate the process for checking those items into the content server, so they can be more widely distributed. You may also find it useful to leverage subscriptions, make notifications, or convert that report to Web-viewable content. In some cases, it may be sufficient to create a small application to copy these reports to a folder controlled by WebDAV or the Oracle Desktop Integration Suite (included with UCM). This way, your reports are automatically checked in with the right metadata, with very little effort. In many cases, an integration with BPEL makes the most sense for simple application-to-application integrations.

In other cases, if you need greater control over the content, you may need a more sophisticated integration. In which case, you should use one of the more sophisticated tools: SOAP, enterprise service busses, or the Content Integration Suite for Java applications.

By the same token, if you would like to extract some content from your strategic repository and insert it into your tactical repository, your options are similar. You can copy the content out of a WebDAV folder, consume an RSS syndication feed, or create a more sophisticated integration with SOAP.

Implementing Federation with the ECM Strategy

Now that you understand what is possible, the next question is how should you get started? Clearly, consolidating all content into one system is the ideal, but sometimes that's not feasible. You may have invested a great deal of time and energy into a heavily customized system, which is running fairly well, and which a migration to a centralized, strategic system may be too costly to justify. This is where a federation as opposed to a consolidation strategy may present the best approach.

As discussed in Chapter 3, the first step is to enumerate all the content repositories in your enterprise, and classify them as strategic, tactical, or replaceable. Strategic and replaceable repositories should be migrated into the UCM as soon as is feasible. Federating ECM with in-context tools is a *temporary* solution to the problem, and should only be used until you have the time and resources to complete the rationalization of your strategic systems. In contrast, a tactical content repository would use federated ECM tools for a more long-term solution. Following the basic rules outlined in Chapter 3, you can use the combination of strategic ECM and federated ECM to implement your pragmatic ECM strategy.

First, remember to keep it simple. If all you need is a lightweight integration with content management, you might be happy creating a custom integration with some of the simpler integration tools: RSS, WebDAV, CMIS, or Oracle Desktop. The functionality in these lightweight integrations is absolutely minimal, however, it is sometimes all you need.

Second, look over the list of federated tools, and see if they fulfill a need that you have in your tactical repositories. You almost certainly have a need for some kind of Secure Enterprise Search, and if you fear the costs of litigation, you should also look into Universal Records Management. An e-mail archiving solution that integrates cleanly with URM is a huge benefit. The IRM and Ensemble tools may fill a need for you as well, depending on how severe your content proliferation and application proliferation problems are.

Enterprise Architecture Requirements

As mentioned before, UCM was built from day one as a service-oriented architecture. Every feature it offers to end users is available as a Web-service. This early adherence to SOAs gives Oracle's UCM system many advantages when it comes to integrating with other applications.

Does this mean you need to adopt a service-oriented architecture throughout your enterprise in order to fully implement a pragmatic ECM strategy? Thankfully, this is not necessary.

As mentioned in the previous chapter, SOAs are extremely useful, but they are simply one of the many tactics to achieve an ECM infrastructure. Because of Oracle's pragmatic approach to federated solutions, it supports multiple kinds of architectures, infrastructures, applications, and languages. This allows it to not only work with your existing infrastructure today, but grow to meet the enterprise infrastructure visions of tomorrow.

Alan Key—the developer who coined the term "object-oriented programming"—once said that the secret to great and growable systems is to focus on *messaging*. Thinking in terms of objects or services is misleading; instead, focus on understanding that messages need to be sent between applications in order to solve your problems. If your systems can send messages to each other in a clear, efficient, robust, secure, and auditable fashion, then you have already achieved most of the messaging goals that SOA delivers. At present, an SOA infrastructure has tremendous advantages over a jumble of federated repositories and enterprise applications. However, the decision of how and when to move to SOA varies by application, system, and department.

Therefore, a pragmatic ECM strategy should never punish you if you do not have the latest enterprise architecture. This approach will still be true in the future, even if another architectural model beyond SOA gains heavy adoption in the enterprise.

In keeping with Oracle's hot-pluggable strategy, there is a great deal of flexibility in how, and in what combination, you deploy these capabilities. Thanks to the SOA architecture at the core of UCM, nearly every single feature that Oracle UCM implements is available as a Web service. This means you can use SOAP to integrate ECM features into any application. As mentioned above, there are also prebuilt integrations that use these Web services, but you can create your own if you need. There is no requirement to use any language, any platform, or any architecture in order to gain the full benefits of ECM.

Security Requirements

Oracle strongly recommends an enterprise-wide, single sign-on system with centralized user management. This will allow your application to easily and securely connect to your ECM system, and manage the security policy in a centralized system. Unfortunately, not all legacy applications support identity management as well as Oracle ECM does, in which case, you may need Information Rights Management to fill in the gaps. These and other security concepts are covered in greater detail in Chapter 6.

Takeaways

■ A pragmatic ECM strategy must account for legacy systems that cannot be moved in a cost-effective way. Instead, provide tools that federate ECM capabilities to these tactical systems.

■ Having all content in one system reduces costs, complexity, and risk. However, consolidation is not free and might also have risks.

■ A federated approach to enterprise content management allows you to gain some benefits of ECM in existing systems, without the need to migrate.

■ Oracle has multiple tools to help with federation:

  ■ Oracle Universal Records Management (URM): centralized enforcement of records and retention policies, no matter where the documents exist.

  ■ Oracle Secure Enterprise Search (SES): securely find content anywhere in your enterprise, whether it's in a repository, file system, or database.

  ■ Oracle Information Rights Management (IRM): encrypt your documents so they are secure both inside and outside your repository.

  ■ Oracle WebCenter Services: Ensemble is an Ajax-based tool that lets you embed any Web application into any other application.

■ Oracle ECM works best with service-oriented architectures, but doesn't require them.

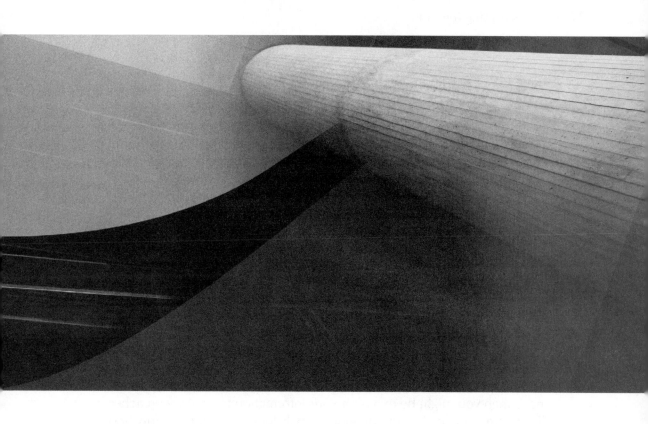

CHAPTER
6

Securing Information
Wherever It Lives

ost experts agree that a good security plan has three pillars: protection, detection, and reaction. You need to protect your information, you need to detect unauthorized access, and you need to react when you suspect a problem. In a pragmatic ECM system, you'll need a combination of applications to implement a coherent information security policy.

The most vital application is a unified approach to user management. You need a centralized repository that manages passwords, access rights, and other user information. Most enterprises use some variety of centralized user management such as Microsoft Active Directory, or any number of enterprise Lightweight Directory Access Protocol (LDAP) solutions. You may also have an enterprise-wide, single sign-on solution to enable instant access to all applications in your enterprise. Beyond these basics, some Identity Management (IdM) systems support access rights auditing, risk management, and syndication of user information.

The security risk here is simple: if information flows from one system to another, the security around that information needs to flow as well. If your security policy cannot be as easily moved from one enterprise system to the next, then you might be exposing your information to security breaches. Therefore, you need a combination of tools that allows the security and the content to move together between systems.

Identity management is a rapidly changing field, and a complete overview is beyond the scope of this book. However, in a pragmatic ECM deployment, we must be mindful about integrating best-of-breed identity management systems. These systems should cleanly integrate with your existing infrastructure, and be a natural extension to your enterprise-wide security policy.

A pragmatic ECM system should never require you to re-create your users or their access rights. That just creates additional maintenance effort, and security holes can hide in the complexity.

It is also important to realize that centralized identity management is not sufficient. Even if the access rights for a content item flow through your enterprise from repository to repository, you are still vulnerable to leaks. This is because a content repository can only secure content when it isn't actually in use! For example, is your content still secure if somebody prints it, copies it, or e-mails it to an individual outside of your domain of control?

Also, let's not forget the importance of monitoring user behavior. Wouldn't you like to know which content items a user downloaded the day before they quit?

A pragmatic ECM system needs to identify all the ways that you need to secure content, and allow you to add it in multiple layers. Instead of focusing all your effort on securing it in one repository, you should also focus on what happens when it flows between repositories, and when people access the item for everyday use. In this chapter we outline what tools Oracle offers that add additional security layers, and how they improve overall content security.

Layers of Security

Within any enterprise there are layers of security to protect information and infrastructure. To be successful, content management needs not only to integrate with that enterprise security model, but extend that model's capabilities.

Information classification, infrastructure access, and application security all play critical roles in the security of enterprise content. Information classification is the high-level categorization placed on data or content. The number of classifications in a given organization is typically small and the categories broad, covering topics such as "internal use only" or "public." Infrastructure access provides the core security underneath enterprise applications. In other words, it prevents unauthorized users from circumventing security by going around the repository application or other enterprise application and accessing the data or content directly in the database, file system, or other medium. Application security is the authentication and authorization of end users when they interact with systems.

Speaking broadly, and using all Oracle tools as examples, a model may look something like this: Users are created, stored, and managed centrally using Oracle Identity Management. This provides a single directory (or, optionally, a single virtual directory) where users can be assigned to groups, such as "employees." Oracle Single Sign On (SSO) provides a common security layer for application access, based on the roles and permissions defined in the common user store (directory). These enterprise applications include E-Business Suite, Siebel, SOA Suite, and Enterprise Service Bus, and, of course, Oracle Enterprise Content Management. Authentication and authorization within those applications can be (and as a matter of implementation, should be) contingent on the credentials supplied by the directory server.

At an infrastructure level the content stored in the system can reside in the Oracle Database using the Oracle Secure Files technology. The information in the database, both the metadata and the content items themselves, can implement Oracle Label Security, an optional feature of the Oracle Database. Label Security enables the database to label the individual rows in the database with an information classification policy. Enabling Label Security means that even at an infrastructure layer, only users provided credentials by the common source (the directory) will have access to those rows. Even if they are accessing the database directly with a proper database login they will need credentials for that information classification to see those rows in the tables.

Additionally, when you download or remove information from any of these systems, you have another layer of security at your disposal. Oracle Information Rights Management (IRM) can enforce the document classification within the very application that you are using to view the content. IRM encrypts the document in a special way—called *sealing*—so that users must authenticate back to a central server to obtain their access rights. Depending on the classification of the document, users may be able to view it, change it, or print it. If users have not been given access to that classification, then they will not be able to decrypt the document for viewing. As before, this authorization and authentication can (and as a matter of implementation, should) be tied to the same directory server.

Under this model, users are provisioned in a single location and provided uniform access to information based on these classification and security policies regardless of the application, repository, or infrastructure. This security even extends to local copies of the information that may have been downloaded or removed from the repository for offline use.

An ECM Stores Content, Not Users

The primary purpose of a content management system is to store content, not users. This means that if your content management system requires you to migrate user names, passwords, and access rights into a content repository, then you have less than a pragmatic ECM solution. Integrations with the latest identity management systems should be seamless, and should never mandate that you store user information twice.

In practice, this usually means a tight integration with Active Directory, or an equivalent LDAP-based authentication server. These systems allow administrators to use standard tools to maintain user information and access rights. A pragmatic ECM system would defer to the user repository for password authentication and access rights authorization. If a user's access rights or password was changed in the central user repository, this change would be quickly reflected in the other enterprise systems.

Centralized identity management is frequently coupled with single sign-on. In effect, once users log in to their workstations, they are granted access tokens to all enterprise applications in their domain. The effect is an invisible login to every enterprise application, including their content management system.

After this, they have access to all the applications in your enterprise without needing to remember additional passwords. Your workstation provides the authentication credentials invisibly to any network application you connect to. Next, the enterprise application connects to your centralized identity management system, to determine what tasks you are authorized to perform.

A centralized identity management system has tremendous benefits for maintaining and auditing your users. However, it comes with some drawbacks. The one people notice first is typically the performance of the enterprise application when it performs authentication. Since the users are not stored locally, and the identity management system might be on the other side of the planet, then each authentication and authorization request could take several seconds. Most enterprise applications create a temporary local copy of the user's authentication credentials to speed things up; however, this is sometimes not enough.

The second problem, seen later on, is due to the tendency of central security policies to sometimes be resistant to change. Since a change to the central policy could alter the access right of any user to every system, the changes need to be thoroughly tested. Assume that for workflow purposes, you'd like the identity management system to store additional information about your users. It might be helpful to know users' peers, their boss, or team leaders on a specific project so the application can properly route a task. However, because of centralized IT policies, it may take weeks or months for them to get approval for this modest change in the global policy.

Both of these problems can be solved with a federated approach to user management. This means setting up multiple identity management repositories in your enterprise, and federating access rights to each of the machines. This way, you can make a copy of a user repository that is geographically close to your enterprise systems, and slightly modify its policy to suit your application's needs. There are several tools that can help you achieve a federated identity management strategy, such as ADAM for Active Directory or Oracle Identity Federation.

There is a great deal of debate over whether a 100 percent centralized system is the best approach, or whether federation should be allowed for anyone in need. A fully centralized system is probably the best approach for some government or research groups, where centralized access control is essential. However, when hundreds of people in two separate organizations need to work together for a project, federated identity management is important for maintaining users and auditing their access rights.

For companies in rapidly changing markets, the optimal approach seems to be "allow but monitor." This means that business units can set up federated systems for better performance, and also adjust the rights for users to access systems in that business unit's domain. When performance is a requirement, federating the repository to a nearby system might also be a good idea. When an application administrator needs to modify the policy to suit their needs, that mapping would best be done inside a federated repository. That allows the systems to be more easily audited by the central security team, but they needn't be bothered every time an application administrator needs to make a minor change to a user's attributes or rights.

Surviving Without Federation

Just because federation is the best approach for you, that doesn't mean your IT department will have it available for you. They may think that the maintenance or auditing effort is not worth the cost, or perhaps they don't believe in the "allow but monitor" philosophy. In which case, you still have one central system, but less control over it.

Although Oracle strongly recommends a centralized approach to user management, it is not a requirement. Through connectors called User Providers, Oracle UCM can connect with an identity management system to do authentication, authorization, or both. This means one system will contain your password, whereas another will contain attributes such as your full name and e-mail address.

In the event that the centralized identity management system is very close to what you need, the content server allows you to perform credential maps. The UCM administrator would create a "map" from a group membership in the identity management system to an access right in the content server. These rights are called *roles* and *accounts*, and are discussed below. You can also map attributes, such as name, e-mail address, and favorite color, just as easily. If you have a need for a complex mapping scheme, you can create a custom User Provider with a small Java customization.

Finally, you can even store passwords, rights, and attributes directly in the content server. This is used mainly for workgroup-level deployments, test servers, or systems where identity management is not an option.

The debate on this matter is not settled. Perhaps in the future new identity management standards will allow easier federation and maintenance of users. The best idea is to remain flexible, so your system can integrate with the next generation of identity management, whenever your IT department chooses to deploy it.

Pragmatic ECM means that your content management strategy needs to be aligned with your identity management strategy. ECM should never be a replacement for your identity management system; they must work together as closely as possible. Deviation is only recommended in specialized situations.

Securing Information in the Database

One of the layers of security that is important within an ECM strategy is the infrastructure layer. As we have discussed, single sign-on and identity management tools can integrate with our ECM systems and our applications to manage users and ensure roles and responsibilities appropriately restrict or provide access to information. Beneath these applications and systems the content resides in an infrastructure layer that must also be secured. While there are device-specific approaches that can be taken depending on your storage hardware, at Oracle we leverage the security of the Oracle Database as part of our overall content security strategy.

Using the capabilities within Oracle Label Security, we can actually secure individual rows and columns in the database using the security model of the ECM system. Label Security limits access to content and metadata to those who have clearance. This clearance can be based on a variety of factors, including the network from which a request is received, the authentication credentials of the user, or system access rules such as time of day. This layer of security enforces compliance with regulatory policies and industry standards and can also be integrated as part of Oracle's Database Vault technology to ensure proper separation of duties and implementation of multifactor security rules.

In practice, this means that when two people look at the same database, they will see different information. This means that you can use one database schema for dozens of different applications, but these applications will never see each other's data.

For example, assume you have a database application with secure content about employees or clients. Your developers and administrators need access to this system so they can test and maintain it, however, they do not have sufficient clearance to view the secure data. Oracle Label Security would allow you to host "sample" content alongside the "secure" content; your administrators would only see the sample data, whereas your secure application sees the sensitive data.

Securing Information Outside a Repository

In addition to securing content access in a repository, a pragmatic ECM strategy should control access to an item even after it's *removed* from a repository. In other words, it should block access by unauthorized users even if the document is outside your organization's firewall, and on the opposite side of the planet. Solving this problem is the duty of Information Rights Management.

Imagine your team is tasked with analyzing all the information pertaining to a new acquisition. Perhaps you are being purchased by a larger company, or perhaps you are the acquiring entity. Some of this information is financial, some of it involves research and development, and some contains employee payroll information.

How can you secure this information, but simultaneously make sure that the fewest people possible know about the relationship? Also, what if the acquisition fails? That would mean a separate entity owns a great deal of competitive information about your company. What's the best possible way to secure this information once it leaves your repository?

Let's first assume you only have a very basic setup. Your content is secure when it's in your repository, but at any point a team member could download it to their desktop. From there, they might accidentally send out sensitive information via e-mail.

To add more security, you could encrypt the e-mail so only the intended user can decrypt it. Or you could set up a collaboration space where teams from both companies can exchange sensitive information. Both are common approaches, but can become a management hassle. Another option is to trust a third party to host all secure information for you. In this case, you trust an expert to set up a secure server with appropriate user access rights. For example, in the energy industry, they have neutral Web sites so anonymous purchasers can exchange information with individuals selling power plants. This solution works if you can find a third party that both entities trust. However, content migration from one secure repository to another can be more time consuming than you first think, and may force everybody to alter their natural workflows.

Each approach is better than the pervious one, but they all have one flaw: they can be described as "brittle" systems. A chain is only as strong as the weakest link, and once you break that link, you break the system. The key question is this: how can I secure my content once it's removed from my repository? How can I keep people from making copies, screenshots, or printing out secure information? Is it even possible to do this?

Information Rights Management

Once content is managed in both traditional ECM systems and non-strategic legacy content stores, companies should also extend their ECM vision to desktops and places beyond their "corporate" reach. In other words, organizations need to secure and track their information wherever it resides, even when copies are sent beyond their own networks or firewalls.

Oracle Information Rights Management (IRM) adds a new layer of content security, by encrypting content and tracking when it is accessed, no matter where it is stored. Unlike typical content security products, which only secure the content while in the repository, IRM secures the content even when removed from the repository. Every copy, no matter if it's inside or outside your firewall, has an extra layer of security.

This is called *information-centric security*, as opposed to traditional repository-centric security. And, as shown in Figure 6-1, it works like this:

1. A user creates a document or an e-mail.

2. Using the IRM plug-in, the user seals the document to a specific classification. In effect, it encrypts the document according to a policy-based security model. The decryption key is stored on the sealing server.

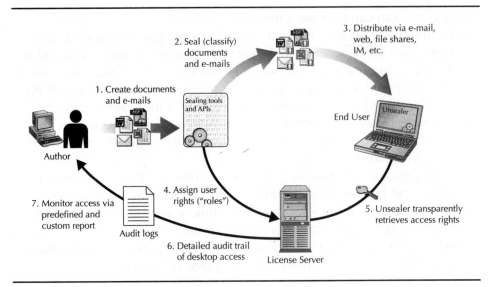

FIGURE 6-1. *The process of securing documents with Information Rights Management*

3. The user distributes the document via e-mail, saves it locally, or places it into a repository.

4. When another user or application need to read the content, an IRM connector contacts the sealing server to access the decryption key. The server logs this access.

5. The server authenticates the user's credentials, and verifies that this user has read access to this specific classification. If so, the server supplies a temporary decryption key.

The IRM desktop unsealer—which is tightly integrated with standard desktop applications—can also prevent people from taking screenshots, printing the document, or using cut-and-paste to move the information to a new document. You can also use the IRM desktop unsealer even if you are not connected to the network. The plug-in securely caches credential data for several hours, allowing users to read documents while on an airplane, or when the Internet is unavailable. In practice, the offline support should be long enough to accommodate travelers, but not too long that it causes additional security risks.

The document access rights are stored separately from the information itself on network-hosted Oracle IRM Servers owned and operated by whomever controls the information. Anybody who wishes to view sealed information must first access this server to obtain a decryption key. This yields several benefits:

- Unauthorized users cannot access the document at all.

- Authorized users can view the document, but may have additional rights restricted. These include modifying the document, printing it, using cut-and-paste, or taking a screenshot.

- All attempts to access sealed information is centrally audited and reported.

- Access to a document can be revoked at any time. This may occur when a contractor leaves, a partner collaboration initiative ends, or the document retention policy calls for the destruction of the document.

These rules apply even if the document is outside your organization's firewall. No matter where the information is in the world, you have control over how it is accessed and used.

For example, assume an employee downloaded a great deal of secure content the night before they turned in their resignation. You can revoke their access on the central server, which means that they would be unable to read the files on their own desktop!

Naturally, once a person has been granted access rights to a document, they could copy it with non-electronic methods. They could use a camera phone to take a photo of the content, they could manually copy it down on paper, or simply memorize it. All good security strategies need to operate in layers and IRM is an excellent layer. You could add another layer of security by restricting cameras and copy machines in your enterprise; however there is little defense against somebody with a photographic memory. IRM is about the right mix of security and usability: it adds a powerful layer without forcing your users to significantly change their habits.

IRM is excellent at preventing accidental disclosure, as well as preventing fully unauthorized access. It also has other uses when it comes to records management, as discussed next.

IRM and Content Management

Sealing services work particularly well when combined with a content management system. For example, there are some documents so essential to the day-to-day operations of your business that your employees keep local copies on their computers. Unfortunately, this document changes every month. How can you ensure that every employee will always have the most recent copy?

As soon as a new revision of a document is checked into the repository, IRM can revoke access to the decryption keys for older revisions. Your users will be unable to open the encrypted document. Instead, your users would

IRM in Practice

We use the Oracle Information Rights Management (IRM) solution for securing and auditing confidential documents related to our mergers and acquisitions (M&A) activities. Since the implementation of IRM, we can ensure that only individuals within Oracle who are authorized to take part in M&A activities are able to see sensitive documents. As new members join the team, as is often required through the diligence process, they can easily be provisioned through business processes without the involvement of Oracle IT. Due to Oracle's classification-based security model, we also do not have to change permissions on the existing documents to provide a new, authorized user access to the information. This is critical to the scalability and maintainability of the solution. Oracle IRM also gives us the ability to centrally de-provision users from all of the information according to our internal policies or to meet specific legal requirements. In addition, access is automatically revoked for users who leave Oracle through our integration with Oracle's Identity Management solution. Should the need arise, we also have the ability to audit document access and usage to ensure proper procedures and guidelines were followed.

Oracle IRM is seamless to our end users, works wherever the documents are located, and provides the critical security needed to keep our M&A activities confidential.

—Doug Kehring
Senior Vice President,
Corporate Development and Strategic Planning
Oracle Corporation

be prompted with a Web page instructing them to download the more recent version.

The Desktop Integration Suite (DIS), covered in Chapter 4, does this with a different approach. The most recent versions of DIS will notice when you are viewing an older version of a document, and then politely recommend that you get the most recent version. In contrast, IRM can enforce the policy that nobody is even allowed to view older revisions.

For example, imagine you are looking at an older revision of the corporate overview document. DIS would allow you to see multiple things about that content item: existing revisions, the metadata, the records management file plan, workflow information, discussion threads about the item, as well as whether or not this is the most recent revision.

In contrast, IRM enables policies around *version enforcement*. Even though DIS politely tells you that you don't have the most recent revision, sometimes the information is too important or too secure to ever allow people to see older revisions. For example, you may wish to block sales people from viewing older versions of a price list to ensure they always give your clients accurate quotes. Another example is for blueprints. There is too much risk if somebody does repair work with out-of-date blueprints, so revocation of access is vital.

IRM and Records Management

Records management systems enforce record retention and disposition policies. For example, a typical disposition rule for critical business records is to retain the document for a specific period (such as seven years), during which time the document cannot be modified. After this point, the document should be destroyed to minimize the risks and costs related to legal discovery.

Unfortunately, just because you delete a document in one repository, that doesn't mean it is gone. It may exist in old e-mail archives. It might exist on old USB thumb drives, or on the desktops of various employees. You may have hundreds of copies scattered around your organization. These items are legally discoverable, especially if you have deployed an enterprise search application.

Alternatively, you should seal the documents with IRM. This yields two primary benefits. First, the documents are tamper-proof, because users are unable to edit them. Also, when time comes to destroy the record, you can configure the IRM server to never supply the decryption keys. All of those extra copies are digitally shredded: without the decryption key, they are totally useless.

Another complication arises when using Records Management Agents. These agents—as discussed earlier—are a part of Oracle's federated approach to content management. You can place an agent in a remote content repository—like Microsoft SharePoint—and still manage the metadata and life cycle from inside Oracle. If the retention policy dictates that an item cannot be deleted for seven years, then the agent will block all attempts to delete it, even if the document resides in SharePoint.

This strategy has one problem: how can we prevent people from altering content in remote repositories? Many legacy systems, including SharePoint, do not have sufficient functionality to prevent alterations to content. Another approach would be to use IRM: create a read-only copy of the document, and leave it in SharePoint. People can access the information in the exact way they are accustomed to, but they will be unable to alter it.

One of the key issues at hand is the question of when a document is legally considered destroyed. What if it exists on a backup tape in an unencrypted format? What if the encryption key is stored on a backup? Can a judge force you to un-delete a deleted document during legal discovery?

The answer to this is complex and dependent on your country's laws about legal discovery. In some countries, backup tapes are not subject to legal discovery. However, this may only apply if you have a rigorous records management policy that is followed, and your backup tapes are used for disaster recovery only.

An even better approach is to encrypt the document, and when it reaches the end of its life cycle, configure your decryption server to never allow that document to be decrypted again. This acts like "digitally shredding" the document: not only did you "destroy" the original, but you also destroyed all copies of it everywhere in the world.

In either case, it should be clear by now that IRM is a natural extension to Oracle's records management and retention management applications. The extra layer of security helps ensure that records are not altered, and that all copies of digital information are properly destroyed.

Creating a Successful IRM Strategy

The key to a successful IRM deployment is the design of a policy-driven method for classifying content. In other words, all documents with a specific classification require the same rights to access. This system has to be complex enough to suit your needs, but simple enough so your end users will make the correct security choices. For example, should a document be Secret, Top Secret, or simply Restricted? Should every department get their own classification scheme, or should it be reserved for just specific departments?

A second advantage to a policy-driven method for classification is better enterprise scalability. All documents with Top Secret classification require identical authorization credentials. This is a much simpler scheme than giving every document in your organization unique access rights. Not only is it a burden on your users, but it seriously hinders the ability to scale your application. As such, you should focus on the fewest possible classification schemes.

A good security policy should focus on the following areas:

- Manageability

- Classification-based rights management

- Standard rights model

- Role-based control of functionality

- Role-based administration

- Auditing

- Infrastructure integration

- Performance

- Scalability

Additionally, your IRM plug-in is able to cache your access rights in the event that you cannot access the Internet. Imagine you need to view sealed documents, but you're about to get on an airplane from New York to Tokyo. If you have an aggressive security policy, you may only have a few minutes to read the document before being forced to reauthenticate with the IRM server. However, it is generally safe to allow a user to cache their credentials for several hours. The primary risks to long caches are stolen laptops and the risks involved with terminated employees. Your business will need to determine for itself what an acceptable level of risk is.

Once your policy-based security scheme is ready, IRM is easily integrated with your existing business processes. Individual users can seal documents manually, or you can have them sealed when checked into a content repository. You can also use the IRM Web service API to seal documents from any application in your enterprise.

When integrating IRM with other applications, be wary of giving that application superuser access to sealed content. This will allow your application to read all sealed content so it can run reports, or create a searchable index, however it can also be a security hole if that application is compromised. However, there are several business cases where it is important to unseal the document, extract data, then reseal the document, so this rule is not absolute.

For example, many documents are sealed to prevent accidental disclosure, or to ensure that when they are opened, users are viewing the most recent copy. In those cases, there is little harm if a trusted application extracts text or creates a thumbnail of the sealed content.

IRM supports heterogeneous environments with multiple types of documents:

■ Microsoft Office 2000–2007, including Word, Excel, and PowerPoint

■ PDFs in Adobe Acrobat or Reader

■ E-mail on Microsoft Outlook, Lotus Notes, Novell GroupWise, and BlackBerry 6.5–7.0

■ HTML and XML on Internet Explorer

Since it works with so many file types, IRM is a natural extension to how most of your users create documents. It will not require a special repository for sealing, so it should fit in quite well with existing workflows.

IRM Outside Your Domain

IRM integrates with your internal Active Directory system, and there are plans to add support for LDAP in the future. You can also do Web-based authentication, which enables support for RSA SecurID or most PKI solutions.

This works great to integrate sealing service inside your enterprise, but what's the best way to add people from outside your domain? What about business partners who have their own user repositories?

As before, the ideal solution is federation. Allow your identity management systems to share information between each other, then use those shared credentials to drive the IRM authorization. However, this level of federation is only worthwhile if you frequently collaborate with a large number of individuals in the other organization.

Alternatively, you can also set up a basic username/password directly into the IRM server. This is not the ideal way to manage users, but it's an important feature if you need to share information with enterprises with less modern infrastructures, or you wish to have total control over the user's passwords and access rights.

In addition, since the IRM plug-in uses the latest security standards, as well as multiple checks to ensure no tampering with the document, you can be assured that your content is safe from all but the most determined and sophisticated hacker.

However, since these documents are outside of your domain of control, you will always have risks. You can disable printing, and cut-and-paste, but you cannot disable a good memory. Even though 100 percent security against determined attack by hackers is impossible, IRM adds extremely useful security layers to protect your documents from tampering, access, and accidental disclosure. It enhances your existing security, by adding features that are simultaneously easy to use and difficult to circumvent.

Securing Information Inside a Repository

Designing a security model from the ground up can be a daunting task. However, if you think in terms of classification of documents, then further restrict classifications by department, the problem can be simpler. You'll need to answer the following questions:

- What content needs to be secured?

- Who needs access to secured content?

- Who would like access, but it's a security problem if they have it?

- Who doesn't need access, but there's not a security risk if they have it?

- Who doesn't need access, and it's a security problem if they have it?

In general, a simpler security model will yield greater security than a complex one. The fewer options you have, the less chance you have to classify something as too secure.

Oracle UCM's Security Model

Oracle's security model for content management was designed from the ground up to integrate cleanly with enterprise-wide identity management systems. It uses a policy-based model, where the document is given a classification, and users are given access rights to specific classification levels.

Specifically, content items belong in security groups. For example, content that everybody can see may belong in the public security group, content for internal employees may be in the internal group, and highly sensitive content would belong in the secure security group.

Users also belong in groups. In the content server, these user groups are signified by a user having a specific role. Each role gets a certain level of access to content items in a specific security group. For example, you may want a role called *contributor* that gives read and write access to items in the public and internal security groups.

In addition to roles and security groups, UCM supports another security layer called *accounts*. These are mainly to allow department-specific classification schemes. For example, it is highly likely that both the Human Resources (HR) department and the Research and Development (R&D) department need to store documents with the secure classification. However, it is unlikely that anybody would need access to both kinds of content.

The solution is to enable accounts, and create one account per department. In this case, you would create an account named HR, and another named RD. To secure R&D content, make sure the security group is secure, and the account is RD. Likewise, secure HR content would have the security group secure, and the account HR. In this case, an R&D executive would have access to content in the secure group, and the RD account, but not secure content in the HR account. Thus, any attempt by this user to view secure documents in the HR account would be blocked and logged.

As mentioned before, this system is designed to work with your enterprise identity management system. In practical terms, your identity management system would place users into groups (such as all people in the HR department), and give them attributes (such as e-mail addresses and user names). When a user logs in, the UCM system will query the identity management system for a list of group membership and attributes. UCM will then translate the user information into an access list of security groups and accounts, as well as user attributes. The user attributes are stored locally; however, the authorization information is only cached for a few minutes.

As mentioned above, UCM can also operate as a workgroup-level solution. In this case, all information about the users is stored in the content server's database. This includes role and account membership, e-mail address, full name, and any custom user metadata that you need. Depending on your security and maintenance needs, this model may work fine on production systems, even if they are very large. Nevertheless, the preferred approach is to take advantage of centralized identity management systems—the advantages to auditing and user management are simply too great to ignore.

It is common to organize your security model according to business units, and have different levels of security within those units. For example, someone with access to secure Human Resources documents usually does not need access to secure Research and Development documents. Likewise a sales manager—while having full access to secure Sales documents— would not access secure HR or R&D documents. The following table shows which role should have access to documents in specific groups:

	HR Docs	Secure HR	R&D Docs	Secure R&D
Executive	Full access	Full access	Full access	Full access
Sales Manager	Read access	No access	Read access	No access
HR Manager	Full access	Full access	Read access	No access
R&D Manager	Read access	No access	Full access	Full access

In some cases, restricting broadly based on department is important to secure your content. On the other hand, if taken too far, it can lead to *content silos.*

In the past, every department kept information hidden from the others in separate repositories. Enterprise content management seeks to break down these silos and manage all content in the same way. However, that goal is easily thwarted by security policies that re-create those silos with overly strict security policies.

If it seems like your security model is becoming too complex and people cannot find what they need, you'll need to reassess if the security is doing more harm than good. Will it be a security risk to give the HR person access to non-restricted R&D documents? If not, then you should avoid the temptation of creating a silo, and allow departments to share mildly restricted data. Avoid the temptation of using security groups to organize content; rather, use your security layer only when there is a legitimate risk.

If there is a legitimate risk in allowing an HR member to view unrestricted R&D documents, then you have three options:

- Avoid giving R&D access to anybody in HR

- Give HR access to R&D, but move the risky documents into another classification

- Add another layer of security to the document to prevent abuse

The additional layers include Access Control Lists or Information Rights Management.

Additional Security Layers

Besides securing your content in a repository and sealing it with IRM, there are a handful of other layers that you can apply. Most of the following can work in combination.

Access Control Lists (ACLs)

An Access Control List (ACL) is a list of individual people who can access a content item, along with their access rights. For example, an ACL in UCM would allow a content creator to directly specify which users have access and what kind of access—read, write, or delete. Then the content server controls access to that content item based on the list provided.

Access Control Lists are very convenient for project spaces. Sometimes people have initial draft versions of content, notes, memos, and documentation that help create content items. None of these draft documents are relevant to most people, and the authors would feel better about keeping them away from others until they are completed. Access Control Lists give the content contributor total control over who gets to see their content.

The downside to access control lists is that they add significantly to the complexity of your security model, making the system slower and more difficult to audit. In general, you should try to keep the security model simple and use mainly roles and accounts. This is because, typically, it is someone's role that gives them access to content. As roles changes and users join or leave the organization, access to documents will need to be updated. If your security model is based on the assignment of roles and the classification of content, the appropriate access to content will automatically be granted or removed when users' roles are changed in the user management system.

If, however, you have utilized ACLs, your security model is based on the explicit granting of permissions to individual users. When roles change you will need to update the individual content items to reflect this new access model. This can create large security holes as users' permissions are not regularly removed from documents to update changes in organizational structures.

Content Cleansing

Most desktop applications store "hidden" content in your documents without your knowledge, such as your name, your company, and in some cases, all previous edits you made of the document. Just because you don't see it, doesn't mean your content is safe.

This hidden content can take even more forms. Most Microsoft Office documents support a feature called "Track Changes," which stores all changes to the document: insertions, deletions, rewording, and who made those changes. In other words, your Microsoft Word documents might contain all the previous iterations.

According to a 2005 study by the security firm Workshare, on an average, 30 percent of all business documents contained sensitive information that they would not want exposed. Unfortunately, 90 percent of companies had no idea that their confidential information was leaking. This is because a great deal of this sensitive information took the form of text that the users thought they deleted.

Perhaps you took an important document, and deleted a section that would be considered confidential, then e-mailed it to a business partner. If that person knew what they were doing, they could uncover the deleted section and view the confidential information you thought you destroyed.

Oracle provides content cleansing filters that strip out this hidden content on the fly. This means you can remove unnecessary information from your documents when they are put into a repository or when downloaded from your site. Cleansing is an important part of the content life cycle, and is a vital part of a pragmatic security policy.

Content Firewalls

Some companies also deploy special hardware to do something similar to content cleansing: a content *firewall*.

Instead of stripping out hidden metadata, these systems inspect documents for keywords before they leave your domain. Whether the documents are sent in an e-mail or uploaded as a file attachment to a Web site, a content firewall can be amazingly helpful at preventing accidental disclosure of information.

Imagine you're involved in a highly sensitive merger. You decided to secure the content correctly: first by cleansing documents of all hidden content, then by sealing them with IRM. You then place them into a secure repository, awaiting review by your team. Your digital files are perfectly safe, but the information is still vulnerable. Why? Because your secure data also exists in the minds of your team, who are—like everybody else—prone to mistakes.

Imagine that one team member is sending a quick update about the merger to the rest of the team. He makes a simple plain text e-mail and types in the addresses of the rest of the team. Unfortunately, he is using an e-mail system that uses an auto-complete feature. When he begins typing an e-mail address, the auto-complete feature suggests an e-mail address for him that is similar to the address of somebody on his team. Without noticing, he accepts the auto-completed e-mail address, which is unfortunately not somebody on the team. Now somebody outside of your organization has this vital information.

This was not malice in any way—it was a simple mistake. Unfortunately, it occurs with extreme regularity. If you had a content firewall, you would be able to scan all outgoing e-mail and block those that contain certain keywords, such as *merger*.

Together, content cleansing and content firewalls can protect the wrong element from seeing your information, whether or not you use IRM.

Dynamic Watermarks

Several applications allow you to apply watermarks to your documents. Typically, you need to convert your documents to PDF, and then you place an image overlay on the document. A common technique is to overlay the word "CONFIDENTIAL" in big, bold letters. However, this by itself is not much of a deterrent. Since you do not know the origin of the document, in the event of a leak, you would have a difficult time tracking down who did it and when.

Instead, some organizations prefer to do the overlay dynamically. When a person views a content item, a watermark is embedded in the PDF document on the fly. In addition to the word "CONFIDENTIAL," you can create a header with the name of the person viewing this document, the time, and which computer they were using.

If this user then prints out this confidential PDF, every single page is branded with who viewed it and when. If the user then forgets to pick up the document at the printing station, it is simple to trace this security violation back to the culprit.

Naturally, these watermarks are only as secure as the PDF encryption, so a determined professional hacker may someday bypass them. However, in many cases it's effective as an additional "shame" layer to prevent accidental and intentional disclosure.

Monitor and Audit Your Users

Each of the tools mentioned above are useful to add security, but most of them deal with *protecting* your content. A coherent security policy also must focus on *detecting* access violations and properly *reacting* to them.

How to react to an access violation is something best left up to the individual security teams. However, Oracle does provide a few more tools to help people detect access violations, so you know when to react.

All UCM components detect and log unauthorized access in their Web logs. Access violations in the Records Management Agents are logged back to the content server logs as well. IRM logs both failed and successful unsealing attempts, but in a different database. Authentication errors, such as incorrect passwords, are usually logged by your identity management system in yet another log file.

In a pragmatic ECM system, you should consolidate these log files into one system, and use auditing tools to analyze the data within. In some cases, security log aggregators are sufficient. In other cases, you may need advanced business intelligence tools to data mine your logs for access violations, as discussed in Chapter 7.

Takeaways

- A comprehensive security policy entails protecting your content from unauthorized access, detecting access when it happens, and reacting to violations. It should also secure content while it is being used and not just when in a repository.

- An enterprise content management system should store content, not users.

  - Keep users in an identity management system that supports federation.

  - Use security roles and rights defined in the user repository to control content access.

  - Map the rights from the central system to the local ECM repository.

- A comprehensive security model comes in layers.

  - Secure content in your repository, based on which users can be trusted with what information.

    - Avoid the temptation of creating content silos based on security.

  - Use Information Rights Management (IRM) to securely seal content.

    - IRM requires authentication to decrypt, view, and modify the content.

    - Sealed content is tracked every time it is accessed.

    - IRM applies no matter where the document is opened.

- Use additional layers when applicable.

    - Layers include content cleansing, watermarks, and content firewalls.

- Information Rights Management is an essential piece of a Universal Records Management strategy.

    - Encrypt the documents in-place, and don't allow anybody to modify them.

    - Make copies of the record in the true ECM system to better monitor its life cycle.

CHAPTER
7

Bringing Structured and Unstructured Strategies Together

As mentioned in Chapter 1, people have a tendency to treat structured and unstructured content differently. Structured content usually means the highly organized data stored in a relational database and accessed from an enterprise application. The purpose of this data is to help access, edit, and manage well-defined processes. Unstructured content is usually about the information that exists outside the process: notes, memos, reports, e-mails, and drafts.

This separation is somewhat artificial. Essentially, all of this is information that needs to be managed, and it's a mistake to think about them differently. Unfortunately, many organizations do exactly that.

The historical separation of structured and unstructured information in different systems has led to the evolution of different capabilities and tools for these two types of systems. While the capabilities of the different toolsets may have been driven by the underlying value proposition of the types of content against which the tools were applied, today there is a good case to use a common set of tools for both structured and unstructured information. Why limit business intelligence tools to structured data, where they have traditionally been focused? Why limit records management or enterprise search to unstructured content when it can be extremely valuable to structured information? Why limit metadata tagging to documents and Web pages, when database records would similarly benefit?

An optimal information management solution should bring these strategies together. This means your enterprise content management strategy should not be designed in a vacuum. It should be a natural extension of currently existing policies for general information management that your enterprise applications use: similar rules for access rights, similar rules to guarantee accuracy, similar rules to conform to compliance regulations.

However, it also means that you should also extend the power of both kinds of applications by taking advantage of information and services that the other offers. Why not access logs in your Siebel CRM system to determine what content items a customer might be interested in? Why not use real-time business intelligence analytics on your Universal Online E-mail Archives? Why not extract structured data from your unstructured content, and allow applications to query it?

This chapter covers how to bring your strategies together, and then shows what can happen when you do.

The Blur Between Structured and Unstructured Content

The content management industry coined the term "unstructured content" to include any content item that contains useful business information, but for whatever reason, the content item lacks structure that would make the information easy to extract. For example, you probably store a list of your customers in a nicely defined set of tables, columns, and rows in your database. This is considered *structured* content. In your database, every customer must have a customer ID, a customer name, a content person, a list of product orders, and the like.

However, an e-mail containing a bullet-point list of the top five high-profile customers would be *unstructured* content. A generated HTML report displaying the list of customers would be *unstructured* content. Even an Excel spreadsheet containing the entire database would be *unstructured* content.

As you can see, the term "unstructured content" is extremely misleading. There is a tremendous amount of structure in all of the above examples of unstructured content. Language is structured, bullet points are structured, HTML tables are structured, and Excel spreadsheets are definitely structured. However, the key difference is *how the content is created*. A structured repository is very strict about what information belongs in which field, and it carefully verifies and strongly enforces this structure. In contrast, unstructured repositories will store any kind of free-form content, regardless of how it is structured, with little to no validation of the format.

To put it another way, structured repositories force contributors to all use the same structure. Unstructured repositories allow contributors to use whatever structure suits them—strict or loose, consistent or inconsistent. Unstructured content enables the user to capture, organize, and present information that best suits the author's needs and the audience's needs. A structured system, on the other hand, requires a user to enter information that best suits the application's needs. Ideally, your database application also serves the needs of your contributors and your audience, however, needs change so frequently it is difficult to close all gaps.

Naturally, there are benefits to each kind of approach. Strongly enforced structures can ensure your data integrity, but they are limited in the number of things they can store. Also, highly structured information systems go against human nature: people prefer simple, usable systems, to do their jobs, because it is the path of least resistance. Unstructured systems can store anything, but if there is no consistency, it will be difficult to find and extract useful information from them.

As a result, the distinction between these kinds of applications is blurred. Structured repositories allow you to store some unstructured information— like scanned images or freely formatted comments—in the database. Unstructured repositories extract what limited structure they can from the free-form content, and encourage people to add further structure with metadata, such as author, title, department, or project.

For another example, it's a common practice to lock away vital information in an enterprise application, with strict access policies and rigid processes for changing data. This is in order to protect the accuracy of the information, as well as its security. However, what if that same information was circulated in a Microsoft Word document? Since that's the data people can access more easily, they will assume it's accurate because they can't access the enterprise application to verify. And what happens if somebody e-mails that report to the wrong person? Suddenly you have a security breach, even though your enterprise application is still running strong.

In order to completely manage your content, you need to understand why people resort to unstructured content solutions instead of structured ones, and try to merge your strategies.

Master Data Management

Before we go too far into the details of bringing your strategies together, it's important to mention a technology that is similar to ECM for structured content repositories: master data management (MDM).

The goals behind MDM are somewhat similar to the goals of enterprise content management. In general, MDM tries to define and manage the non-transactional portions of structured content repositories. This includes things like customer names, project names, the list of services your company provides, the list of offices in your company, important dates, a calendar of events, and any other kind of useful reference data. In general, multiple applications in your enterprise will use this "reference" data to drive application logic, or present user interfaces.

Unfortunately, for very large applications, it sometimes becomes difficult to locate the authoritative—or *master*—copy of the reference data. For small organizations, managing the master data is simple, because the number of enterprise applications is small. However, for larger enterprises, or enterprises that reuse the master data in multiple systems, managing this "master data" can be problematic.

Do you use a unique customer ID across all systems? What happens when you acquire or merge with another organization that uses a different identification scheme? Do all of your applications refer to the master data before making decisions? Is your copy of the master data up to date? Is it of sufficient quality for your needs? Can you consistently identify and classify your data?

Similar to ECM, there are many applications available that provide MDM. Also similar to ECM, each one solves the problem in a subtly different way. In which case, an MDM solution that works fine for one department or application might not be sufficient for everything. There are both tactical and strategic MDM deployments, and a pragmatic MDM strategy might need multiple MDM applications.

All together, this means that the people in charge of your MDM strategy might be asking the same questions as your ECM Center of Excellence. What naming convention should we use? What terminology can everybody agree with? How often should we publish the "single source of truth" to remote repositories? How should we integrate an enterprise-wide solution with a tactical point solution?

In any event, when it comes to bringing strategies together, your ECM Center of Excellence should keep in close contact with those designing your MDM strategy. You may be able to reuse some of the same technical skill sets across projects. Also, the high-level executives in your Center of Excellence could be important for pushing forward politically difficult decisions for both ECM and MDM.

The Value of a Unified Strategy

As mentioned in the previous section, bringing your strategies together is difficult, both politically and technically, for many organizations. In many cases, people treat structured and unstructured applications so differently that the teams barely even communicate. They may not recognize the value in each other's applications or in how much effort would be involved in replicating the functionality. It is not uncommon for a misguided middleware developer familiar with ECM to believe he can re-create a customer relationship management application from scratch. Likewise, a misguided product information management administrator may believe their application is wholly capable of enterprise content management.

Ultimately, the best strategy is to assemble an ecosystem of enterprise applications that work together in a way that maximizes the strengths of each. Some of the primary value propositions of a unified strategy are

- **Security**   Most applications can only secure data inside their own repository. However, data moves from application to application, and many times it isn't in *any* repository. To truly secure your data, you need a unified strategy to control and audit data access, whether or not the data is in a repository.

- **Information Access and Reuse**   If you make your content easy to reuse, whether it is structured or unstructured, other applications will be able to gain value.

- **Service Access and Reuse**   Similar to content reuse, service reuse means that you don't have to keep reinventing the wheel. Applications can focus on their strengths and offer functionality as services to other applications, ensuring better interoperability and consistent best-of-breed technologies.

- **Extracting Structure from Unstructured Content**   Creating value with unstructured content sometimes requires finding and extracting the embedded structure. This includes automatic extraction of keywords, converting documents into a more searchable XML format, or data mining content for embedded structure.

There are many names for these kinds of blended approaches. Some call them *content-enabled vertical applications*, meaning a structured content application specific to an industry that also supports unstructured content. Other analysts use the term *content-centric applications*, which implies that it is a solution focused mainly on unstructured content, but enhanced with structured data and services.

In contrast, Oracle uses the term Fusion Applications to not only include the above two categories, but all solutions that include both structured and unstructured content, covered in the next section.

Oracle Fusion Applications

Middleware is used not only to build custom application and modernize legacy infrastructure, but also to enhance packaged enterprise applications. Oracle has a strategy around enterprise applications that extensively leverages middleware to extend, compliment, and even provide new features to enterprise applications. This strategy makes obvious sense when viewed in the context of Oracle's acquisitions over the past couple of years.

Using ECM as an example, Oracle has acquired several enterprise applications that in some way or another include content management. A few instances of this, but by no means an extensive list, are the PeopleSoft attachments framework and the Siebel Files technology, in addition to Oracle's E-Business Suite and its attachments framework. So while Oracle is building its next generation of applications, called Fusion Applications, based on Fusion Middleware, it is also building on and extending the existing applications through a program called Applications Unlimited. In order to efficiently do so, Oracle leverages Fusion Middleware technologies, such as content management, both for Fusion Applications and to enhance Applications Unlimited products.

This means that the work of building a best-in-breed content management system is leveraged as a product feature (at some point) within the Applications Unlimited products and as a core building block for Fusion Applications. This middleware-centric strategy, shown in Figure 7-1, also allows customers to utilize Fusion Middleware today, with their existing applications, in a way that is inline with the future strategy of both the Applications Unlimited product(s)

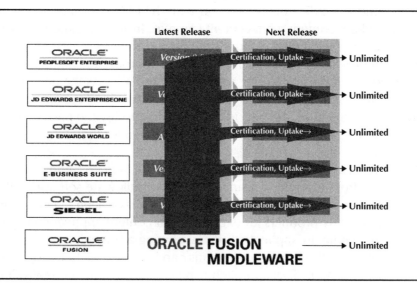

FIGURE 7-1. *Oracle Fusion Applications uses Fusion Middleware at its core.*

they are running today and the Fusion Applications that Oracle is building for the future.

Content management plays a critical role in Fusion Applications. Oracle ECM is the foundation for the knowledge management framework, which is the mechanism by which unstructured information is stored, managed, secured, and consumed by Fusion Applications. Oracle ECM supports both knowledge workers and process workers with the same system. Process workers care about unstructured attachments to traditionally structured data, such as a scanned image of an invoice attached to the Accounts Payables entry. Knowledge workers care more about collaborative capabilities such as sharing sales presentations and individual PowerPoint slides amongst a sales team. The knowledge worker's system can be further enhanced with information from the process worker's system, such as updating the content of the sales slides based on raw data in a sales force automation application.

The latter was part of a demonstration done at Oracle Open World 2007 in which the new Fusion Sales Force Automation was shown. In the demonstration Oracle's extensive business intelligence capabilities were used in conjunction with sales data to not just produce a sales forecast and manage contacts (as traditional sales force automation tools do), but to also show a sales person what types of products are selling in other sales territories and to what types of customers. Once that data was available the sales person was shown a list of targets with contacts in their territory that had the same key indicators for success with the identified products.

This is where content management came in. Instead of simply showing the products and the target accounts, the Fusion Sales Force Automation application provided the salesperson with the appropriate collateral, such as presentations and datasheets, for approaching the sale. As the final part of the demo, the salesperson was able to not only download the appropriate, up-to-date presentation, but also to dynamically modify the presentation with additional slides to customize the presentation for their intended audience.

It is in this capacity that some of the largest gains in cost and efficiency can be made from leveraging a strategic ECM middleware solution. Often these applications have their own repositories or have been integrated with different third-party products for each different content application or content area within an application. By leveraging a strategic ECM middleware layer, these multiple systems can be consolidated into a single, cost-effective solution. This approach can also add significant new value to an enterprise application.

Enterprise content management is not limited to Fusion Applications. With Oracle's Applications Unlimited strategy, the applications in use today are being certified with Fusion Middleware, allowing users of those applications to immediately take advantage of Fusion Middleware.

Fusion Middleware is also "hot pluggable" with other enterprise applications, allowing the tools discussed here (and in other areas of Fusion Middleware) to be leveraged not only by Oracle applications but also by third-party applications, such as SAP.

Bringing Strategies Together Pragmatically

In order to bring together your strategies, you need to play to the strengths of each application. With a service-oriented architecture as a backbone, your structured applications will be able to consume services from your unstructured applications and vice versa. This means that ideally, any unstructured content in your solution belongs in your strategic ECM repository, so others can manage and reuse it. There are four general ways to bring strategies together:

- Unify your security policy (as was discussed in Chapter 6).

- Bring unstructured services to structured applications.

- Bring structured services to unstructured applications.

- Extract structure from unstructured content.

Of course, this raises several questions. When does your data belong in an ECM repository, and when should it be stored alongside the rest of your structured data? Naturally, if all you are storing is a "description" field, you probably don't need content management.

But what about the future? Will you need to edit this unstructured data frequently? Who will need to change it? Who will approve those changes? How do they like to edit content? Will it be reused in other applications? How? Will you need to audit when the information was accessed and by whom? Will it need to conform to regulatory compliance? Will you need to transform the information? Revision it? Put it through a workflow process when added or changed? What if you get sued? Can you be certain your content complies with HIPPA, Sarbanes-Oxley, and other industry regulations?

Overall, the goal is simplification:

- One tool for data mining structured and unstructured content

- One tool for business intelligence

- One tool for tracking user behavior and making suggestions

- One tool for security policy management and enforcement

- One tool for records management

- One tool for searching content repositories

- One tool for managing and browsing Web sites

It's very early on in this next stage of ECM evolution, but the authors believe Oracle's products to be ahead of the curve. Not only does Oracle have all the required ECM components, but Oracle also has the most comprehensive set of popular enterprise applications, middleware tools, and database features. Oracle is also dedicated to creating integrations between all these applications, to reduce the costs of deployment and maintenance.

Integrate Strategically or Tactically?

Like any other application, you need to do a cost-benefit analysis to determine what kind of integration makes the most sense. Should this integration be tactical or strategic? In other words, how much of the unstructured content belongs in your strategic ECM repository? All, some, or none? When you bring services from one kind of application to another, what kind of integration makes sense?

When unifying your security policy, it is ideal to think strategically. All of your applications should be able to adhere to a global security policy and support auditable exceptions to that policy. The problem here is that it is not always cost effective to fully integrate your application with a global identity management system. Therefore, you will need tools that allow you to integrate tactically, such as Information Rights Management, or perhaps the perimeter-based security offered by Ensemble.

When bringing unstructured services to structured applications, you should almost always integrate strategically. Your ECM system should act as the single source of truth for unstructured content in all your structured applications, as discussed in the following sections. The best option is to integrate content services directly into your enterprise applications. In some cases, the best option is to integrate the strategic ECM repository directly with the structured application. However, in many cases the best solution would be to use middleware to host the blended application.

When bringing structure to unstructured application, the question is more difficult. A strategic integration would mean that you would need to extend the back-end of your ECM infrastructure to integrate with structured data and services. This is ideal when those services should be considered a natural extension of what a content item is, such as ratings, user-suggested keywords, or recommendations.

Remember, the goal is a single source of truth to support your unstructured content needs. You want dozens of enterprise applications to connect to one single repository to get all information about that item. If practical, you should store this structured data in the unstructured repository, so access to the enhanced data is fast and easy. In other cases, the strategic ECM system should be an invisible proxy to the structured system. This means that when an end user requests information about a content item, the ECM system returns what information it has, then connects to the structured system to access additional information, and returns the entire bundle to the end user.

When extracting structure from unstructured content, your integration will almost certainly be strategic. This functionality is a natural extension of what ECM is, and where many ECM systems will be going in the future. Therefore, any technology along these lines should have a tight integration with your strategic ECM system, and may someday be bundled with it.

Unify Your Security Policy

Unifying your security policy is the only way to fully secure your data. If the primary goal is to secure your data, then securing your repository is only part of the problem. It doesn't matter how secure your structured repository is; what matters is how the data *flows* from your repository to the user. If the data is ever used, that means it must at some point leave your system, which means it leaves your sphere of control, which means it might become vulnerable. Unfortunately, most employees have incentive to access and share information, rather than keep it secure. Therefore, in a high-performance environment that focuses strongly on innovation, odds are your employees actually have incentive to violate the security policy!

Therefore, unifying your security policy is a daunting task. If the administrators of your structured repositories set the security policy, they might make it too restrictive for your knowledge workers to function.

Ironically, in many cases the raw data in your structured repository has *lower* security needs than the same data in an unstructured repository. For example, which of the following two documents would be more valuable to your competitors:

■ A raw data dump of your product lines and sales totals, or

■ One-tenth of that data in a Word document, along with analysis of which product lines will be the focus of next quarter's sales initiatives.

Clearly, if your competitors acquired your raw data, they would be able to perform several analyses on it to make a guess at your strategy. The Word document has only a small fraction of the data, so it is of less value for raw data analysis. However, it already comes with one very useful analysis, giving your competitors full access to your strategy. Losing your raw data means that your competitors can do multiple kinds of analysis on their own, but losing the Word document is handing them critical strategy information on a silver platter. In this case, the odds are good that the unstructured Word document should be treated with more care than your raw data. However, the odds are also good that it is currently treated with *less* care.

As covered in Chapter 6, the best way to implement this is with a global security policy that empowers your users to safely share information. You should also use Information Rights Management as an additional layer of security, both to audit access to content, and to encrypt content while it isn't in use. This will help you add the extra layers that you need to secure your unstructured content as much or more than your raw data.

Bring Unstructured Services to Structured Applications

The entire purpose behind having a strategic ECM infrastructure is so that you can bring unstructured content and services to other applications. These may be client-facing applications—like the Desktop Integration Suite mentioned in Chapter 4—or they may be structured content repositories. These structured repositories may be existing enterprise applications or they may be new middleware applications.

In either case, these applications are likely to have similar unstructured content needs:

- Content display and annotation

- Metadata services, including folksonomy and tagging

- Search services

- Archiving services

- Content transformation services

- Records management services and adapters

- Managing content on Web sites, portals, and extranets

- Tracking usage and popularity of content

The ideal solution is to do a tight integration between your structured application and the strategic ECM infrastructure. However, this is not always cost effective. According to Oracle, 40 percent of IT budgets is spent on integrations, so anything that helps reduce this cost would be strongly encouraged.

There are several off-the-shelf applications that help you with this integration, as discussed in the following sections. Some of these are direct integrations, others use standard connectors such as SOA and BPEL. If you need to create your own integration, you should refer to the customization tools listed in Chapter 4.

Oracle Imaging and Process Management

The IPM application is a good way to deliver a small subset of unstructured content services to your structured enterprise applications. Its focus is on managing business process flow, from a scanned document to a structured repository, and image-enable your back-end systems. As mentioned in Chapter 4, IPM has connectors to several major systems:

- Oracle E-Business Suite

- Oracle Financials

- PeopleSoft Enterprise
- JD Edwards World
- JD Edwards OneWorld
- SAP

IPM is mainly for transactional content. A typical transaction starts with a process worker scanning a document and submitting the image to IPM. IPM uses applications that support optical character recognition (OCR) technology to extract some structured information embedded in the scanned document, such as invoice numbers, dates, names, and dollar amounts. Next, IPM uses its connectors to submit the structured data to one of the above enterprise applications. This all takes place inside of a custom designed workflow process for the transaction, which can orchestrate the data flow between people and applications, and deal with any discrepancies. IPM also stores the original scanned document in your strategic ECM infrastructure, for future reference or reuse by other applications.

IPM comes with a viewer that runs in context with the enterprise applications above, allowing these systems to query the content repository, view documents, and perform annotations on the documents. This is very useful when there is a discrepancy, or during an audit, and process workers need to refer back to the original.

If you have an existing enterprise application and need general support for viewing images, the IPM application may be the most cost-effective solution. If your needs include a wider variety of unstructured content services, then you may need a different approach.

BPEL Workflows with UCM

If you have integration needs beyond what IPM offers, but you would like to use as many prebuilt integrations as possible, then using UCM in combination with Business Process Execution Language (BPEL) workflows might be the best option. This will allow you to create most of the data-flow portion of the application using visually designed BPEL workflows. Since BPEL workflows use the SOAP infrastructure built-in to Oracle UCM, it is very easy to make application-to-application integrations with BPEL.

When your application needs something beyond what is easy to do with BPEL—such as image viewing, metadata tagging, comments, or annotations—then you can create a custom integration by executing UCM services directly. You can use the SOAP or Java APIs described in Chapter 4, or you could even use the Ensemble mashup APIs described in Chapters 5 and 8.

Business Intelligence Publisher

Oracle ECM frequently needs to integrate with legacy reporting systems. Such applications typically analyze database tables and output a report based on the data. Most enterprises have several of these applications and would like to make their output more accessible via the Web. In general, an integration would require a custom integration with WebDAV, SOAP, or one of the other tools discussed in Chapter 4. Alternatively, you could update your report generation system with a more modern business intelligence application that already integrates with Oracle UCM.

One such application is Oracle Business Intelligence Publisher (BI Publisher), formerly called XML Publisher. This is an application specialized in centralized report generation. With it, you design how you would like to present your data with a native application like Microsoft Word. Next, you configure BI Publisher to download information from one or several data sources. Finally, BI Publisher renders the data into the template and generates the report in the specified output format, such as HTML, XML, PDF, or even Flash.

The final step is to send this information to a specific output destination, such as a printer, e-mail, fax, or into a content management system. Oracle UCM has a native plug-in to BI Publisher, so it can be used as the destination repository. Once the report is a managed content item in UCM, it can be securely stored, versioned, managed, and distributed. The distribution of the reports can leverage the document transformation capabilities in a variety of outputs including HTML, PDF, XML, and mobile outputs such as lightweight HTML or WML for handheld devices allowing the reports to be integrated across multiple Web sites and applications.

Siebel Files

Another good example of bringing structured and unstructured information together is in enterprise customer relationship management (CRM) systems. Siebel, an Oracle enterprise CRM application, allows organizations to centrally manage and store everything they know about their customers. For obvious reasons this centralization enables the organization to better understand its customers, provide them with better service, and ultimately retain them as customers while selling them additional products and services. This centralization requires that both the structured information about the customer (customer ID, transaction history, contact information, etc.) be combined with unstructured information (e-mail correspondence, scanned documents, etc.).

Siebel ships a basic document store as part of the application, called Siebel Files, which allows users to attach unstructured documents to transactions or records in the Siebel system. Now, as part of Oracle's Applications Unlimited strategy of using Fusion Middleware to enhance Oracle's enterprise applications, Siebel can be connected to Oracle Universal Content Management to provide ECM capabilities from within the context of Siebel. This also allows the Siebel content to be integrated with the rest of the enterprise content as part of a pragmatic ECM strategy.

The Siebel connector to Oracle UCM is a native integration into Siebel, meaning a Siebel component using Web services to connect to UCM from directly inside Siebel. Users can check in new documents, update information, and work with document metadata from the Siebel interface, the UCM desktop integration, the UCM Web application, or from any other application that has access to the UCM repository. Content within the system utilizes all of the capabilities of UCM, so it can be tagged with profiles-driven metadata, full-text indexed, searched, transformed to PDF or Web formats, sealed via Information Rights Management, and managed via enterprise records and retention policies.

The Future: Sales Force Automation

At present, business intelligence tools are based on highly structured information. The next generation of tools will blend structured and unstructured content to give a richer and more powerful interface. They will take advantage of how UCM manages Web sites, as well as PowerPoint presentations, in order to empower your sales people to be more productive.

For example, when your sales people log into your sales portal, they will see information about which campaigns are successful in regions similar to theirs. It will show the top three products and the contact information for three potential clients. It will also present links to promotional Web sites, marketing literature, and several slides from successful PowerPoint presentations.

How does this help sales? Assume that your company has a general purpose product, which has now added features specific to a certain industry. They begin a promotion by data mining your customer base for people in this industry, and they present this information in your sales portal.

Next, your saleswoman places a call to a few of these clients. She discovers that these clients are indeed frustrated because of the lack of products that satisfy their needs, and the clients want information more specific to their industry. Luckily, your organization has exactly what this customer needs. The old method would be to download the default marketing literature, and present this in person to the client. The new method would be to use more powerful sales force automation tools.

Starting from your portal, your saleswoman creates a more targeted PowerPoint presentation, based on the general promotional slides created by the marketing department. She eliminates the ones that are irrelevant to the client's industry and removes any distracting clutter.

She then creates an entirely new page on the promotional Web site. This page will have the exact same look and feel of the other pages, but it speaks directly to the needs of that specific group of clients. It mentions their industry by name, and has a clear message about how the product will help them. This needn't be a formalized white paper: a few paragraphs of text with bullet points may be sufficient.

Naturally, this new Web page may need to go through a workflow process to make sure the quality is high enough to be placed on the promotional Web site. You will also need auditing to keep track of what promises were made to satisfy the legal department and future auditors. However, having your sales promise directly reflected on an official Web page will lend additional authenticity to the saleswoman's claims.

Your saleswoman can also use the next-generation sales force automation to download scripts of how to pitch the new product. These may contain messaging that works, tactics that have helped sell, and tactics that should be avoided. These scripts also contain competitive information about your competition, with traps to set and traps to avoid. They can be further customized by noting which tactics have worked in this industry, and not just general tips.

Finally, after the site is complete, the saleswoman follows up with her prospects in the neglected industry. Armed with a new PowerPoint presentation, a newly launched Web site, and a sales script, she is certain to impress.

Bring Structured Services to Unstructured Applications

Naturally, the next best way to bring your strategies together is to tap into structured data and services to enrich the value of unstructured content. Sometimes this enrichment means using structured data about users and their history to present a more useful interface for the end user. Sometimes it means using services and applications normally reserved for structured content, and adjust them to also consume unstructured content.

ECM and "Next Best Activity"

Once you store a massive amount of information in your repository, your content access problem is mostly solved. The problem now shifts to the question, how do I help my users to find new content? Should I create an easily browseable interface so they can actively find content, or should I push relevant related documents so my users can passively find content?

Sometimes this problem is simple: if a content item belongs to a specific project group, and a user views that item, the odds are good that they may be interested in more information about that project. Therefore, you may wish to display a sidebar with links to popular content in that project: download pages, whitepapers, or FAQs. If you organize content items into a taxonomy, the odds are similarly good that you'll be interested in items that are close to that item according to your taxonomy. Similarly, many Web pages contain a list of "related articles" arranged by topics that are manually controlled.

However, this is just the tip of the iceberg. It is still too focused on the content and isn't considering the context, nor the user's needs. For example, based on this user's search history, which of the documents might be more important? When searching for documents about Project Alpha, would the user be more interested in marketing literature, sales reports, or research documents? Would he desire different documents depending on the time of year, or on what campaigns are currently running? What would you like to "push" to the user so they don't have to spend any energy looking for new information at all? In short, how do you convert a "search" into a "find?"

Perhaps the most powerful combination here is between Oracle Universal Content Management and Oracle Real-Time Decisions. Oracle Real-Time Decisions is a business intelligence product that makes recommendations based on a predictive analytics model. When combined with enterprise content management, a predictive analytics engine can aggregate data from multiple data sources to provide a personalized, persuasive content to customers, suppliers, or employees.

In the customer relationship management (CRM) world, this type of technology can play a major role in a concept often called "next best activity." *Next best activity* is essentially the ability of a company or organization to know what the ideal proposition or interaction is with any given customer, at any given time, or any channel of communication. For this to be accomplished, we must know all of the options available for the interaction, have knowledge of previous interactions, be aware of the customer's data in our various systems, and ideally know the customer's preferences about the types of offers we may make during this interaction.

In practice, the Real-Time Decisions (RTD) engine acts as an adaptive, learning-based personalization engine, as shown in Figure 7-2. Based on data available in enterprise databases, cookies, and other sources, RTD will recommend a specific item from a list of available options to an end user in order to achieve business objectives. The engine monitors the success of different options against success criteria and proactively adapts the rules it uses

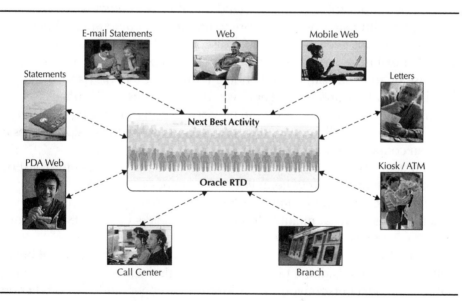

FIGURE 7-2. *Oracle Real-Time Decisions helps determine the next best activity on Site Studio Web sites.*

to make recommendations to optimize the output of the recommendations. This is a key element of customer services initiatives known as "next best activity."

In other words, RTD gathers information from your Siebel call center, analytics from your public-facing Web site, your data warehouse, and other available sources in order to suggest what the next best activity would be for this specific customer, partner, or employee. These recommendations can be used to drive persuasive content to users about new services or products that may apply to them, billing or account options that may be relevant, or simply educational information that is targeted to the users.

Traditionally, this type of personalization was done via hard-coded rules and programs established by marketing teams. While these rules did provide some personalization, they required a very manual process of analyzing log files and trend reports to see which offers are working, then manually adjusting the hard-coded rules based on those results. Using a predictive analytics engine, we can use a great deal more data while also eliminating the time delay and manual intensiveness of hard-coded personalization rules.

Because RTD works across a wide range of data sources, we also have personalization capabilities that can span the organization and customer touch points. Our rules can understand that if the customer is calling our call center with issues, we may want to offer them a different product or services, perhaps even with a sale or discount, when they visit our Web site next. For example, assume that a cell phone customer called his provider because of an issue with his old phone. It turns out that his hands-free headset is broken, and no longer covered by warranty, so he needs to purchase a new one. The next time he visits your public-facing Web site, your RTD engine will know of this history, and ensure the customer sees ads or even coupons for new headsets.

In practice, this means significantly less work than maintaining a list of "related content" for every item: you use analytics to determine what is popular, instead of employing an administrator to do market analysis and make guesses on what might be popular. This works whether the audience is your customers, your partners, or your employees.

Naturally, this application is only as good as the historical data it begins with. In other words, if the first person cannot find a piece of content, odds are that the next person won't be able to find it either, and your prediction engine will not have enough information to be useful. Therefore, it is still a good idea to spend time making your site easy to browse and easy to search.

ECM and the Culture of Information Sharing

"People, process, and technology"—the phrase is a part of so many mission statements, it's almost a truism. Yet the expression is particularly apt when the topic of discussion is ECM technology. ECM makes it easier for people to share information, whether internally (with other departments) or externally (with customers, business partners, or constituents). In turn, this ability to share information accelerates business processes; in particular, processes that cross departmental boundaries. But the introduction of ECM also changes the way people work. That's why successful ECM initiatives also address the need for change management to help create a corporate culture of information sharing.

—Jeetu Patel
Executive Vice President, Doculabs, Inc.

You may also want exceptions to the next best activity rule, so you can promote specific products or services. However, after this initial set-up, Real-Time Decisions can significantly ease the burden of maintenance for determining related content and activities.

Oracle UCM and Oracle RTD can be used in conjunction and as part of our SOA strategy to provide targeted content to both internal and external users. This combines the structured data stored in relational databases with decision logic and the ability to transform and present content to users across various different touch points, such as a Web site, a kiosk, or even a help desk application.

Customer Communications Management

Just as we use Oracle Real-Time Decisions to recommend content to customers, we can leverage additional information in our systems to enrich the ways we already interact with our customers, partners, and employees. While RTD can provide a powerful analytics engine and predictive capabilities for determining what information to present a user, Oracle UCM provides the ability to reuse content across multiple channels through the extensive transformation capabilities in the product. Content can be combined with data and presented to users across multiple channels.

These channels can include Web applications, kiosks, e-mail, letters, billing and statements, or interactions with employees at storefront terminals, on call center phones, or even via real-time online chat. The important thing is that information be consistently available from all of these sources and presented coherently to the customer across each channel.

We have discussed throughout the book electronic transformation and delivery, such as presenting information consistently across multiple Web sites. To truly manage our customer interactions consistently, we will also need to include our print and e-mail interactions as part of our overall customer communications management strategy. Often this capability is referred to as document output management (DOM). In 2008, Oracle acquired Skywire software, which was a leader in DOM, and it has rapidly become a strategic piece of Oracle's ECM offering.

DOM manages the integration of data and content in the document creation process and manages the high-volume output of those documents for distribution. An example is your bank statement, which has your transaction information from a relational database combined with branding and content from the bank. Ideally, this content is integrated with the messaging and promotions being utilized across other media, such as e-mail campaigns or the Web site, as shown in Figure 7-3.

As part of our pragmatic ECM strategy, we need to enable DOM systems and other customer correspondence management systems to leverage our

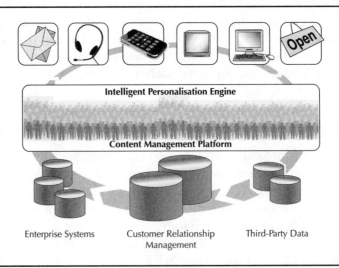

FIGURE 7-3. *Document Output Management combines structured and unstructured content into your communication channels.*

strategic ECM infrastructure and share content across multiple customer touch-points.

The Future: Business Intelligence and Analytics

Business intelligence systems analyze recent and historical metrics, in order to better enable business decision-making. The analysis is culled from any and every kind of metric that your business can reliably take:

- Historical sales data, broken down by region, product, and department
- Sales estimates
- Customer complaints
- The time required to perform a specific task

Since these systems typically work with structured content, your analytics will be limited to what is stored in the database. For Oracle UCM, this includes metadata about the content, historical records about content creation and workflows, as well as access logs. Analytics of unstructured content can help you create dashboards for what content is popular, and what is not. This may help you determine where to spend your resources when it comes to updating older content. It can also help drive user acceptance by making content popularity a competition, as discussed in Chapter 3.

Another more interesting possibility is to use business intelligence and analytics on e-mail archives. Most e-mail archiving solutions store e-mails in backup tapes, which are difficult to analyze. In contrast, the Universal Online Archive stores e-mail in an always-online database, as discussed in Chapter 4. That means that your archives are always available to do real-time analytics on the data in the e-mail.

In an instant, you will have information about who e-mailed whom, when, and did they use any suspicious terms? This kind of functionality is vital in the financial industry in order to monitor and block any potential wrongdoing or insider trading.

Of course, business intelligence and analytics is only practical when analyzing structured content. In order to get the most out of your unstructured content repository, it would be ideal to first extract the structured content embedded in the documents and perform additional analysis on that.

Extract Structure from Unstructured Content

As mentioned many times before, the term "unstructured content" is a bit misleading. Obviously, all useful information has some kind of definable structure. Regardless, this category applies to any content item with a non-rigid structure: e-mails, Microsoft Word documents, spreadsheets with tables and graphs, images, video files, scanned paper documents, and the like.

Most unstructured content items have structured characteristics in common: titles, authors, sections, sub-sections, diagrams, tables, and images. It is certainly possible to create a database schema to store a Microsoft Word document in such atomic units. However, would this be of value to your end users? You could define a document template using XML, store your content as nodes in the database, and force your business users to switch from Microsoft Word to an XML authoring tool. However, would your users prefer this tool to e-mail or Microsoft Word? The value is in letting your knowledge workers use the tools that maximize their own productivity. This means allowing them to create content with little to no explicit structure, and trying to add structure in a different "enhancement" step.

There are three main ways to add structure to unstructured content. The first, covered in previous chapters, is for the author of the content item to supply metadata about this item. This metadata sometimes takes the form of describing what a content item is, such as its title, author, and project. Other times this metadata helps describe the state of the item, or who might want to find it. This process was covered in detail in Chapters 2 and 3.

Good metadata is probably the best way to organize unstructured content. However, users do not enjoy filling out metadata forms. If they do not see immediate value in providing metadata, and are not trained to use metadata, and are not given incentive to use metadata, then they will supply very poor metadata. This can become a problem, because if you use metadata to organize your content, poor metadata can quickly overwhelm good metadata, making it even more difficult to find content.

Another option is to allow end users to enhance content items that were authored by other people. The most straightforward approach is to associate end-user comments with the document. People can also use annotations to draw their comments onto the document. These annotations are stored as separate layers, so they do not affect the original item. End users can also give ratings on content items, mark items as "favorites," or tag them with custom keywords that they find useful. Annotations and comments were covered in previous chapters, and custom keywords—also folksonomies—are covered in detail in Chapter 8.

Folksonomies are helpful, because even if a contributor is not good at filling out metadata, the consumers can still sort and organize the content in their own way. However, not everybody uses the same terms, so by itself it isn't sufficient for organizing all content.

Finally, you can also extract structured information from these unstructured content items. This process is more complicated, because of the simple fact that different users will add structure to their documents in different ways. Sometimes documents have a standard structure, and it is easy to extract titles and dates from them. In other cases, you need to use complex algorithms to extract keywords and commonly used terms, and try to associate them with a globally organized thesaurus. If you can get your users to follow some basic conventions—such as contributing Word documents based on a specific template, or using similar conventions throughout their documents—then this process can be easier. However, very loosely structured content is very difficult to work with, and at best you could only extract metadata keywords and tabular information.

The rest of this section covers this last approach: trying to extract structured data after the content has already been created.

Auto Categorization and Semistructured Content

One of the problems with metadata is that relatively few people care about properly setting metadata values. Worse yet, few of these people are particularly good at selecting metadata values.

There are many solutions to this problem, which are mostly cultural. You should teach your users the importance of metadata, and create some kind of metric to measure popular content and content with good metadata. This allows you to harness the natural competitive nature of your users in order to get them to make better metadata.

Probably the best way to make sure your users supply good metadata, is if they are given incentive to supply good metadata so that they themselves are able to find the content again. If they are forced to supply metadata, they will only do the minimum, whereas if the metadata directly helps them, they will be incented to do more. To this end, user-supplied keywords are more trustable if they come in the form of folksonomies, compared to taxonomies. However, folksonomies alone are not sufficient: you also need some kind of controlled taxonomy or controlled thesaurus so that you have a standard way of using terms that everybody can agree on.

Following a rigid taxonomy can be a lot more difficult for the average user, because you need to understand the "right way" to classify content. In contrast, a controlled thesaurus may be easier, because every "preferred" term has several "non-preferred" variants. For example, assume that one department uses the term "Project Alpha," whereas another department uses the term "The Seattle Project" to refer to the same initiative. If you used a controlled thesaurus, this would allow both teams to use the words they are most familiar with in order to tag their content, and find similar content.

Therefore, in lieu of training and incentives, you may find value with an auto-categorization engine. Oracle UCM comes with the Content Categorizer functionality, which allows your users to extract titles, keyword, and other metadata from well-structured content items. There are also several features built-in to Secure Enterprise Search that allow you to take advantage of a controlled thesaurus, so your users can more easily find content.

In practice, auto-categorization and controlled thesauri are not superior to a user trained in the value of metadata. However, it is vastly superior to a user who doesn't understand metadata. It can also be helpful when doing large migrations of content, where you want the information to be accessible, but don't have time to generate keywords for all items.

Auto categorization engines need user feedback. In some cases, this is as simple as having the engine perform a "first pass analysis" of the content and extract keywords. If a human verifies that the keywords are accurate, then they can be stored alongside the content item. Any time a human agrees that the terms are correct, then the rules that extracted those terms should be reinforced. Every time that a human rejects the suggested terms, then that rule should be used less often.

In addition, behavior analysis tools like Oracle Real-Time Decisions may have an important role to play in the future of auto—categorization engines. In other words, the next generation of auto—categorization engines may care less about the "correct" terms to use for a content item; rather, they may monitor user behavior and feedback to see which terms were most helpful to people similar to the current user. In the future, these systems may focus less on what a content item is about, and more on what items a statistically similar user found helpful.

Microformats

Another way to add structure to unstructured content is with microformats. In essence, a microformat is somewhere between a technology standard and a social convention.

For example, assume you have a document that contains an important calendar event. This could be a meeting, a seminar, or a trade show. If everybody followed a basic convention for structuring the data that describes an "event," then you could embed that data in your unstructured documents, extract it, and effortlessly add it to your online calendar application.

This doesn't mean that all "event" descriptions would look the same, or that everybody would have to create event notices with a verbose XML template. By using a microformat convention, it becomes much easier to extract structured data from an unstructured content item.

The value in this is that your documents will continue to have this structure even if the content is migrated from one system to another, or from one format to another. Unlike auto-categorization engines, the metadata about this document is embedded in the document itself. Therefore, whenever you move content from one repository to another, or send it to a friend via e-mail, the metadata will still be there.

Microformats are a natural extension of what a lot of applications already do to content items. For example, digital cameras embed a great deal of metadata into every photo they take, such as the format, the resolution, and the time the photo was taken. Some people are hopeful that newer cell phone cameras will be able to embed metadata about the latitude and longitude of where the photo was taken as well. This is called *geotagging*. It allows people to submit their photos to public Web sites, and allow users to easily search for photos that are nearby a specific address.

Microsoft Word already has the power to embed metadata in your documents. However, this is only one piece of the puzzle. This would only allow you to "tag" the entire document, as opposed to tagging different sections of the document. For example, imagine you had some convention that allowed your users to highlight areas of their documents like so:

- This sentence is important!

- This sentence is an assumption!

- This sentence has implications that affect our sales!

- This sentence is opinion!

- This sentence is a cold, hard, fact!

- This sentence is confidential, and must never be shared!

Now, imagine your search engine knew about these conventions and could rapidly extract these sections from your documents. With one query, you could get a list of all documents that might affect sales, or all facts about a specific product initiative.

You are not required to convert your documents to XML in order to take advantage of microformats. All that is needed is some kind of additional rich markup, such as HTML or even Microsoft Word styles. Examples are in the following sections.

Metadata Microformats

There already is a commonly used microformat convention for metadata, called the rel-tag format. In HTML, you would signify that a metadata tag—such as "technology"—is relevant to the current item by placing the following HTML into it:

```
<a href='http://company.com/technology' rel='tag'>technology</a>
```

The above code is an HTML link. On the page, users would see the link as the word "technology." If they clicked on the link, it would take them to the Web location http://company.com/technology, which probably contains lots of other content items relevant to technology. The exact Web site does not matter; the microformat standard only cares about the last word in the URL, which is "technology." This, plus the extra "rel='tag'" code in the link, signifies that this page is about "technology."

In other applications, such as Microsoft Word, your options are more limited. At some time in the future, Microsoft may add support for microformats. However, at present you are limited to creating your own convention. One suggestion that we propose is a global convention of named Microsoft styles. Styles are a feature of Microsoft Word that allow you to apply the same kind of formatting multiple times; when you change the style, all instances change.

For example, say you wanted all bulleted lists to have the same indenting, padding, and symbols for the bullet. You would define a style named "Bulleted List," define it with the specific format you need, and apply this style to all your lists. Then, if you ever wanted to change the formatting, you change it once in the style, and all bulleted lists in your document change.

For a metadata microformat, the process would be equally simple. If you wanted to tag a document with the word "technology" in Word, you could apply a style named this:

```
uF:tag:technology
```

The letters "uF" are a common abbreviation for microformat. This is then followed with the word "tag," meaning that you are applying a metadata tag to the document. Finally, the word "technology" is the metadata tag that would apply to this document.

The style doesn't need to apply any special formatting to your document. It could highlight it yellow, or behave like normal text. The only important thing is the name of the microformat, which is sufficient enough to follow the convention.

In practice, your users would start by embedding a metadata microformat in their Word documents. Once the document is converted into HTML, you could automatically convert the Word microformat into an HTML microformat.

Fact, Opinion, and Important Microformats

The metadata format is just the tip of the iceberg. What if you could also embed tags all over your document, calling out specific paragraphs, words, or bullet points? As mentioned above, perhaps some data should be called out as being risks, facts, or confidential. A confidential microformat would be of tremendous use when it comes time to redact documents for consumption by different audiences, whereas fact microformats would be useful for search engines trying to extract information at the micro-level from documents, in order to enhance data mining or quick viewing.

At present, these kinds of microformats are not common conventions on the Web. However, that should not prevent you from using them internally to help you find the content you need. For example, a fact microformat might look something like this in HTML:

```
<div class='fact'>Sales increased by 20% in the third quarter of
2008.</div>
```

In this case, the semantic HTML uses the special "class='fact'" attribute in order to signify that this sentence is a "fact." In Microsoft Word, you would use a similar approach, and tag all "facts" in your document with the following style:

```
uF:fact
```

Naturally, it is very early on in the microformats movement. These conventions may or may not achieve great success on the Internet. However, there is still a great deal of value in using them on your internal systems to provide additional semantic markup to your documents. This will aid in not only finding content more quickly, but also in being able to more accurately data mine your content repository.

The Future: Data Mining Unstructured Content

Every time we add structured content into an unstructured document, we open up the possibilities of data mining the unstructured repository for useful, hidden information. The easy part of this problem is analyzing the popularity of content or common keywords. More sophisticated data mining would be able to analyze the full-text repository for keywords and trends, or extracting the data in embedded tables, lists, or microformats.

Data mining unstructured content is a very recent concept; besides keyword extraction, there are few tools available that help you with this. In the future, we anticipate that the demand for this functionality will lead to new innovations.

Some believe that you need to convert all content into a semantically rich format—such as XML—before you can extract the structured content. This is true if you wish to extract data from embedded tables and charts, but less true if all you want are keywords and microformats. Others believe that the search engine's index itself is the place to target for the data mining of unstructured content. Since the search engine has already extracted keywords, and counted how often they are used, it's a natural place to do trend analysis, as well as semantic analysis to analyze what a document is "about." Unfortunately, getting a computer to "understand" what a document is "about" is a very difficult problem to solve, which explains why there are so few new innovations in this area.

We believe that data mining is most useful when it is accompanied with context-rich popularity analysis. Software like Oracle Real-Time Decisions can help your users find the content they need, but the software doesn't need to try to understand what the content is. In other words, the software doesn't need to understand what content items contain; it only needs to know that most users who viewed content item A also wanted to view content item B.

Metadata, keyword analysis, and data mining can help get this process started. However, in environments with a long search history, analyzing behavior to recommend content is a much easier problem to solve. If you add in features like folksonomy and identity management, then you might get even better results than you would with an ideal data mining application alone.

Takeaways

- The line between structured and unstructured content is becoming more blurred.

    - A pragmatic ECM strategy needs to be aligned with your structured content strategy, such as master data management initiatives.

- Unifying your security policy across all applications is the only way to ensure the security and integrity of your data.

- You should enhance structured enterprise applications with unstructured content and services.

    - Imaging and Process Management (IPM) and BPEL workflows can bring documents, workflows, and searches to enterprise applications.

    - Siebel Files and Business Intelligence Publisher can integrate directly with your strategic ECM infrastructure.

- You should enhance your ECM applications with structured content and services.

  - Use Real-Time Decisions to determine what content users might want to see.

  - Use document output management to manage high-volume printing, e-mail, and customer communication.

- Extracting the structured content out of unstructured documents yields a rich environment for finding new information.

  - Convert content to XML to extract data in embedded tables, or other structured data embedded in the document.

  - Use microformats to embed easily extracted "tags" and "facts" from your content.

  - Auto-categorization and data mining are useful, but are difficult problems to solve, and new innovations come along slowly. Analytics of user behavior can fill in the gaps.

CHAPTER
8

ECM and
Enterprise 2.0

he term "Enterprise 2.0" is often used and misused. In general, the term tries to describe a fundamental shift in both the technology and the culture of the enterprise. Unfortunately, there is a lack of expert guidance explaining what exactly Enterprise 2.0 means.

This lack of guidance is not necessarily a bad thing; one of the primary concepts behind Enterprise 2.0 is to help create *systems* that solve problems, instead of having to always rely on one single self-appointed expert, or documenting every minute detail of your business. Enterprise 2.0 is about experimentation, creation, and flexibility, and will therefore be very different across industries. Nevertheless, in order to be successful with Enterprise 2.0, most people will need guidance in what works and what doesn't.

Some claim that Enterprise 2.0 is simply about taking popular Web 2.0 collaboration tools—such as blogs and wikis—and scaling them up to the enterprise. This would mean quicker and easier collaboration, and the ability to keep connected with other's information.

Others say it's about bringing Web 2.0 *philosophies* to the next generation of enterprise tools. That means concepts such as openness, ease of use, connectivity, and community should be implemented into identity management systems, ERP systems, and CRM systems, then used through your service-oriented architectures. In other words, it's about breaking down application silos, and allowing reuse in a safe and open way.

Still others—most notably Wikipedia throughout 2008—think that there is no difference between Enterprise 2.0, and enterprise social software. In other words, these people believe that Enterprise 2.0 is little more than a clone of MySpace, Facebook, or LinkedIn, plus some enterprise-specific applications. This means that the crowd currently believes Enterprise 2.0 is only about getting people connected, and little else.

The authors believe that Enterprise 2.0 is a combination of all three. While it includes information management, connectivity to services, and engaging people, Enterprise 2.0 is at its core a strategy for helping enterprises know when and how to evolve. This means connecting the right people to the right information, and having the right infrastructure to safely empower the enterprise to be agile and adopt to meet new challenges, both known and unknown.

Naturally, there is a lot of well-founded excitement about the possibilities. However, we would like to remind people that some caution is warranted: unless you remain mindful about why the Knowledge Management movement failed 20 years ago, you are doomed to repeat the same mistakes with Enterprise 2.0. You must always keep in mind the limitations of technology; without the proper culture, Enterprise 2.0 could cause more problems than it solves.

In this final chapter, we'd like to discuss how you should use enterprise content management (ECM) tools and philosophies in your Enterprise 2.0 strategy. Since Enterprise 2.0 covers the management of information, services, and people, some of your strategies will have nothing to do with ECM. We feel that the service-empowerment aspect of Enterprise 2.0 is best accomplished with a service-oriented architecture, as discussed in Chapters 3 and 5. Below, we will discuss how ECM plays a major role by connecting people to information, but more of a supporting role for connecting people to each other.

Pragmatic Enterprise 2.0

There is no universally accepted formal definition of Enterprise 2.0, nor should there be. However, we believe the following is a reasonable approximation:

> Enterprise 2.0 is an emerging social and technical movement towards helping your business practices *evolve*. At its heart, its goals are to empower the right kind of change by connecting decision makers to *information*, to *services* and to *people*.

When we say "emerging," we mean that it will never be fully formed. New ideas, new technologies, and new social trends will mean your strategy will need to change rapidly. However, we believe it is fair to say that at its heart, the goals are to connect people with information, services, and each other. This also includes ensuring that your systems provide the proper context for each. When you connect people to information and each other, you also need to provide the context for direct feedback and participation in sharing new ideas.

Enterprise 2.0 is also about creating a business culture that can survive and thrive in a hyper-connected world. Being hyper-connected means that you will need to make important decisions more quickly, but it also means that your decisions have a higher probability of causing negative effects to people outside of your immediate control. In a word, the optimal culture is one that encourages *entrepreneurialism,* by all employees and on all levels.

A culture of entrepreneurialism means you need to teach your employees that their knowledge and creativity is essential to the future success of the company. The process does not control them; they have the power to modify the process when it is inefficient. If they choose to teach people what they know, then their influence grows. Also, no longer should the CEO be the only well-connected person in the company. All employees need to feel connected with other employees in other departments. This builds trust and understanding, and ultimately leads to better decisions that help the company as a whole. All employees should feel that they are a part of something bigger than themselves, and they should trust those around them to also make good decisions. This means they are more likely to make good decisions, and more likely to change their behavior when they notice how their good decisions negatively affect other departments.

Naturally, there is probably a large gap between the ideal culture and your current reality. That is why you need to proceed with caution with your Enterprise 2.0 initiative. Your tools can help demonstrate the value of an entrepreneurial culture, but the odds are good that many employees will need more incentives and education.

The reason why social connectivity is so important is because Enterprise 2.0 tools give everybody a voice. Somebody may come up with what they believe to be a great idea, and it might be hugely popular, but overall it would be bad for the company. This is because most of your employees only think tactically; how does this decision affect me, my pet projects, or my department? This is why bottom-up initiatives always help one single department, but frequently are detrimental for the company as a whole. Instead, you need a system that helps people get connected with people outside their department. They need to build friendships and trust, so that they can gain a better understanding about how their ideas affect others.

Since Enterprise 2.0 is a *strategy* more than a product or application, it means that there are multiple paths to these goals. A pragmatic Enterprise 2.0 strategy needs to understand this fact, and not try to control too tightly what is essentially an emerging set of best-practices. Indeed, Enterprise 2.0 is highly evolutionary in nature. Since the "right way" to implement it could change over time, a rigid system is exactly the opposite of what you need. So what kinds of technology would make sense?

Connecting people with information is primarily the realm of enterprise content management. Connecting people with services is the realm of next-generation enterprise architectures, such as SOAs, identity management, and complex event processing. However, Enterprise 2.0 is also a social phenomenon, so it must include social software that allows employees to get connected, generate "social capital," and get things done more efficiently.

However, are these technologies absolutely necessary? Perhaps you don't want enterprise content management, and are fine with a patchwork of content silos that only support collaboration with wikis. Perhaps you don't want service-oriented architectures, and instead use alternative approaches like resource-oriented architectures, or Representational State Transfer (ReST). Perhaps you don't want a single "walled garden" like Facebook in your enterprise, and instead use a patchwork of smaller systems that each manage different kinds of connections: friends, coworkers, clients, prospects, and partners. This is certainly possible, but a patchwork of applications usually requires more maintenance than a strategically deployed system.

For those who choose to implement a more strategic Enterprise 2.0 plan, you may still encounter problems similar to those that plagued Knowledge Management 20 years ago if you are not mindful of the lessons that have been learned. As mentioned in Chapter 1, the biggest mistake that first-generation Knowledge Management systems made was assuming that access to information was the primary problem. In other words, once the information broker—the person who shielded you from the information you needed— was eliminated, content silos would collapse and innovation would soon follow. Unfortunately, even though the information broker occasionally kept useful information away from you, the broker's primary job was to keep *useless* information away from you. Eliminating the broker caused a flood of information that few users are able to handle.

In the same way, some Enterprise 2.0 vendors are claiming that access to services and people are the main problem, and once all barriers go away, innovation is inevitable. Unfortunately, this is not quite correct.

For example, many of your business services are hidden for a very good reason: it is sometimes dangerous to execute services out of order. Many of these services were never properly designed for use by novices, and therefore side effects are sometimes inevitable. Enterprise 2.0 needs to have a broker to ensure people use the *right* services at the right *time*. In effect, an SOA initiative without SOA governance can lead to chaos.

Similarly, access to people is not a cure-all. Busy people frequently have gatekeepers, whose job is to prevent random solicitations from distracting the busy person. In order to protect that resource's valuable time and make sure the company functions smoothly, solicitors must follow a formal escalation process before talking to that busy resource. Does this prevent useful information from getting to the resource? Of course. But remember: that process exists for a reason, and getting rid of it without fully understanding why it currently exists will inevitably lead to problems.

Also, your exceptional employees—the ones who you need the most in your social software applications—are the least likely to adopt new systems for staying connected. Why? They are already extremely busy, and they already have systems that work well for them. They don't have the time to learn new software applications, just so they can have the privilege of processing even more requests, and doing even more work. Without some kind of gatekeeper, or social broker, these software systems will never reach their full potential.

The problems with Knowledge Management were not apparent at first, because early adopters did have reasonable success. However, their success had more to do with their *culture* than because of any specific technology. Many information brokers were genuinely dedicated to *teaching* their knowledge—instead of merely *sharing* their information—and thus were happy to have new tools that made them more efficient.

However, once more and more people started using these systems, the flood of irrelevant information became worse. Organizations without a culture of teaching their knowledge expected the software to solve all their problems, which almost never works. The contributors shifted from people who were dedicated and talented information brokers, to those who knew very little about how to share information. They knew little about metadata, taxonomy, or findability, and they didn't care to learn. Thus began an endless cycle: contributors don't know how to make content findable, and now they don't have time to learn, because they're spending so much of their time trying to find content!

The only reason enterprise content management exists is because Knowledge Management vendors failed to realize the truth: without the information broker, people will inevitably be flooded with useless, outdated, and just plain false information. This created infoglut, which then requires effort if you want to transform it into useful business assets.

Enterprise 2.0 is at the beginning stages of this same path. Early adopters of blogs, wikis, and social software find tremendous value in them, because these organizations are dedicated to staying connected with information and important business contacts. But what happens when everybody uses it? What happens when the human gateways to other humans disappear? Are you replacing individual gateways with "social" gateways? Will people be inundated with irrelevant "friend" connections as well as irrelevant information? Are all blogs equally important? Are all wikis equally authoritative? Are all services equally safe? Are all social connections equally strong? And finally, how do you plan on funding and maintaining these systems that are supposed to be collective property?

It is clear that Enterprise 2.0 tools and philosophies will spur innovation, and they are too useful for business units to ignore them. However, unless your strategy is approached with a clear understanding of what killed Knowledge Management, you may experience even more information overload then you do right now. Some of these challenges are solved by bringing back the human information broker, and giving them the tools they need to be more efficient. In other cases, it involves engaging your audience to become the information broker by ranking people and ideas before your busy resource sees them. It also includes empowering your audience to "tag" content items with relevant keywords, so others can more easily find them. Overall, this is an expansion of who the information broker is, and can be the best of both worlds, but only if you can also create a culture of information sharing.

Pragmatic Enterprise 2.0 is not just about connecting to information, services, and people; instead it's about connecting to the right information, the right combination of services, and the right people. As such, your Enterprise 2.0 team would do well to engage your ECM Center of Excellence, who had to solve very similar problems in the past. They should be able to help you not only transform your infoglut, but also prevent the next generation of socialglut.

Drivers for Enterprise 2.0

The primary driver for Enterprise 2.0 is to enable your business to evolve and execute in a way that generates competitive advantage.

Bluntly, it doesn't matter what your business is doing right now; if you're still in business you're obviously doing something right! Instead, what matters is whether you will know when it is time to change, what to change, and whether you can implement that change efficiently. Businesses do not fail because they do the wrong thing; they fail because they do the right thing for too long. Obviously, empowering the right kind of change is both a technical and a social problem.

The first promise of Enterprise 2.0 is to ensure that decision makers—both at the top and the bottom—have both the information and connections necessary to know when and what to change. The second promise is to ensure that your enterprise architecture can easily adjust to the necessary change. Changing your accounting policies will not require a full redesign of your system; your enterprise will be agile enough to make changes both small and large as needed.

Empowering All Decision Makers

The primary difference between Enterprise 1.0 and Enterprise 2.0 is in who the decision maker is. Enterprise 1.0 was strictly a top-down endeavor: executives spent a great deal of time and energy designing a process optimized for their business, and enforced compliance all the way down to the process workers. These processes were rigid, and difficult to change. Deviation from the process was forbidden for good reasons: it might temporarily make one department more efficient, but others would become less efficient, and the overall business would suffer.

Enterprise 2.0 combines bottom-up with top-down: knowledge workers get connected and share their ideas, then take advantage of existing re-usable services to help the process evolve. Instead of blocking process change, executives combine top-down initiatives with bottom-up feedback. Analytics of strategic business indicators—in contrast to tactical system-level indicators—help ensure that efficiency improvements in one department do not have negative side effects elsewhere.

Despite the newness of the term "Enterprise 2.0," the challenge of gathering and using bottom-up information is nothing new to the business world. It's the same age old dilemma: *when should you empower your employees to take the initiative?* When can you trust that they will make the right decisions? What should you do to recover if they make the wrong one? Are their goals inline with the strategic initiatives of the executive team? Getting your employees the right information can only do so much: you must also have a process for reconciling top-down strategies with bottom-up efforts. Once you have this, you can safely allow your business practices to evolve to take maximum advantage of the present opportunities.

Hiring and Retaining Young Talent

A secondary driver for Enterprise 2.0 is to hire and retain young talent. The newest generation of workers has never known a world without reality television, e-mail, or the Internet. They blog regularly, communicate via social networking sites, text message instead of talk, and believe wikis are the best way to find accurate information. They have *always* suffered from information overload, and they believe Web 2.0 tools are an important part of the solution. A 2008 survey by IT services provider Telindus reported that 39 percent of 18-to-24-year-olds would consider leaving their jobs if their bosses banned access to Facebook—currently the most popular social software application. To them, an employer without access to Web 2.0 tools is as absurd as one without access to e-mail.

Unfortunately, even with all their passion and talent, the new generation often doesn't understand how you currently do business. They have a strong desire to help you change your business for the better, and they likely have a lot of great ideas. However, they are the opposite side of the Enterprise 1.0 problem: they may try to get you to change your business too aggressively, perhaps in ways your overall business model cannot support. If you try to change too quickly into "what is next," but neglect "what you are," your business will suffer.

Building "Social Capital"

Another driver is simply getting your employees to socialize with each other, and helping them make useful connections within your enterprise. In the past, organizations have relied on hallway conversations, company picnics, all-day meetings, and team-building exercises to help connect people with each other. Unfortunately, because of the trend towards telecommuting, satellite offices, global business units, and outsourcing, these kinds of informal connections are becoming less common. It is impossible to have a hallway conversation with somebody who is seven time zones away. Technologies like teleconferencing and telepresence attempt to bridge this gap, but they can only do so much.

The primary goal of inter-office networking is to generate "social capital," which is a fancy word for the tendency people have to do favors for their friends that they wouldn't ordinarily do for random people. You are also more likely to listen to your friend's idea without prejudice, and you are more likely to bend the rules to help out a friend. As a result, social capital helps people communicate better, it helps streamline a slow business process, and it helps people understand how their decisions affect people in other departments.

Most importantly, it enables feedback between two departments that might not ordinarily communicate. It helps the CEO get the "on the ground" perspective of the employees, and it helps the employees understand why the CEO made a specific strategic decision. Both top-down and bottom-up initiatives benefit greatly from this enhanced perspective.

On the Internet, most people use social software to connect with people they would normally socialize with. In contrast, your Enterprise 2.0 applications should help connect you with people you would *never* socialize with: strong connections with existing friends are less useful to the enterprise than lightweight connections with people who might help you in the future. The ideal would be if every employee could find one "buddy" in every other department in your organization, although in practice this is uncommon.

Bypassing the official process does have risks, but people with the most kinds of connections will also see firsthand what the consequences of their actions are. As a result, they will be better able to measure the risks of their actions on the enterprise as a whole.

What holds these "buddies" together need not be much; it can be as simple as watching the same movies, following the same sports teams, or gossiping about the same celebrities. In many cases, that is all it takes to make them feel like a team. In other words, it is not a bad thing if employees use internal resources to discuss movies, sports, or celebrity gossip. If it helps them build relationships with people whom they do not normally socialize with, then you are helping create vital social capital.

How ECM Fits into Enterprise 2.0

The Enterprise 2.0 goals are around sharing information, reusing services, and connecting people. As stated before, there are multiple paths to achieve these goals, and Oracle offers multiple products to achieve these goals.

Since one of the goals behind Enterprise 2.0 is to connect people with information, an important component of any Enterprise 2.0 strategy is enterprise content management. You can extend your strategic ECM repository to support the content needs of your Enterprise 2.0 applications. This means empowering ECM to deliver or integrate with the newest breed of collaboration application.

Some of the newer Enterprise 2.0 applications are a natural extension of what ECM does, so a tight integration makes a great deal of sense. Other times, ECM takes more of a supporting role. The following sections outline what these new technologies are, why you may need them, and how Oracle ECM fits in.

When it comes to the services aspect of Enterprise 2.0, your ECM system should cleanly integrate with your enterprise architecture. For example, if your architecture is SOA-based, then your strategic ECM should offer easy-to-use content services. It should also cleanly integrate with your service governance model and your global security policy. As stated in Chapters 4 and 6, Oracle ECM can fit in nicely with your service governance model.

When it comes to connecting people to each other, your ECM plays more of a supporting role. If your social software needs to store unstructured content so people can reuse it—such as photos, notes, and blog posts—then it makes sense to store it in your strategic ECM system. Also, your ECM system has a lot of information about emerging trends, based on the popularity of search terms and pages. The final sections of this chapter discuss why enterprise social software is important, and how ECM could play this supporting role.

Limitations of Enterprise 2.0

All of this Enterprise 2.0 technology is very exciting, and incredibly useful. However, it's important to reemphasize that it is *both* a social and technological movement. In order to get maximum value out of these tools, you also need to create a culture of sharing information, services, and connections. This can be difficult if you have departments that prefer to hoard access to information, or protect their employees from information in other departments.

Enterprise 2.0 will not get off the ground in your organization without the proper system of rules, rewards, incentives, and accountability. It may be official policy to share information and connections, but are people properly motivated to do so? It may be official policy to encourage risk takers, but do you properly motivate the risk takers regardless of whether they succeed or fail?

Not All Connections Are Equally Strong

One problem that is common to a lot of social software is the question of how should we define a connection. When sites like LinkedIn and MySpace were new, early adopters wanted to have as many connections as possible, regardless of whether or not you had ever interacted. This led to the illusion that these individuals were "well connected," when in reality they were not.

Truly well-connected individuals do favors for their connections: find them jobs, share insights and information, and actively get them connected with other people who might help them. In contrast, people who are well connected on LinkedIn are takers, and not givers. They are not building social capital, they are only consuming it.

A good Enterprise 2.0 initiative should be mindful of this reality. Simply because two people are connected, doesn't mean that the connection is strong. People need to communicate with each other to strengthen connections, and do favors for one another. If they do not, then connections should eventually expire.

Also, just because you have a lot of connections, doesn't mean that you are well connected. Imagine a business that has ten departments, with 100 people per department. Further imagine that in one department, there is a person connected with all 100 people in her department, but not connected with anyone outside her department. Compare her against a coworker who is only connected to one person in each of the ten departments. The former has 100 connections, the latter has ten connections. Who is better connected?

Arguably, the employee with only ten connections is better connected than the one with 100 connections. Why? Because the one who knows a greater variety of people is more likely to have a better sense of what is going on across the entire company. The person who is very well connected—but only with people like her—will have a very narrow view of what is going on.

It is therefore important to encourage your employees to connect with many different *kinds* of people. The people with cross-departmental connections usually have a better grasp of what is happening across the organization. By making these connections and being genuinely helpful to others, your employees will gain both influence and knowledge that they otherwise would lack.

Extending ECM with Web 2.0 Technologies

The primary role of ECM in an Enterprise 2.0 strategy is to be a repository for the unstructured content created by whatever new systems that your enterprise adopts. Some Web 2.0 applications are a natural extension of what ECM does, and thus should be tightly integrated. Other technologies have functionality that is far removed from the problem of storing unstructured content, so ECM's role is more limited.

The term "Web 2.0" is an often misused and misunderstood term. It is not simply the latest generation of Web technology. In fact, some of the technologies that analysts include in the Web 2.0 stack—such as instant messaging, e-mail lists, and bulletin boards—were invented many years before the Web even existed. In fact, instant messaging dates back to the 1960s.

Therefore, it's important to understand that Web 2.0 is more of a *social* phenomenon than a technological breakthrough. The old model was one of broadcasting: create a Web site or broadcast a message and your audience was supposed to passively consume your data. However, in the era of information overload, people crave more control over their data. They crave faster ways to give feedback, and to improve the information of third-party content. People also want to build communities around ideas, products, or services that they liked. Simply put, the strength of such a community ensured the long-term health of their idea, and gave them influence over the direction of products and services.

Following is a description about some of the more popular Web 2.0 technologies, and how ECM can deliver or support these technologies.

Instant Messaging

Instant messaging is a form of real-time text-based communication that two or more people use to exchange quick messages over the Internet. Unlike e-mail, you usually only type in one line of text, and quickly send to another person. You can also create private chat rooms, where multiple people can engage in the dialog.

Essentially, instant messaging fills in a gap between e-mail and the telephone. You can have instant back-and-forth communication like the telephone, but it creates a running dialog that you can save or refer to later. Some instant message clients can sends files, photos, and links as well. Others, like Skype, allow you to do both instant messaging and the telephone with the same system.

Also, since instant messaging doesn't require the full attention that a phone does, it is easier to perform multiple tasks while using instant messaging. You can engage people in a chat, then read an e-mail, then listen to a voicemail, then check the instant message conversation again. Since most people can read faster than they can type, you can usually stay caught up. However, splitting your attention across too many places isn't always an overall productivity boost, so it should be done in moderation.

Instant messaging might be the Web 2.0 tool that has the most value to your business. According to a 2007 survey by Forrester, 37 percent of IT decision makers said that instant messaging delivered substantial business value, compared to just 16 percent on average for other Web 2.0 tools. This could be because it is a familiar blend of the phone, and e-mail. As a result, it's probably easier for business users to adapt socially to instant messaging, since they do not need to significantly alter their behavior to see value in the technology.

How does ECM fit into this picture? There is a tremendous amount of useful information in those IM conversations, so you may want to allow people to search through them. The easy way to do this is to have your instant messaging server log all chat messages, and save them in your strategic ECM system for later discovery and consumption. Most of this text probably belongs in your archive. However, some content—like the pictures, documents, and digital files embedded in the message—probably belong in your active repository.

There are two dangers to storing all of your instant message data. The first is technical: how much data will this be, and can your system handle it? Can it handle the volume of data, and the problems with people searching the archives for information? How much value is in recording these conversations, and how much are you increasing or decreasing your business risk by keeping it forever?

The second problem is social. If people know their instant message chat rooms are being monitored, then they might avoid instant messaging and just use the phone, or face-to-face meetings. The younger generation of workers probably will not have a problem with permanent logs, however, others may be a bit more wary of every outburst and misspelling being stored in a permanent archive. Also, your legal department might be wary of allowing your IM logs to be discoverable, so they may insist that they be destroyed after a matter of a few weeks.

Wikis

A wiki is a collection of Web pages that can be easily edited by a community. They are typically authored in a simplified version of HTML—called Wiki Markup—so that non-experts can create heavily linked Web pages.

From a social perspective, a wiki is a place where the authoritative version of a knowledge-base document slowly evolves. This process encourages both experts and non-experts to edit the content, in order to make it more readable, more precise, and more authoritative. Experts add value by making sure that the latest information is properly presented. Non-experts help by making sure that the page is clear to those who are just learning about a topic and do not have expert knowledge.

Wikis take advantage of a common social problem with knowledge sharing: people do not like creating documents from scratch, rather they prefer to modify existing ones. On a wiki, a page normally starts out as a stub, then an outline, which eventually is edited by enough people that it becomes useful. You should never expect your page to go unedited for long.

Because of the community-editing aspect of wikis, it is vital that wikis only contain information from a neutral point of view. Wikis are not the place for opinion, propaganda, or persuasion. Justin Kestelyn from Oracle sums up this philosophy nicely:

"A wiki is not the place for opinion, because opinion does not invite editing, only response."

Additionally, wikis have other features such as the easy ability to link to other wiki pages, to place wiki pages in categories, to have discussions about wiki pages, view differences, and roll back to older revisions. The original wikis required their users to know "wiki markup" in order to edit the page. Unfortunately, this simply meant that all your contributors had to learn something that was nearly as complex as HTML, but with less power. More modern wikis use WYSIWYG controls to let people edit the HTML with tools that look more like Microsoft Word.

From a technology perspective, you may notice that there isn't much difference between what a wiki does, and what the Site Studio application within Oracle UCM does: easy HTML editing, categorization of pages, navigation, and link management.

Since wikis are a natural extension of ECM, there are three ways to implement a wiki with your strategic content management infrastructure. The first is to extend Oracle UCM and implement a wiki directly in the standard interface of your UCM application. This is already available in the Content Server Blogs and Wikis Components, which is bundled with the most recent version of Oracle UCM. This is shown in Figure 8-1. Another option is to create a wiki using middleware tools and use UCM to store the unstructured wiki markup. A third option is to extend Open WCM to support wiki markup, and wiki contribution.

All three options have merit. The simplest solution is to use the wiki functionality embedded in Oracle UCM. However, by extending Open

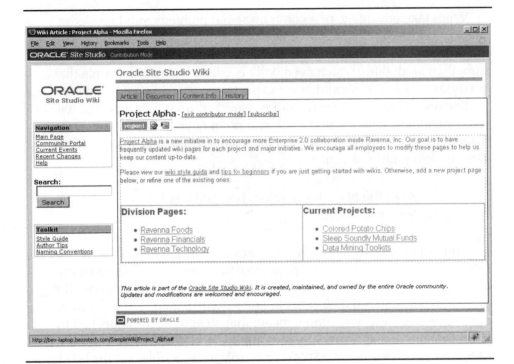

FIGURE 8-1. *Oracle UCM offers wiki functionality to make content pages easy to edit.*

WCM to add the wiki functionality you need, then you gain several other advantages. The first is that you can embed your wiki on any application server page in your enterprise. Perhaps you'd like the authoritative wiki about "company help-desk policy" to be embedded on every Web application in your enterprise, both JEE portal servers, and .NET SharePoint systems. Using Open WCM, you can embed the wiki in both places, so everybody can view the policy, no matter which application they use on a day-to-day basis. Combined with Oracle Ensemble—as discussed in Chapter 6—you could embed an Open WCM wiki on nearly any Web application in your enterprise.

However, a pragmatic ECM strategy does not require you to build all these features directly in your ECM repository. If you have a compelling reason to build a wiki in middleware, then ECM can manage your unstructured content with the connectors we discussed in Chapter 4. If you have already installed a stand-alone wiki application, and it is not cost effective to do a strategic integration, then you should manage it with the federation tools discussed in Chapter 5.

Blogs

One of the primary goals behind Web content management is to make it easier for non-technical people to add and edit Web content. A "blog," short for web log, is a great example of a Web site that is extremely easy to update and maintain. A blog is a simplified version of a Web page, designed to empower users to make rapid commentary of ideas or descriptions of events as they occur. They frequently support images, video, audio (sometimes called a Podcast), as well as multiple ways to submit content: via e-mail, text message, or simplified Web forms.

The primary value of blogs is their simplicity: it takes very little effort to create and post a new article. This encourages people to update their sites more often, even if their prose is less than perfect. It also takes very little effort to create an entirely new blog site. Thus, when you begin a new project, you can quickly create a new blog for it and enable lightweight project management. Most blogs support comments threads, so your audience can make suggestions or add relevant tips.

The proper use of blogs in the enterprise requires a blend of structured and unstructured content. For example, assume you are managing a very large project. You will no doubt be using tools that help you schedule time and resources. Your managers will need to use strict progress reports to monitor milestones and resource usage. Unfortunately, non-managers strongly dislike creating formal progress reports, especially when a project is behind schedule. They force your employees to shift gears, and direct their focus away from solving the problem, towards trying to communicate what the problem is. This context-shift reduces productivity more than most managers realize.

If you simplify the problem down to a blog, it will be easier for your employees to do a quick brain dump and move on with solving the problem. Perhaps an employee discovered a trick on his project that might be useful on two current projects. If he mentions this in a daily progress report, it will go into the reporting system, probably never to be seen by his peers again. Perhaps instead he should just place it on his blog, which is more likely to be read by his peers. Then his audience could tag it and comment on it, enabling even more people to find the diamonds in the rough.

However, now the problem is over-simplified. A blog is too loosely structured. Even with extensive use of tags, you are missing information on milestones, deliverables, and the time it takes to complete a project. In practice, you will always need both: rigid, structured tools that enable the manager, plus flexible tools that encourage your resources to become engaged in the process, but not overburdened by the process.

Oracle ECM can support blogs in the same way that it supports wikis: either by building blog support into the strategic repository itself, or by supporting middleware tools that host blogs. Also similar to wikis, you may see multiple parallels between Oracle Site Studio and blogs. In fact, a blog like the one shown in Figure 8-2 is a highly simplified version of what Oracle Site Studio has done for years: easy contribution, navigation, contribution from multiple channels, video, audio, and archives. As mentioned earlier, blog support is already built-in to Oracle UCM in the Content Server Blogs and Wikis Components. However, you could also implement blogs using Open WCM, or middleware.

Same as with wikis, if you use Oracle Open WCM or Oracle Ensemble, you could embed your blog in any Web application in your enterprise. This means that for the example above, you could embed your project blog in the Web interface of the project management application, as well as embedding it on an employee portal. That way, your managers could easily create a dashboard to view the metrics and the war stories in the same interface, while other employees would see it in whatever context they are familiar.

Some would argue that *syndication* can also solve this problem, which is covered in later sections. In other words, publish the content of the blog to multiple locations, and expose it to a wider audience. However, this breaks one of the primary rules of a blog: it is supposed to be a *conversation* between a speaker and the audience. If you publish the content of the blog to four places, then the conversation is split into four different places as well. This means that people may be wasting energy raising and discussing objections in one place, even though the problem was already resolved in a different conversation.

Instead, by using Open WCM or Oracle Ensemble, you can embed the blog as well as its comments anywhere in your enterprise. The conversation looks exactly the same, no matter which interface you used to view the blog.

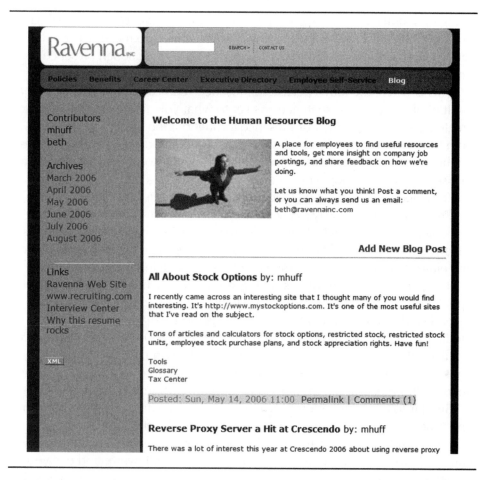

FIGURE 8-2. *Blogs are a quick and easy way to create and update Web sites.*

That helps keep the discussion in one place and make sure everybody gets up-to-date information.

Microblogging and Persistent Presence

One of the more socially interesting subcategories of blogging is *microblogging*, also known as *persistent presence*. Instead of writing an entire page about your opinions and ideas, you simply blog the answer to one question: what am I doing right *now*? Twitter is the most commonly cited example of microblogging; however, other sites like Jaiku and Pownce have emerged recently to do the same. Other sites like Facebook and MySpace have since added presence functionality, but call them instead "status updates."

This is where the term "persistent presence" comes from. If you make it a habit of blogging a one-sentence answer to what you are currently doing, you create a persistent log of your presence throughout the day. This empowers both the ability of your "followers" to get real-time updates of your activities on their own Web pages or on portable devices. By storing this stream of data in a search engine, people can scan your presence at a later date to see if you're working on something that they are also curious about.

Presence is an easy way to encourage collaboration. What task are you working on right now? What problems are you having right now? What tricks have you discovered right now? Your team members can get real-time updates, and either give you advice, or implement your advice in other projects.

The persistent monitoring is useful in situations when fast real-time updates are important and need to be logged for a log time. For example, several studies have shown that Twitter was more reliable than blogs or the media to track the California wildfires in October 2007. The Red Cross even has a Twitter account so you can keep up to date on their relief efforts. Twitter allowed people to exchange links, maps, and directions, as well as keep multiple people up to date on a minute-by-minute basis.

Similar to blogging, microblogging is a natural extension of Site Studio and Open WCM. There are two primary technical differences: updating followers and storing a searchable log of your persistence. Alternatively, you can implement the entire presence engine with middleware, and use your strategic ECM repository as the content storage mechanism. That way, you can tag and rate messages so people can find them more easily, as well as move your presence logs to an archive once they are no longer needed.

However, limiting presence to text-based updates is horribly unimaginative. Why not do video updates instead? How about sending a voicemail memo to your presence engine? This would allow for faster and more frequent updates, without requiring your users to become wizards at text-messaging from their phones. You can use the digital asset management feature in Oracle UCM to extract the text, and make both of them part of the persistent presence.

Syndication Feeds: RSS and Atom

Content syndication is similar to content publishing: it means moving content out of a repository and into a separate system, which then delivers the content to multiple targets. The most common kind of syndication is an RSS feed, which originally derived its name from the term "Really Simple Syndication." Instead of using a complex publication protocol, RSS feeds chose to keep it simple: an XML file with minimal additional formatting, which you could access over the Web, and which included links to the original content and limited metadata.

RSS feeds first became popular when blogs began to proliferate. Most blogs were not focused on selling products or advertising, so they were perfectly happy to repurpose the content on their sites into easily digested RSS feeds. It wasn't long after this that e-mail readers began offering RSS "subscription" features: whenever a new item appeared on the blog, you would get the equivalent of an e-mail in your inbox containing the new article. This did not work the same way as e-mail, however. Instead of the Web site sending you the RSS feed, your e-mail client would constantly connect to the Web site and look to see if any new content was published in the RSS feed. This "polling" occurs as often as the client wants: every day, every hour, or every minute.

Subscribing to RSS feeds help people stay immediately up to date on multiple blogs, even if new content was published very rarely. Also, they never have to supply their e-mail address to these Web sites, which therefore cuts down on the amount of unwanted "spam" e-mail. Other tools—called *feed aggregators*—could consume multiple RSS feeds and combine them together into one Web interface. These aggregators usually collect feeds based on specific themes, such as personal travel advice, software trends, or news items about specific companies.

Because the RSS format is so simple, it is trivial to take any list of data—news releases on a Web site, recent blog posts, error messages—and turn it into an RSS feed. In 2006, Universal Content Management added secure RSS feeds to virtually all of the lists it produces, including arbitrary search results (see Figure 8-3), arbitrary lists on any Site Studio page, and secure lists of a user's workflow tasks.

Because syndication feeds are simple to read, many applications treat them as a de-facto publishing standard. For example, if all of your enterprise applications published error messages as RSS feeds, it would be trivial to

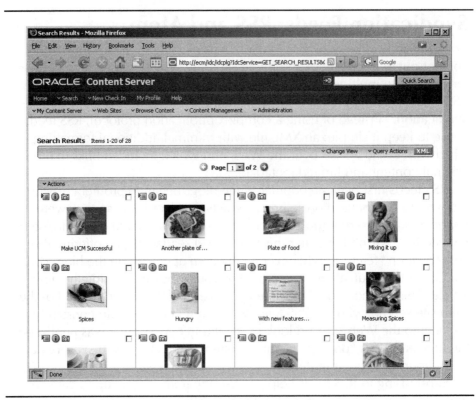

FIGURE 8-3. *A standard search result displays a list of items as HTML, but you can also access it as an RSS feed by selecting the XML button.*

syndicate them to a central monitoring system. From an end-user perspective, you can publish RSS feeds of UCM lists into alternate applications. This may include a custom Flash animation that helps you visualize your results. A good example of this technique is free Pic Lense integration, shown in Figure 8-4, which uses an RSS feed of a search result as an input so that a user can more easily select an image based on a thumbnail.

The RSS format has several limitations, and unfortunately fixing some of them would break backwards compatibility. Since the standard was frozen by the copyright owner, many people felt that it was time to start over with a new, more extensible standard: Atom. The new Atom standard has gained in

FIGURE 8-4.   *The Pic Lense viewer uses this RSS feed to give a richer viewing context.*

popularity significantly since 2006, and is endorsed by the IETF standards body, so it is only a matter of time before RSS feeds are completely displaced by Atom feeds. This is good, because even though neither Atom nor RSS implicitly support important content management concepts, at least Atom is extensible enough to add them.

Unfortunately, syndication feeds in general have severe problems when it comes to large numbers of users. For example, assume you have a popular syndication feed that has one million viewers on the Internet. You only update the contents of this feed daily, but you do not have control over how often your one million clients connect to your Web site to see if your feed has changed. In other words, your site should only be getting one million hits per day, but because of RSS readers, you might be getting over one million hits *per minute*. This can cause severe performance problems if done improperly, so you should be aware of how to make a scalable polling architecture before starting a large-scale RSS initiative.

Also, syndication feeds do not scale when it comes to large *amounts* of content. Again, assume that you have a popular RSS feed that displays the top 20 most recent news items on your home page. You have a million viewers, but this time they only download your feed once per day. On some particularly busy days, your company may update the news articles 50 times. Unfortunately, since your RSS feed only displays the most recent 20 items, your users missed out on 30 important news items that day. This is irritating for users, but it can cause critical failures if you use RSS feeds for moving content between two applications.

Despite these limitations, syndication feeds will be a useful part of your pragmatic ECM strategy. They are useful as a lightweight publishing standard, but there are a lot of features missing, such as search, in-context editing, and scalability. However, if you understand and accept these limitations, they can sometimes make tactical integrations a lot easier.

Enterprise Mashups

As covered in Chapter 5, a "mashup" is a blend of two web applications in a single application. In effect, you are "mashing" two applications into one. In general, mashups require very little server-side code; they use mostly JavaScript and dynamic HTML to make composite applications.

The most frequently cited example of a mashup is probably HousingMaps.com, shown in Figure 8-5. They were one of the first to realize that Google Maps had a JavaScript API that supported embedding a Google map on sites other than Google. This API also allowed them to inject custom HTML into their Google Map interface. Specifically, HousingMaps.com extracted information from CraigsList.com about what houses were for sale, their cost, a description, and their address. Using the house address, HousingMaps.com draws a Google Map of the location, along with extra HTML containing a description of the home.

We should emphasize here that this interface is drawn *entirely* with JavaScript. This means that the user's browser and Google Maps are doing most of the work to draw the presentation layer. In practice, the browser downloads static JavaScript and image files from Google Maps, then dynamically draws the interface based on static JavaScript and XML files on HousingMaps.com. This means that most of the performance, uptime, and stability issues with their application have already been solved by Google Maps; the maintainers of HousingMaps barely need to know anything about

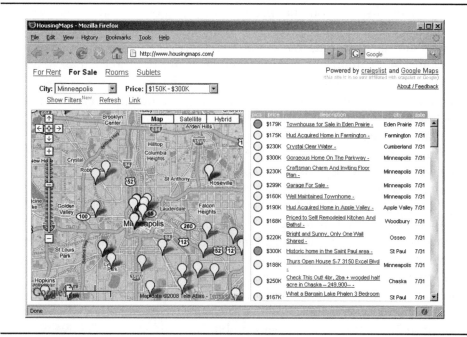

FIGURE 8-5. *HousingMaps.com is an excellent example of a mashup.*

enterprise-class software in order to create a robust and stable interface to the existing information.

Imagine if you could always create applications in this manner. If you have a true service-oriented architecture, complex Java middleware tools are not required. Your Web designers could use pure JavaScript APIs to connect to enterprise-class resources to download information and execute remote services.

The implications to your enterprise are huge. Instead of having your enterprise-class developers spend time on the user interaction layer, they can instead focus on making their services and information easier to reuse. This means focusing on solving the security, stability, and scalability problems, and allowing your Web developers to focus on just the interface.

This is the big promise behind enterprise mashups: they allow ordinary developers to create enterprise-class applications. In theory, with mashups you no longer need your developers to understand complex portal frameworks in order to create user interfaces to back-end information and services. Instead, you only need your developers to understand new Web 2.0 techniques like Ajax and dynamic HTML. If your enterprise architecture supports reusable services and reusable information, enterprise mashups are a natural end result. We covered mashups in Chapter 5, when we discussed the Ensemble feature in the Oracle WebCenter Services product. The beauty of Ensemble is that you could quickly create a fairly functional mashup API to most existing Web applications. This allows you to create mashups for systems that were never intended to operate as mashups. However, Ensemble is not a magic bullet. As mentioned before, all requests need to be proxied through the Ensemble server, in order for Ensemble to provide the mashup API.

Proxying all requests through Ensemble is great if you'd like to create perimeter-based security to legacy applications, or if you'd like to limit access to legacy systems that might not be able to handle the excess load. However, some enterprise applications in the future may wish to supply their own mashup API. Also, a direct JavaScript API to your enterprise applications may sometimes perform better than always being forced to go through a proxy. Nevertheless, Ensemble plays a vital role in a pragmatic Enterprise 2.0 strategy, because it's probably the most cost-effective way to create a mashup API to existing applications.

From an ECM standpoint, Oracle should follow the same rules for creating mashups that all applications do: use Ensemble, unless a low-level API gives you more functionality. Oracle UCM has two JavaScript APIs that may be more useful than Ensemble for some applications. One of them is called the "Schema" interface, which offers a fast JavaScript API to run predefined secure queries on UCM's database tables. Through special configuration, you can allow secure read-access to any data in the database: user information, workflow information, metadata, or even entire documents.

The second API was discussed briefly in Chapter 4. Oracle UCM has a SOAP interface, and any request that you make can return a SOAP response. By adding the parameter "IsSoap=1" into any URL to the content server, you can get back a SOAP response. This means that you can make a content server request through Ajax, pass this extra flag, and get an XML response. Then, in typical Ajax fashion, you can read the XML response in JavaScript, and draw the response data to the Web page. We should emphasize here that the only language used is JavaScript: no knowledge of Java, .NET, PHP, or JEE portals is needed to create an interface.

Full technical coverage of these APIs is beyond the scope of this book. Please refer to Oracle's documentation for more information and examples.

SOA and the User Interface Layer: Essential Components for Enterprise Mashups

As mentioned briefly above, service-oriented architectures allow us to reuse the underlying application functionality by encapsulating the business logic in reusable pieces. This is sometimes called the "business logic" layer of the application. Most enterprise applications try to encapsulate as much functionality as possible in this layer, in order to maximize the reusability of the logic.

However, when we talk about the movement around Enterprise 2.0, we are focused not just on the services, but also the user engagement model and participatory paradigm of the application. In other words, it's not just about resources like services and information: it's also about the people. How do they currently interact with these resources? How would you like them to interact? How would they like to interact?

As we have discussed, the primary thing that makes a blog interesting is not the technology; it's the user interaction model and participation model. Therefore, if we are to properly bring Enterprise 2.0 features into applications, then we need an SOA-like approach to the user interaction layer as well. This layer cannot be buried beneath layer upon layer of complex arcane frameworks. The logic of how you draw your user interface needs to be as portable as the services and data that it interacts with.

In other words, technology like SOA makes services portable. Technology like ECM makes content portable. Technology like mashups makes the user interface portable.

This is where the power of tools such as Oracle's WebCenter Services and Ensemble come into play. Using these capabilities, we can wrap the user interaction around a set of services or application functionality and deliver that entire component—UI and all—to multiple applications, whether it is a JEE portal server, a .NET application server, a legacy PHP application, or a cutting edge iPhone application.

Portable information, portable services, and portable user interfaces. All together, these are the building blocks that you will need for next-generation Enterprise 2.0 applications.

> ## Web 2.0 Needs an ECM Foundation
>
> Web 2.0 tools and attitudes have already become part of the fabric of our technological expectations. It is not whether blogs *will be* used by a senior executive, they are. It is not whether ratings, feedback, and tagging *will be* implemented by business units, they are. It is not whether project deliverables *will be* shared via wikis and presence, they are. The common thread that runs through all Web 2.0 interactions is unstructured information. For this reason, it is imperative that, in enterprise settings, this information be stored, managed, and controlled. Web 2.0 systems that do not rest upon the fundamental pillar of enterprise content management will likely be doomed to obsolescence and obscurity.
>
> —Billy Cripe
> Coauthor of *Reshaping Your Business with Web 2.0*

Folksonomy and Shared Bookmarks

One of the primary challenges of organizing information is determining a taxonomy structure so your audience can easily browse your system to find what's important to them. Consumers and contributors almost always speak different languages; they call things by different names, and they browse for information differently. As such, your information architecture is a constant struggle to satisfy multiple audiences at the same time. This usually means multiple taxonomies, and a controlled thesaurus to manage preferred and non-preferred terms. These are sometimes dependent on who the audience is, or what task is being performed. However, even with expert help, these systems are difficult to keep up to date. The auto-categorization engines discussed in Chapter 7 can help, but they cannot fill in all the gaps.

In contrast to an expert-oriented taxonomy, a *folksonomy* is a content organization structure created and maintained by ordinary "folks," instead of experts. Your content consumers can add metadata tags to Web pages, reports, or any Web-accessible resource in your enterprise. Your consumers get to describe what this resource is, what it contains, or perhaps why you would want to use it.

In short, a folksonomy is a task-oriented taxonomy that is maintained by the consumers of information. Common folksonomy sites on the Web include Del.icio.us for organizing Web sites, and Flickr for organizing photos.

In practice, users would browse to find content via the normal ways: by browsing your digital library through the expert-maintained hierarchy, by searching based on keywords, or perhaps by following links from another page. Once the user finds content that they consider useful, they can submit a form to recommend keywords that are relevant to this item. This is called "tagging." The folksonomy application stores a list of all the items you tag in an online list of "bookmarks," so you can easily find your items of interest based on the keywords you think are important. If the user chooses to make these bookmarks public, they are usually listed on publicly accessible pages for all to see.

Sometimes these "tags" are words used inside the document, and therefore they act as user-verified keywords that are relevant to the document. For example, a document about recent sales wins might be tagged with the words "sales," "revenue," or even the names of new clients. Other times, the folksonomy tags are never used in the document itself, but instead reflect what the audience *feels* about the item. In this case, your recent sales wins might be tagged with terms like "surprising," "important," or "financial."

Some may say that using both the tags "financial" and "revenue" would be redundant; thus your administrators should pick one and train all taggers to use it exclusively. However, this would be missing the point of a folksonomy: people search for information in different ways. One group might search with the term "financial," the other might use "revenue." It is not important which term is correct; rather it's about helping people quickly find what they need. Only after this will they be receptive to changing their terminology.

Advanced usage includes tags that represent actions that this user wants to take on the item, like "to read," "to buy," or "to do." One technique that is gaining popularity is tagging items with the names of people or groups that may be interested in this item. For example, if you think Bob might be interested in an item, you can tag it with the keyword "@bob". If you think the New York sales team might want to read it, you can tag it with a group name like "@ny-sales". The "@" symbol is a Web 2.0 convention for saying that a tag or a message is intended for a specific person or group, and can be very useful for instant messaging, microblogging, and folksonomies.

As you can see, the data in a folksonomy system is incredibly useful when it comes to helping people find content they previously tagged, and in helping new users find items of interest. Folksonomy can be incredibly helpful for making recommendations to users running an enterprise search. It is also useful to help validate that your navigation and taxonomy structure is satisfying the needs of your users.

Besides finding content, a folksonomy can tell you a great deal about your audience. When somebody bookmarks a page and tags it with "important," that tells you multiple things at the same time:

- Who tagged this resource? In other words, what do we currently know about this person? Their department? Their position? Are they a customer, prospect, or partner?

- What tags did they use to describe this resource? In other words, how should we categorize this content in the future, so similar people can find it?

- What keyword does this user tag content with most often? In other words, in the past what kinds of content were most important to this user?

- What tags have they used in the past week? In other words, what content is important to this user right now?

As you can see, a proper folksonomy system can store a great deal of information about what your users find interesting, what they think is important, and at what time. The historical collection of metadata tags say more about a user than a typical user survey. Also, since this information is gathered passively, it is constantly up to date, and is gathered for all users instead of only those that submit audience surveys.

This collection of metadata tags is sometimes called a *tag cloud*. This is a visual representation of all the tags used to describe the item, based on how often the tag was used. These can be used on a per-item basis, or you can analyze the tag cloud for an entire Web site. Tag clouds are useful to see what kinds of content a blog or an intranet site typically contains. For example, in Figure 8-6, more people tagged content on this site with the word "Oracle" than the word "mobile," so the word "Oracle" is in larger font. A tag cloud for a content item shows what tags were used to describe that one item. In addition, a tag cloud for a person could say one of two things. It either displays the tags that this user uses most frequently, or in some cases it may represent what keywords other people have tagged this user with.

From an ECM perspective, adding metadata tags to URLs is a natural extension of adding metadata to content items. Therefore, by extending UCM to become your folksonomy engine, you can take advantage of the robust metadata management capabilities that UCM offers. Another possibility

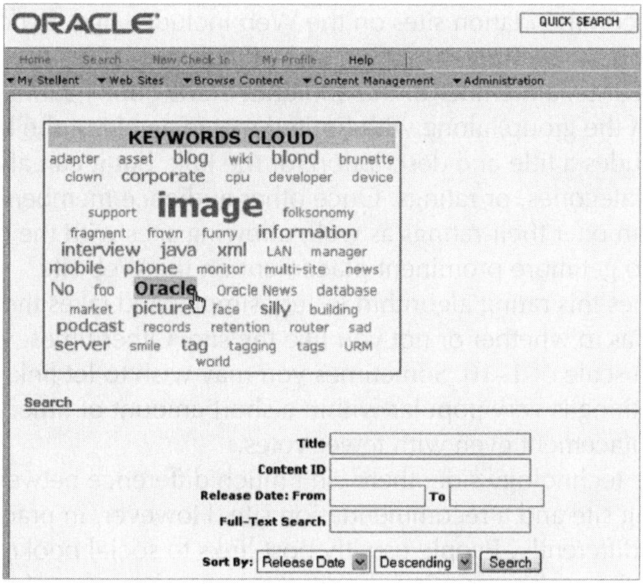

FIGURE 8-6. *Tag clouds can give you a "feel" for what kind of content a site contains, according to the most popular keywords.*

would be to create a folksonomy application from scratch by using middleware, and integrate it with your strategic ECM system.

In either case, it makes sense to store all metadata about a content item directly in your strategic ECM system. That way, other enterprise applications only need a strategic integration with ECM in order to extract all metadata and tags for the item. It would be an unnecessary burden for your enterprise applications to connect to two systems in order to gather a complete set of metadata. Ultimately, it doesn't matter whether the folksonomy user interface resides in your strategic ECM system, or in middleware. However, it is very important for all content, metadata, and metadata services to be served by your strategic ECM system.

Recommendation Sites

A recommendation site is a Web application that allows the audience to submit links to other Web sites, which others in the audience might find interesting. Naturally, the usefulness of a recommendation site is directly proportional to the dedication of this audience. Therefore, these are a great example of how Enterprise 2.0 is both about culture and about technology. Common recommendation sites on the Web include Digg, Reddit, and StumbleUpon.

On most sites, a member of the audience starts out by submitting a link to the rest of the group, along with limited metadata about the link. This usually includes a title and description for the link, but it can also include keywords, categories, or ratings. Once other audience members view the link, they can offer their ratings as well, allowing sites with the highest popularity to get more prominent placement on the Web site.

Sometimes this rating algorithm is very simple, and takes the form of a yes/no vote as to whether or not you like the site. Other times, you can rank the site on a scale of 1–10. Sometimes you may wish to let links "age," so that if something is very popular within a short amount of time, it gets prominent placement even with fewer votes.

From the technology side, there isn't much difference between a social bookmarking site and a recommendation site. However, in practice they are used much differently. People usually post links to social bookmarking sites so that they themselves can find the site again at a later date. In other words, sharing links with others is a secondary function of social bookmarking. Therefore, social bookmarking sites usually have an infinite number of supported keywords and tags, allowing anybody to organize anything in any way.

In contrast, the primary goal of a recommendation site is to help others discover new information. Therefore, recommendation sites need a much smaller number of categories in order to simplify this discovery process. You may not be able to tag sites with specific keywords such as "profitability," "sales," or "revenue," instead you may be forced to use the broad category "finance." However, if your recommendation application knows about your folksonomy application, and it knows you frequently use the tag "sales," then it might be able to make better recommendations. It can even use information about what tags you used this morning in order to give you time-relevant recommendations.

The role of ECM in this depends on how you create your recommendation engine. If you only need a simple voting mechanism on top of a folksonomy application, then you would benefit from a similar architecture. In other words, store the information about a site's "rank" alongside all other metadata on that item. Where you create the user interaction layer is up to you, however, any metadata about a content item should also be stored inside your strategic ECM repository to ensure the "single source of truth."

Alternatively, you may wish to base your recommendations on a great deal more information than simply this user's tag cloud. If you take advantage of information in your ERP or CRM applications, then you may benefit from an application like Real-Time Decisions, as mentioned in Chapter 7, in which case, you may need to create a much more robust application using middleware tools.

Idea Mining Applications

Recommendation sites do not need to limit themselves to Web sites or content items. One important sub-category is called *idea mining*. Instead of forcing people to submit links to external blog posts or Web sites, users submit "ideas" directly to the application, and others vote on just the information in the idea description.

For example, perhaps you are having a difficult time deciding what features to put into the next product? Your research team wants the features that are the most fun to design, your sales team wants the features that sell the best right now, and your marketing team wants the features that best position you for the future. An idea mining system would allow everybody to see what features different people want, as well as their reasoning. This creates a nice, easily referenced history of why your team made a specific decision and why.

There is also tremendous value in integrating an idea mining system with a project management system or a task management system. If your audience makes it clear that a certain idea is worth looking into, the next step could be to promote this informal idea to a more formal system, where experts can sketch out an initial list of tasks and needed resources.

For example, "we should have a space colony on Mars" is a good idea, and many people would vote in favor. However, it would require the careful hand of a professional to determine what would be needed for the implementation. After people understand the time, expenses, and lost opportunities involved with pursuing this idea, they might change their votes. Taking this extra step towards documenting the trade-offs is essential if you wish to achieve the blend of top-down and bottom-up analysis essential to Enterprise 2.0.

The biggest problem with idea mining is not in the technology, but in the culture. Should everybody use these systems, or just the ones with the best ideas? Do the people who get the most votes really have the best ideas, or do they simply have the most free time? Are all votes equal, or should some votes be more heavily weighted because of the voters' rank, influence, and history of accomplishments? Will this system actually harm your ability to get things done, because too many resources just want to relax and be "the idea guy?"

From a business perspective, you should consider an idea management system to be a Web-enabled extension to your existing suggestion box. Ideas that are popular are not always best, but it is very useful to know who voted for each idea, and why. Also, people should be discouraged from submitting too many ideas, lest they stop doing their normal job and keep making work for others. Finally, when a decision maker needs to reject a popular idea, she should fully document the required tasks and trade-offs of the idea, so it is clear to all why the idea had to be rejected.

Idea mining systems are an excellent way to avoid informational meetings where people present ideas, but never seem to create action items. Instead of putting your entire team in a room to endlessly discuss what could be done, first put these ideas into your idea mining system, and let your team discuss and vote at their leisure. Then, when the top few ideas have bubbled to the top, it is now the responsibility of the team leader to get everybody to agree on one course of action. Never forget: idea mining systems are useful, but they can never replace a good manager with leadership skills.

Enterprise Social Software

As mentioned in the beginning of this chapter, there is a blurred line between the terms Web 2.0, Enterprise 2.0, and enterprise social software. For the purposes of this book, when we talk about enterprise social software we mean primarily the applications that help connect people with each other. As such, social software is one-third of the Enterprise 2.0 problem, and provides critical support for other Enterprise 2.0 applications and services. Social software gives a much richer context to the blogs, wikis, idea mining applications, and mashups mentioned in the previous sections.

The first steps in using social software involve creating an online profile for yourself, and then seeing which of your friends are already in the system. If they are already there, you can get connected to them and include them in your "friends" list. You can also join specific online "groups," to try to connect with people of similar interests. Good social software constantly tries to increase your number of connections by introducing you to friends of friends with whom you have something in common. Perhaps you both like biking, travel, the same sports teams, and your mutual friend describes you both as "good with computers."

You can use these connections to find their blogs, their shared bookmarks, or the ideas they rank as most important. Some social software requires you to use them as your blogging and wiki platform. Others are more extensible, and allow you to share your list of connections with other Web 2.0 applications, running elsewhere on the Internet.

Perhaps the biggest question to ask about social software is: why bother?

Why on earth would an enterprise care about giving their users a system to find friends, rank each other, play online games, and chat about fantasy football? Don't your employees waste enough time already? Wouldn't this actually hurt productivity? Not necessarily. In fact, having an online place to socialize is the best tool your company has to quickly build social capital. Especially in a world where project teams have members on opposite sides of the planet, what better option could there be for team building?

As mentioned earlier, building social capital is vital for a successful Enterprise 2.0 initiative. Without it, your initiative is likely to do more harm than good. Imagine you deploy an idea mining application to solicit ideas from your employees. Imagine an idea is well thought out and popular, but it is too tactical. It greatly benefits one group or department, but overall would hurt the company.

If you reject this idea, you could cause hurt feelings and bitterness. Even if you successfully explain how the idea is harmful, resentment is inevitable. Why? Because the people who had the good idea are disconnected from those that they would negatively effect. Therefore, they may not even care if they cause harm to another department; they might even relish the opportunity! In contrast, if the team with the good idea was well connected to the other teams, and they liked and trusted the other team, they would be more likely to understand when you explain the negative side effects of their idea.

As such, getting people connected to each other is vital for both bottom-up and top-down initiatives. It gives the top-down decision makers—like the CEO—a greater amount of information with which to make a decision. It gives bottom-up decision makers—like the people who set IT policies and procedures—enough high-level feedback so they can see any negative consequences of their actions.

How ECM Fits In

As mentioned many times in the above sections, unstructured content belongs in your unstructured content repository, in order to guarantee a single source of truth. For some kinds of Enterprise 2.0 applications, your strategic ECM infrastructure should host the content, the services, and also the interface. This holds true for most blogs, wikis, and RSS feeds. In other cases, it makes sense for the ECM repository to supply content and services to middleware applications, and allow the middleware to present the user interface. This holds true for some blogs, some wikis, folksonomy tags, and some kinds of recommendation sites. For other kinds of Enterprise 2.0 systems, your strategic ECM infrastructure only plays a minor role. This includes mashups and instant messaging.

Likewise, when it comes to storing social information about connections, enterprise content management should play a very minor role. As stated in Chapter 6, an ECM system should store content; not users. In our belief, most of this information about your users belongs in an identity management system. Ideally, your identity management system would also host your social software services. However, the list of useful services changes so rapidly, that it will likely take years before identity management systems will be able to implement them all. As a result, frequently the information, services, and user interface for social software is implemented in middleware.

However, enterprise content management can play a supporting role when it comes to data mining your unstructured content repositories, in order to discover these initial social connections.

Data Mining E-mail Archives for Connections

As discussed above, not all connections are equal. Some connections are very one-way and are less strong than others. You should also be mindful of the fact that your users are busier than ever, and probably do not want to spend a great deal of time setting up a network of "friends."

Therefore, you should do your best to set up a decent "social map" of who is connected to whom before you unleash social software on your employees. You should try to guess who is connected to whom, if they are friends or merely coworkers, and how strong the connection is.

This may sound like a daunting task, but you have an excellent tool at your disposal that can help you get started: your e-mail archives. It will not be perfect, but it will help answer the following questions:

- Who do you send e-mails to? These are the people you claim to be connected to.

- Does this person reply to your e-mails? If so, the connection is mutual.

■ How often do you e-mail? A one-time e-mail is probably not a connection, but a weekly e-mail might be a strong connection.

■ How long does it take them to reply to you? A faster reply usually means your communications get priority to them, and they feel a stronger connection to you.

■ How long do you take to reply to them? Again, a faster reply from you means that their communications get priority from you, meaning you feel a strong connection as well.

■ Does one person usually do all of the initiation of new e-mails? If so, then this might be a lopsided friendship, or it might just mean that one person has more free time.

■ What are the topics of conversation? If it's only work, then you probably don't have a strong connection. If you also discuss gossip, news, sports, or trivia, then you probably have a stronger connection.

■ What is the flow of e-mail from one department to another? If it's peer-to-peer, then these departments are comfortable sharing information. If it always goes through the chain of command, then these departments are socially isolated.

■ Who do you e-mail outside the company? If an employee in the marketing department e-mailed a friend who works at the company Ravenna, and your sales person is trying to connect with somebody at Ravenna, then these two employees should probably connect.

Unfortunately, many employers have a policy against using company e-mail for personal communications. Ironically, this policy could hurt the employer in the long run, because analyzing the violations of that policy are frequently the best way to determine who is well connected in your company!

Is it possible to efficiently data mine your e-mail archives? Unfortunately, e-mail archives are on backup tapes that are difficult to analyze. However, if you use the Universal Online Archive for your e-mail archive system, then you will have an "always on" archive of your e-mail in your database. This means you can use business intelligence or custom analytics to determine who is connected to whom, and how strongly.

You can also analyze this list of connections for "influencers" and "bottlenecks." Specifically, an influencer would be somebody who has strong connections to many people in multiple departments, and doesn't follow the chain of command to communicate with them. In contrast, a "bottleneck" would be somebody in management who insists that e-mail follows the chain of command, and is in charge of a team that has few connections outside their department. Influencers are not necessarily good, and bottlenecks are not necessarily bad, nevertheless this information is useful for determining problems with the flow of information.

It may also be a good idea to constantly keep your social network up to date with weekly analysis of your e-mail archives. This will help your users keep their connections up to date by simply using the e-mail tools they are already familiar with.

How Identity Management Fits In

Enterprise social software relies heavily on identifying users, and associating things like "tags" and "connections" to them. In other words, Joe from accounting is the guy to talk to about expense reports—he's highly professional and he's friends with many sales folks. Where should this information be stored?

This information is valuable to every application in your enterprise. It is vital to give context for enterprise searches, or human resources applications, or customer relationship management systems. Therefore, this information is too vital to be embedded in a social software silo, where it is locked away in a walled garden.

Who do you know? Who knows you? What are your skills? How do your peers rate you in those skills? What are your interests? What is your favorite sports team? Arguably, all this information should be stored in your enterprise-wide identity management system, and all services to get or change this data should likewise be directed there.

Once this data is in your identity management system, all applications will be able to use this rich context in order to enhance the interface for the end user. Your list of contacts and connections will not be restricted to your blog: all your enterprise applications could utilize this data and enhance the functionality of the system.

Naturally, this opens up many possibilities, and many privacy issues. Also, as mentioned before, social software is changing so rapidly that it might take a long time for identity management to catch up. In the mean time, we may need to host the data, services, and user interface for social software in middleware applications. However, within a few years the data and services will probably be hosted in next-generation identity management systems.

A full description of what's next in identity management is beyond the scope of this book. However, if you plan to roll out a multi-year initiative for social software, you need to be mindful of the latest advances in identity management as well.

The Future of Pragmatic ECM

The importance of enterprise content management as part of our IT infrastructure, our applications, and our overall use of enterprise technology should be apparent due to the recent acquisitions in the ECM marketplace, as well as the entrance of new products by several high-profile vendors. Content management and user-enablement are major themes of new applications and the extension of existing tools. The term "ECM" is expanding while the major vendors that make up the marketplace are consolidating. Therefore, content management is growing in both importance and scope.

Even when viewed against the backdrop of the software market generally moving towards platform players, ECM companies have been acquired at a pretty amazing rate. ECM is now viewed as a critical component of an enterprise stack. As mentioned throughout the book, it is becoming more infrastructure and middleware, rather than point solutions or niche applications.

Throughout this consolidation, the ECM value proposition has also been growing. New market demands, driven by users and by regulators, are bringing more and more requirements into the ECM fold. Access to information by employees, partners, and customers is now expected over a much wider area of devices and channels. Compliance and knowledge transfer are pushing traditional content storage mediums towards ECM solutions.

Because the current trends on the ECM market are towards consolidation and infrastructure, the future will probably hold new kinds of standards for ECM—some better than others. If one standard becomes widely adopted, this will cause some people to think of ECM as a commodity, creating even greater pressure for ECM vendors to differentiate themselves in the market. Some may focus on tighter integrations with enterprise applications and middleware, whereas others may focus more on specific features for vertical applications.

These trends are going to continue for some time. Therefore, what you need is a pragmatic strategy that provides you with the flexibility you need to adopt these new technologies as they emerge. Our strategy allows you to adapt as this market changes, and take advantage of new capabilities that supplement the applications in your enterprise. You do not have to continuously migrate your content from one system to another simply because a newer one has slightly more features; you can use tactical integrations and ECM tools to take advantage of these new innovations when needed. The pragmatic strategy is about the flexibility and agility you need to take advantage of the best technology in this quickly evolving market.

Even with this flexible, pragmatic strategy, ECM needs to continue to focus on users and context in order to remain useful. This means two primary things for the future.

Firstly, ECM will continue to become more "social," which includes a lot of the trends that we talked about in this chapter. These trends include simplified contribution with blogs and wikis, and also better metadata context with folksonomies. Since a pragmatic ECM system stores content, not users, it should fit right in with both your identity management strategy, and your social software strategy.

Secondly, ECM will continue to become more "contextual." This includes a lot of the things we discussed in the previous chapter, such as using middleware tools to bring content management into as many places as possible: enterprise applications, desktop applications, composite applications, and Web portals. It also means analyzing the behavior of your users across multiple systems, in order to make a better guess about what content they are likely to want. Because of information overload, we think it is vital to place information as close as possible, and with as much context as possible, to the end user. Likewise, analyzing what content is popular and why will likely be the future of "smart" enterprise search.

Oracle is in a unique position to tackle these technical problems. With the recent BEA acquisition, it already has the best-in-breed middleware, and multiple ways to provide ECM in context with your applications. It also has the best-in-breed business intelligence applications that are critical to analyzing what information is popular and why. Oracle also has an incentive to champion ECM as comprehensive middleware, since it has a strong desire to integrate ECM with as many of its own applications as possible. This is in addition to Oracle's ability to bridge the gap between structured and unstructured content systems, because of its leadership in enterprise applications and database systems.

Naturally, all this technology will not be sufficient in and of itself to solve your content management problems. The current issue with infoglut is as much a social problem as it is a technical problem. Ultimately, what matters is satisfying the information needs of end users, in the context of the applications they use every day. Also, you need to use caution when deploying the latest Enterprise 2.0 technologies: a social software strategy without an ECM strategy will only *increase* your information management problems. In the absence of the right technology and the right culture, information sharing merely causes the flood of information to be redirected to another channel. When scaled to the enterprise, this ultimately degrades the effectiveness of new Web 2.0 technologies, despite any early success you may have.

In other words, just as "meeting overload" led to "e-mail overload," so too will "e-mail overload" lead to "blog overload." The best culture is not one of hoarding information; nor is it one of sharing information. The best culture is one of *teaching* information, and using new knowledge to drive innovation at every level.

In addition to the right technology and the right culture, you need the right strategy to blend the two. You need to think strategically, but implement tactically. In other words, your mantra should be "think big, focus narrow, and move quickly!" This means you need to look ahead to what technology will soon be available, but also be mindful of what you need for immediate operational success.

We hope this book will help you take advantage of a pragmatic strategy for approaching ECM. The idea is to help you roll out strategic ECM, while still taking advantage of tactical repositories you have in-house. While this isn't a step-by-step prescription, we believe it is an overall model for transforming infoglut into the strategic business assets you need.

Takeaways

- Enterprise 2.0 is a fundamental shift in both enterprise technology and culture.

  - The proper technology connects people to services, to information, and to each other.

  - The proper culture should encourage universal entrepreneurialism.

- You will need an Enterprise 2.0 initiative to better empower decision makers, hire and retain talent, and build the social connections that make your business run more smoothly.

- Some Enterprise 2.0 tools are a natural extension of ECM, and should be a part of your strategic ECM infrastructure:

  - Blogs, wikis, syndication feeds (RSS), and folksonomy.

- Other Enterprise 2.0 technologies use ECM more as a supporting application:

  - Instant messaging, enterprise mashups, and enterprise social software.

- The future of ECM is to become more contextual and more social.

Index

GET YOUR FREE SUBSCRIPTION
TO *ORACLE MAGAZINE*

Oracle Magazine is essential gear for today's information technology professionals. Stay informed and increase your productivity with every issue of *Oracle Magazine*. Inside each free bimonthly issue you'll get:

- Up-to-date information on Oracle Database, Oracle Application Server, Web development, enterprise grid computing, database technology, and business trends
- Third-party news and announcements
- Technical articles on Oracle and partner products, technologies, and operating environments
- Development and administration tips
- Real-world customer stories

If there are other Oracle users at your location who would like to receive their own subscription to *Oracle Magazine*, please photocopy this form and pass it along.

Three easy ways to subscribe:

① Web
Visit our Web site at **oracle.com/oraclemagazine**
You'll find a subscription form there, plus much more

② Fax
Complete the questionnaire on the back of this card and fax the questionnaire side only to **+1.847.763.9638**

③ Mail
Complete the questionnaire on the back of this card and mail it to **P.O. Box 1263, Skokie, IL 60076-8263**

ORACLE®

Want your own FREE subscription?

To receive a free subscription to *Oracle Magazine*, you must fill out the entire card, sign it, and date it (incomplete cards cannot be processed or acknowledged). You can also fax your application to +1.847.763.9638. **Or subscribe at our Web site at oracle.com/oraclemagazine**

○ **Yes, please send me a FREE subscription** *Oracle Magazine*.   ○ No.

○ From time to time, Oracle Publishing allows our partners exclusive access to our e-mail addresses for special promotions and announcements. To be included in this program, please check this circle. If you do not wish to be included, you will only receive notices about your subscription via e-mail.

○ Oracle Publishing allows sharing of our postal mailing list with selected third parties. If you prefer your mailing address not to be included in this program, please check this circle.

If at any time you would like to be removed from either mailing list, please contact Customer Service at +1.847.763.9635 or send an e-mail to oracle@halldata.com. If you opt in to the sharing of information, Oracle may also provide you with e-mail related to Oracle products, services, and events. If you want to completely unsubscribe from any e-mail communication from Oracle, please send an e-mail to: unsubscribe@oracle-mail.com with the following in the subject line: REMOVE [your e-mail address]. For complete information on Oracle Publishing's privacy practices, please visit oracle.com/html/privacy/html

X _____
signature (required)   date

name   title

company   e-mail address

street/p.o. box

city/state/zip or postal code   telephone

country   fax

Would you like to receive your free subscription in digital format instead of print if it becomes available? ○ Yes ○ No

---

YOU MUST ANSWER ALL 10 QUESTIONS BELOW.

① WHAT IS THE PRIMARY BUSINESS ACTIVITY OF YOUR FIRM AT THIS LOCATION? (check one only)
- □ 01 Aerospace and Defense Manufacturing
- □ 02 Application Service Provider
- □ 03 Automotive Manufacturing
- □ 04 Chemicals
- □ 05 Media and Entertainment
- □ 06 Construction/Engineering
- □ 07 Consumer Sector/Consumer Packaged Goods
- □ 08 Education
- □ 09 Financial Services/Insurance
- □ 10 Health Care
- □ 11 High Technology Manufacturing, OEM
- □ 12 Industrial Manufacturing
- □ 13 Independent Software Vendor
- □ 14 Life Sciences (biotech, pharmaceuticals)
- □ 15 Natural Resources
- □ 16 Oil and Gas
- □ 17 Professional Services
- □ 18 Public Sector (government)
- □ 19 Research
- □ 20 Retail/Wholesale/Distribution
- □ 21 Systems Integrator, VAR/VAD
- □ 22 Telecommunications
- □ 23 Travel and Transportation
- □ 24 Utilities (electric, gas, sanitation, water)
- □ 98 Other Business and Services _____

② WHICH OF THE FOLLOWING BEST DESCRIBES YOUR PRIMARY JOB FUNCTION? (check one only)

CORPORATE MANAGEMENT/STAFF
- □ 01 Executive Management (President, Chair, CEO, CFO, Owner, Partner, Principal)
- □ 02 Finance/Administrative Management (VP/Director/Manager/Controller, Purchasing, Administration)
- □ 03 Sales/Marketing Management (VP/Director/Manager)
- □ 04 Computer Systems/Operations Management (CIO/VP/Director/Manager MIS/IS/IT, Ops)

IS/IT STAFF
- □ 05 Application Development/Programming Management
- □ 06 Application Development/Programming Staff
- □ 07 Consulting
- □ 08 DBA/Systems Administrator
- □ 09 Education/Training
- □ 10 Technical Support Director/Manager
- □ 11 Other Technical Management/Staff
- □ 98 Other

③ WHAT IS YOUR CURRENT PRIMARY OPERATING PLATFORM (check all that apply)
- □ 01 Digital Equipment Corp UNIX/VAX/VMS
- □ 02 HP UNIX
- □ 03 IBM AIX
- □ 04 IBM UNIX
- □ 05 Linux (Red Hat)
- □ 06 Linux (SUSE)
- □ 07 Linux (Oracle Enterprise)
- □ 08 Linux (other)
- □ 09 Macintosh
- □ 10 MVS
- □ 11 Netware
- □ 12 Network Computing
- □ 13 SCO UNIX
- □ 14 Sun Solaris/SunOS
- □ 15 Windows
- □ 16 Other UNIX
- □ 98 Other
- □ 99 None of the Above

④ DO YOU EVALUATE, SPECIFY, RECOMMEND, OR AUTHORIZE THE PURCHASE OF ANY OF THE FOLLOWING? (check all that apply)
- □ 01 Hardware
- □ 02 Business Applications (ERP, CRM, etc.)
- □ 03 Application Development Tools
- □ 04 Database Products
- □ 05 Internet or Intranet Products
- □ 06 Other Software
- □ 07 Middleware Products
- □ 99 None of the Above

⑤ IN YOUR JOB, DO YOU USE OR PLAN TO PURCHASE ANY OF THE FOLLOWING PRODUCTS? (check all that apply)

SOFTWARE
- □ 01 CAD/CAE/CAM
- □ 02 Collaboration Software
- □ 03 Communications
- □ 04 Database Management
- □ 05 File Management
- □ 06 Finance
- □ 07 Java
- □ 08 Multimedia Authoring
- □ 09 Networking
- □ 10 Programming
- □ 11 Project Management
- □ 12 Scientific and Engineering
- □ 13 Systems Management
- □ 14 Workflow

HARDWARE
- □ 15 Macintosh
- □ 16 Mainframe
- □ 17 Massively Parallel Processing

- □ 18 Minicomputer
- □ 19 Intel x86(32)
- □ 20 Intel x86(64)
- □ 21 Network Computer
- □ 22 Symmetric Multiprocessing
- □ 23 Workstation Services

SERVICES
- □ 24 Consulting
- □ 25 Education/Training
- □ 26 Maintenance
- □ 27 Online Database
- □ 28 Support
- □ 29 Technology-Based Training
- □ 30 Other
- □ 99 None of the Above

⑥ WHAT IS YOUR COMPANY'S SIZE? (check one only)
- □ 01 More than 25,000 Employees
- □ 02 10,001 to 25,000 Employees
- □ 03 5,001 to 10,000 Employees
- □ 04 1,001 to 5,000 Employees
- □ 05 101 to 1,000 Employees
- □ 06 Fewer than 100 Employees

⑦ DURING THE NEXT 12 MONTHS, HOW MUCH DO YOU ANTICIPATE YOUR ORGANIZATION WILL SPEND ON COMPUTER HARDWARE, SOFTWARE, PERIPHERALS, AND SERVICES FOR YOUR LOCATION? (check one only)
- □ 01 Less than $10,000
- □ 02 $10,000 to $49,999
- □ 03 $50,000 to $99,999
- □ 04 $100,000 to $499,999
- □ 05 $500,000 to $999,999
- □ 06 $1,000,000 and Over

⑧ WHAT IS YOUR COMPANY'S YEARLY SALES REVENUE? (check one only)
- □ 01 $500, 000, 000 and above
- □ 02 $100, 000, 000 to $500, 000, 000
- □ 03 $50, 000, 000 to $100, 000, 000
- □ 04 $5, 000, 000 to $50, 000, 000
- □ 05 $1, 000, 000 to $5, 000, 000

⑨ WHAT LANGUAGES AND FRAMEWORKS DO YOU USE? (check all that apply)
- □ 01 Ajax
- □ 02 C
- □ 03 C++
- □ 04 C#
- □ 13 Python
- □ 14 Ruby/Rails
- □ 15 Spring
- □ 16 Struts
- □ 05 Hibernate
- □ 06 J++/J#
- □ 07 Java
- □ 08 JSP
- □ 09 .NET
- □ 10 Perl
- □ 11 PHP
- □ 12 PL/SQL
- □ 17 SQL
- □ 18 Visual Basic
- □ 98 Other

⑩ WHAT ORACLE PRODUCTS ARE IN USE AT YOUR SITE? (check all that apply)

ORACLE DATABASE
- □ 01 Oracle Database 11*g*
- □ 02 Oracle Database 10*g*
- □ 03 Oracle9*i* Database
- □ 04 Oracle Embedded Database (Oracle Lite, Times Ten, Berkeley DB)
- □ 05 Other Oracle Database Release

ORACLE FUSION MIDDLEWARE
- □ 06 Oracle Application Server
- □ 07 Oracle Portal
- □ 08 Oracle Enterprise Manager
- □ 09 Oracle BPEL Process Manager
- □ 10 Oracle Identity Management
- □ 11 Oracle SOA Suite
- □ 12 Oracle Data Hubs

ORACLE DEVELOPMENT TOOLS
- □ 13 Oracle JDeveloper
- □ 14 Oracle Forms
- □ 15 Oracle Reports
- □ 16 Oracle Designer
- □ 17 Oracle Discoverer
- □ 18 Oracle BI Beans
- □ 19 Oracle Warehouse Builder
- □ 20 Oracle WebCenter
- □ 21 Oracle Application Express

ORACLE APPLICATIONS
- □ 22 Oracle E-Business Suite
- □ 23 PeopleSoft Enterprise
- □ 24 JD Edwards EnterpriseOne
- □ 25 JD Edwards World
- □ 26 Oracle Fusion
- □ 27 Hyperion
- □ 28 Siebel CRM

ORACLE SERVICES
- □ 28 Oracle E-Business Suite On Demand
- □ 29 Oracle Technology On Demand
- □ 30 Siebel CRM On Demand
- □ 31 Oracle Consulting
- □ 32 Oracle Education
- □ 33 Oracle Support
- □ 98 Other
- □ 99 None of the Above

08014004